ROUTLEDGE LIBRARY EDITIONS:
RELIGION IN AMERICA

Volume 2

FAITH AND ECONOMIC PRACTICE

FAITH AND ECONOMIC PRACTICE
Protestant Businessmen in Chicago, 1900–1920

PAUL HENRY HEIDEBRECHT

Routledge
Taylor & Francis Group

LONDON AND NEW YORK

First published in 1989 by Garland Publishing, Inc.

This edition first published in 2021
by Routledge
2 Park Square, Milton Park, Abingdon, Oxon OX14 4RN

and by Routledge
52 Vanderbilt Avenue, New York, NY 10017

Routledge is an imprint of the Taylor & Francis Group, an informa business

British Library Cataloguing in Publication Data
A catalogue record for this book is available from the British Library

ISBN: 978-0-367-49869-6 (Set)
ISBN: 978-1-00-308009-1 (Set) (ebk)
ISBN: 978-0-367-53007-5 (Volume 2) (hbk)
ISBN: 978-1-00-308008-4 (Volume 2) (ebk)

Publisher's Note
The publisher has gone to great lengths to ensure the quality of this reprint but
points out that some imperfections in the original copies may be apparent.

Disclaimer
The publisher has made every effort to trace copyright holders and would welcome
correspondence from those they have been unable to trace.

Faith and Economic Practice

Protestant Businessmen
in Chicago, 1900–1920

Paul Henry Heidebrecht

Garland Publishing, Inc.
New York & London
1989

Library of Congress Cataloging-in-Publication Data

Heidebrecht, Paul Henry, 1950–
Faith and economic practice : Protestant businessmen in Chicago,
1900–1920 / Paul Henry Heidebrecht.
p. cm. — (Garland studies in entrepreneurship)
Originally presented as the author's thesis (Ph. D.)—University of Illinois at
Urbana-Champaign, 1986.
Includes bibliographical references.
ISBN 0-8240-4162-3 (alk. paper)
1. Chicago Sunday Evening Club—History. 2. Businessmen—Illinois—Chicago—Religious life. 3. Civic improvement—Illinois—Chicago—History—20th
century. 4. Capitalism—Religious aspects—Protestant churches—History of
doctrines—20th century. 5. Cities and towns—Religious aspects—Christianity—
History of doctrines—20th century. 6. Chicago (Ill.)—Church history—20th
century.
I. Title. II. Series.
BR560.C4H45 1989
280'.4'0977311—dc20   89-37997

Printed on acid-free, 250-year-life paper

Manufactured in the United States of America

ACKNOWLEDGEMENTS

My final duty is certainly the most delightful: to say thanks to all who have helped me in ways small and large. I have been blessed with many friends. I have been fortunate to work closely with first-rate scholars; their examples were powerful influences and their personal interest in my work encouraged me at every turn.

I owe a special debt of gratitude to my advisor, Clarence Karier. As a friend and mentor, he introduced me to the field of educational history and aroused a fascination for its scope and depth that I expect I will never lose. Most importantly, he blended his outstanding scholarship with genuine compassion for human beings and a keen desire for justice; I only hope I can achieve this high standard in some modest measure.

Much the same can be said for other faculty members in Educational Policy Studies, especially Paul Violas, Jim Anderson and Steve Tozer. My brief sojourn with all the fine people in this department will be one that I will always remember fondly. Several scholars from other fields were most helpful to me: in particular, I wish to mention Mark Noll, Cliff Christians, Tim Van Laar and Mark Fackler.

Like every historian, I have developed a high regard for archivists. In my case, I relied heavily upon several major collections located in the Chicago area. Without fail, I received able assistance from the staffs of the Chicago Historical Society, Newberry Library, McCormick Theological Seminary and the Billy Graham Center.

Finally, I am grateful to my family: first, to my parents, who taught me by precept and example the ways of quiet but determined Christian living; then, to my three children, Kecia, Caleb and Andrew, who have always kept me honest and humble and around whom the bulk of my life gravitates; and last and most deeply, to my wife, Priscilla, who joined me willingly on this adventure and sustained through the many years of labor. To her I dedicate this work with love.

TABLE OF CONTENTS

INTRODUCTION

The following study has been conducted at a time when there appears to be a religious resurgence in American society. Such phenomena as the Moral Majority, television preachers, prayer breakfasts, parochial schools, brainwashing cults, anti-pornography campaigns and organizations established for the purpose of restoring Judeo-Christian values indicate that religion maintains an aggressive stance in the public arena. They hint at a renewed power among the religiously-inclined, a determination to fight back against secularity, and a desire to regain lost turf.

In this context, questions about the role that religion plays in North American society in the 20th century arise. To probe these questions profitably, one must examine both the religious milieu and the larger environment in which it functions. More specifically, one must look for the interactions between particular religious expressions and the economic order, the cultural milieu and the political system. Of all these interactions, in this writer's opinion, the most fundamental are those that account for the division of Americans into classes, separating those with wealth and power from those without. This underlying feature of the capitalist society in the United States outweighs all other factors in explaining social reality.

The role of religion in capitalism has generated its share of discussion. Some have viewed religion as incidental to capitalist enterprise, a private matter at best, and most adequately explained in psychological categories. Others have boldly linked capitalist activity with the highest virtues of religion, calling "free enterprise" Christian, Biblical, ordained of God. None have disputed the fact that more than a few "successful capitalists" have been deeply pious, heavily involved in religious causes, and quite prepared to acknowledge divine blessing as one reason for their abundant wealth.

One individual who looms large in the background of this debate is Max Weber, the German sociologist who from the vantage point of the early 20th century, traced the impact of Protestant religion upon the rise of a capitalist economic order in Western society. Weber's lasting contribution was to identify the dynamic relationship of religious values and economic practice.

The following study takes its cue from this Weberian model but moves on to explore another dimension of Protestant religious life within a capitalist society. That dimension is the manner in which Protestant religion was shaped and utilized by capitalist entrepreneurs. As will be shown, religion was serious business to these individuals and through their efforts, the faith of 19th century America was reshaped into a modern religion that produced tangible, measurable results.

Max Weber's use of psychological mechanisms as the connecting link between religious doctrines and economic practices is set aside in this discussion. In place of this type of explanation, the concept of ideology is introduced, defined as a configuration of symbols, images and assumptions employed by a ruling class to legitimize its position in the economic order (and one that all classes tacitly endorse). Ideology serves as a more comprehensive tool that interacts with both religious traditions and economic activities.

The particular subjects of this study are members of a business class who were both leading actors in a capitalist society and Protestant church members with personal religious agendas. Together as a group, these bankers, manufacturers, lawyers and corporation executives made common cause in their business enterprises and in their efforts to improve urban life using religion as a primary solution. Though the record of their personal views on religious matters and social issues is limited, their associations with particular agencies and individuals provide definite clues to their ideology. Furthermore, their actions in the marketplace reveal the manner in which they applied their religious convictions.

The fact that these individuals lived and operated in Chicago during the decades before and after 1900 made the task of historical analysis more fascinating. Chicago author Nelson Algren aptly described his native town as a place for both "squares" and "hustlers." Locked in perpetual combat, religion and corruption had to be aggressive if they were to avoid each other's clutches. Chicago was also a town where capitalists and workers did battle; by the turn of the century, some of the worst incidents were past but the struggle for control of the workplace was far from over. The subjects of this study were major figures in this struggle; their collective stories illustrate what religious fervor and money can accomplish.

At least two important themes emerge from the research on these Chicago businessmen. First, the religious views they espoused were fundamentally shaped by their business experience and their social outlook as the wealthy elite of the city. They created what might be called a businessman's religion. Such a faith was pragmatic, activist, and geared to measurable results. It was a Protestantism that above all else was efficient.

Secondly, the ideology of this business class carried significant religious baggage. The vocabulary and elements of Protestant doctrine were incorporated into a larger ideology which featured business entrepreneurs as folk heroes and America as the Promised Land for ambitious "men on the make."

No writer of religious history can escape his own personal judgments, for religion has its way of compelling one to take sides. The questions that haunt this author are the same ones that burdened the late William Stringfellow. Where is Babylon? he asked, and where is Jerusalem? If America is Babylon, as Stringfellow claimed, then where is Jerusalem? If

America is a scene of man's Fall, where self is idolized and death is glorified, then where are the citizens of Jerusalem? Not in the churches, argues Stringfellow, for ecclesiastical institutions for the most part have turned their backs on the biblical witness and given in to the wily temptations of America's materialistic goddesses. Under Stringfellow's harsh condemnation, even activist Protestantism such as that displayed in the subjects of this study would be Babylonian.

If Stringfellow is right, then the account that follows is a story of failure. For the sake of those who live in Babylon, and who wrongly believe it is Jerusalem, such a story must be told.

CHAPTER 1

THE CHICAGO SUNDAY EVENING CLUB

On February 24, 1908, a group of prominent Chicago businessmen, bankers and lawyers gathered at the Union League Club to form "an organization of Christian business men to promote the moral and religious welfare of the city."[1] Calling it the Chicago Sunday Evening Club, they proposed to rent Orchestra Hall and conduct Sunday evening services featuring well-known speakers, music and a Bible lesson.

The prime mover behind this program was Clifford Barnes, a former clergyman who had gained financial independence when he married into a family that owned a large grocery merchandising firm. Barnes eventually became manager of the family estate and a civic reformer with intimate connections to the Chicago business community. He was president of the Sunday Evening Club until his death in 1944.[2]

Barnes had several motives in launching the Club. One was to provide evening services in the Loop business area for the convenience of travelling businessmen and for the thousands of young men living and working in the downtown area. The services were clearly intended as an alternative to the decadent night life of the city. But Barnes had even more lofty aspirations. He perceived the Club as a solution to the problems of labor and capital. This, however, did not imply that the Sunday evening programs were to be a forum for workers and employers to engage in dialog. Rather, the meetings were to offer a religious message that would inspire the listeners and encourage the application of Christian values to contemporary problems. Apparently, for Barnes, the "ethics of Christianity" which he saw as "the touchstone of politics, industry, trade, social service and culture"[3] were obvious to everyone; what was lacking was the motivation to live according to those ethics. Captivating speakers and the friendly environment would serve to create this motivation.

From the beginning, the Club was a project of the religiously-motivated business community.[4] Except for Barnes himself, no clergyman was even considered for membership. This reflected Barnes' desire to be nonsectarian and "religious in a broad sense."[5] But it also reflected the priorities of businessmen on the matter of religion. When Bruce Barton reported on the Club in the Home Herald, he noted that the Club trustees were "associated with huge enterprises during the week and they did not believe in running their religion on any little plan on Sunday." The Club was an instant success because the representatives of "big business have determined that it shall, and are willing to sacrifice to make it."[6]

The story of Barnes, the Club trustees and the speakers whom they invited to promote a Christian ethic for an urban, industrial environment will be the subject of this first chapter.

Clifford Barnes was born in 1864 in Correy, Pennsylvania, into a devout Baptist home. Through his grandfather who had close ties with the Baptist theological seminary in Rochester (N.Y.), the young Barnes met numerous leading clergymen; not surprisingly, he sensed a specific vocational call to the ministry. Eventually, Barnes made his way to Yale where his religious inclinations were given outlets for expression, such as the city mission work in New Haven. Like other New England colleges, Yale in the 1880s offered the aspiring young man far more than academic credentials. In fact, intellectual pursuits in themselves were of little value compared to the creation of upper-class interests and contacts, not to mention the gentlemanly pleasures of fraternity life and football. As a student, Barnes established the relationships that largely determined the course of his life.

Through his involvement with the student YMCA movement at Yale, Barnes met such future church leaders as Robert Speer and John R. Mott. He attended summer student conferences at D.L. Moody's Northfield (Mass.) home where he learned to know many major figures of Anglo-American Protestantism. He also worked as a student assistant to William Rainey Harper, then a professor of biblical literature at Yale Divinity School, and spent a summer with Harper at the Chautauqua Institute in upper state New York.

Barnes followed Harper to Chicago and became one of the first divinity students at the University. While a student, he made acquaintances with Jane Addams and eventually occupied a room at Hull House where he gained an appreciation for community action by concerned citizens.[7] By 1893, Barnes had entered city mission work as a minister, beginning at the Ewing Street Mission around the corner from Hull House. Two of his parishioners were Addams, and her colleague, Ellen Starr. A year later, Barnes moved to the Sedgwick Street Mission which included a settlement house. There he garnered his first newspaper headlines, when as the sanitary inspector for the 22nd ward, he was commended for his diligent efforts to keep the streets and allies clean. The young parson rode the allies every morning on horseback to check for any violations.

In 1896, Barnes began the Christ Chapel Mission under the auspices of the prestigious Fourth Presbyterian Church, through which he made the friendship of reaper manufacturer, Cyrus McCormick. By this point in his career, Barnes knew well how to assist the wealthy in fulfilling their philanthropic obligations. His ability to translate vision into organization earned him a favorable reputation among Chicago's elite.

A few years later, Barnes became an instructor in Social Science at the University of Chicago. Shortly thereafter the Harper protege was surprised by an offer from Illinois College to become its president. Whether Harper engineered the invitation is not known, but Barnes went with Harper's blessing. He inherited a debt-ridden college with aged faculty and a somewhat dispirited student body. Barnes proved to be an effective manager and an able recruiter of distinguished faculty. He also developed close friendships with several Chicago businessmen who were trustees of the College.[8]

Never one to stay too long in any one place, Barnes stepped down in 1904 to once again follow Harper, this time as the executive director of the fledgling Religious Education Association. The R.E.A. represented an ambitious dream of Harper's to bring together all educators, professional and lay, on behalf of moral and religious education which he viewed as fundamental to the future of American democracy.[9] The elements of this vision included the upgrading of Sunday school instruction to conform with modern pedagogical practices, the application of scientific methods in all forms of moral education and the popularization of scholarly biblical research among ordinary church people. The R.E.A. was deliberately modeled after the National Education Association and functioned initially within the orbit of Harper's constellation of university-related educational experiments.

Barnes had attended the first convention in 1903 (along with numerous leading figures of American Protestantism and of American education, including John Dewey) and identified with Harper's goal for "a federation of the educational leadership of

the religious forces."[10] By the time Barnes assumed leadership
of the Association, Harper was gravely ill but he maintained the
euphoric optimism that Harper had generated.

The R.E.A. aimed to focus attention on the religious
instinct that all young men shared (women were not considered in
the domain of the Association's calling). Said Barnes, the
R.E.A. would "bring young American manhood back to the ideals of
our forefathers."[11] Religious partisanship was not to be
tolerated. The Association would be "so broad every creed will
be able to join."[12] Barnes made sure there was a Jew and a
Catholic on the directorate though they remained tokens for many
years.

More interestingly, the R.E.A. enjoyed early support from
numerous businessmen who were active proponents of various
schemes of commercial, vocational, and character education.[13]
Barnes noted that the R.E.A. was "supported by businessmen who
are concerned about employees with good moral character and
religious convictions" who wanted to "install in Amercian
schools and colleges modern courses of study that will give
young men moral and religious training (that would) keep pace
with academic and commercial education."[14]

In his new position, Barnes travelled to Europe to
observe moral and religious training and to participate in an
"international inquiry into character-forming influences of
schools in various nations."[15] He returned convinced that the
United States had failed to systematically instruct its children

in the vital truths of religion and morality. One result of this failure was that students were not equipped to become "effective economic units."[16] European nations were far ahead of the U.S. in this regard.

The R.E.A. experiment did not work, however. Harper died in 1906, the Association accumulated huge debts (like other Harper projects) and Sunday school leaders were never attracted to the Association and its ideal of scientific religious pedagogy. The membership dwindled to a small band of professional educators, almost all of them liberal Protestants who were enamored with George Albert Coe's social theory of religious education that equated the Christian faith with the democratic ideal.[17] Barnes resigned in 1906 citing inadequate finances as the reason.

Though he was some steps removed from Coe, whose "democracy of God" notion emphasized social salvation rather than individual conversion to Christian faith, Barnes had given priority to the social utility of religion. For him, the Bible was not to be used for theological debates. Rather it was a foundation for the upbuilding of righteousness in the nation. The basis for cooperation in an agency like the R.E.A. was the "moral efficiency" of the Bible.[18] In later years, he would continue to articulate the linkage of religion and morality and the importance of religion in the public arena for the mainte- nance of civic vitality.

Barnes' Battles for Civic Righteousness

Barnes was hardly deterred by his short-lived involvement with the R.E.A. In fact, he embarked on the most significant period of his career in which he began to implement his own plans for the moral and religious betterment of Chicago.

The first opportunity came when he was asked in 1907 to take over the Legislative Voters' League, a watchdog organization that scrutinized legislation in Springfield and labored for reformist legislators. The League had been founded by Club trustee George E. Cole in 1901 as an offshoot of the relatively successful Municipal Voters' League in Chicago, which under Cole's autocratic leadership had eliminated a host of boodlers on the City Council during the late 1890s. The battle against political corruption moved to the state level where street railway legislation offered countless opportunities for graft. By 1903, the League was promoting its preferred candidates for election, often on the front pages of several city newspapers.

Barnes became involved when the League established its own bureau in Springfield to lobby against "unwise legislation."[19] He led the League's fight in 1910 for a direct primary law that passed but proved disappointing in its ability to keep corrupt officials out of government.[20] In the tangled web of municipal and state politics, it was difficult for the "millionaire reformers and uplifters" like Barnes to escape the charge of hypocrisy and the impression of representing corporation interests, despite their claims to be non-partisan, ordinary citizens whose sole concern was clean government. Eventually, the reformers found themselves playing politics in the same manner as their opponents. Barnes' predecessor and friend, Cole, articulated this strategy of fighting fire with fire when he said, "God helps those who fight like the devil, and to hell with the libel suits. We'll make this fight with facts alone."[21]

Barnes himself slipped into political infighting when he participated in the protracted struggle to expel William Lorimer from the U.S. Senate.[22] The Lorimer affair began shortly after he was elected to the Senate in 1909 by a close vote in the state legislature. Evidence emerged that several representatives had received bribes to vote for Lorimer; an ensuing investigation was unable to link the acts of bribery to Lorimer himself. The odor of corruption remained but there was no convincing evidence.

Barnes kept the fight alive, when on behalf of the League, he presented a memorial to the U.S. Senate for a full investigation of Lorimer's election. For Barnes, the infamous Chicago Republican typified the greedy gang of scoundrels and thieves who dominated the political scene in Illinois. He went so far as to say, "Lorimer personifies unrighteousness to us as Roosevelt personifies righteousness."[23] Barnes' alternative was to encourage "good level headed business men" to become active in political affairs "for running a state is a big business."[24]

Those who were successful in the world of business seemed to possess a higher degree of morality and intelligence. As Barnes noted, "Isn't it time for common citizens to call a halt upon the all-prevalent practice of nominating men for legislature who couldn't pass a mental test for ditch digger?"[25]

That personification of righteousness, Theodore Roosevelt, came to the aid of Barnes' cause when he refused to attend a dinner in Chicago after he discovered that Lorimer planned to attend. Barnes, who belonged to the Commerce Association which hosted the dinner, was able to consult with Roosevelt privately. This snub of Lorimer reawakened public indignation and a Senate investigation was launched which in the long run led to Lorimer's removal from the Senate.[26]

Another investigation, this one in the state senate, began in early 1911 when Chicago lumber retailer, Edward Hines, was accused of setting up a jackpot fund out of which the Lorimer bribes were paid. Hines did not deny the existence of the fund but argued that he was following the normal practice of gathering corporate donations to support specific candidates. Lorimer himself had not solicited nor directed the use of these funds; he was only the fortunate recipient of their influence.

But by this time, Lorimer had become a national symbol of corrupt bossism and he was marked for elimination. Another U.S. Senate investigation followed and by the summer of 1912, Lorimer was expelled. The Republicans, whose party had been shattered by Roosevelt's departure to the Progressives the month before,

could not afford to have a figure like Lorimer around. The
Senators, whose money ties with corporate giants easily dwarfed
those of Lorimer's, were content to let him suffer the public's
wrath.

The defeat of Lorimer was a victory of "good men" over
the "gang" from Barnes' point of view. Character was what
distinguished the one from the other. But the determination of
character was made by political means. With every election, the
League published its list of approved candidates, all of whom
had voted properly or supported specific pieces of legislation
(e.g., direct primary law). One offended state senator asked for
a debate with Barnes because he had been rejected by the League.
The senator asked, "Do you approve of my record on the coal
miners' bill? Do you consider my vote making ten hours a legal
day's work for women progressive or otherwise?" Barnes
dismissed him as a "relic of the old combine."[27]

The forces of righteousness always had to be aggressive
in order to "get Chicago religiously right" as Barnes put it.[28]
The services of the Sunday Evening Club were but one example of
this. During this same period, Barnes and a small host of
businessmen and reformers engaged in a prolonged war against
vice, a battle that he eventually lost.

In 1911, he organized the Committee of Fifteen to "aid
public authorities in the enforcement of all laws against pan-
dering and to take measures calculated to suppress 'white slave'
traffic."[29] The Committee was a self-appointed group of

individuals whose real enemies turned out to be Mayor Carter
Harrison and the police department.[30] Prompted by what they
considered the "civic spirit" and great generosity in offering
their services free of charge, the Committee members took upon
themselves the task of investigating the notorious South Side
levee district and initiating prosecution of known violators.

Their greatest difficulty was that the public authorities
whom they wanted to aid did not want to be aided. Harrison took
a more pragmatic view of Chicago's vice districts: If they
could be contained in certain sections of the city away from
respectable neighborhoods, this was the best that could be
expected. Proponents of segregation played on the public's fears
by asking, "Would you like this class of vice in your
neighborhood?"[31] When some of the vice districts were closed
down, that "class of vice" did move into other neighborhoods
sparking greater support for segregation.

However, segregated vice districts had their problems and
these were the object of the Committee's attacks. First, the
districts tended to encourage corruption on the police force.
Redlight resort owners, in effect, purchased police protection
with appropriate pay-offs. Secondly, juvenile girls were prime
targets for recruitment by commercialized vice. The Committee
was partly mobilized by a national campaign to stop the white
slave traffic, an effort led by the American Vigilance
Association which its president, David Starr Jordan, called "the
biggest campaign against white slavery launched by business

interests."[32] A third factor in the war against vice districts
was the close tie of prostitution with liquor saloons. Many of
the violations which the Committee fought were over the
enforcement of closing hours for the sale of liquor.

As the local campaign gained momentum, Harrison and
Barnes soon locked horns. Harrison had little use for the
"puritanical narrow-mindedness" of the Protestant reformers.[33]
A nominal Catholic at best, he had built his political base on
the ethnic vote and showed a sincere appreciation for "old world
cultures." He also knew how to follow the political winds. "I
have tried to keep close to the trend of public opinion," he
said, "and whenever I thought I knew what the public wanted, I
have not hesitated to lead."[34] Barnes blasted Harrison for
protecting certain saloon-keepers and refusing to discipline the
police force. Repeatedly, the Committee published long lists of
saloons, dance halls and brothels that were in violation of city
ordinances. Harrison and the police responded sluggishly to
these exposes but closed down literally hundreds of places. The
Committee claimed full credit for this progress since it was
their hired detectives who uncovered the violations and their
lawyers who pressed the charges.

Yet the business community behind the anti-vice campaign
was not all of one mind on the suppression of vice. When Barnes
and his colleagues began to publish the names of the owners of
the property on which the illegal resorts were located, there
were a few surprises. Said one embarrassed landlord: "Good

people can't live in that neighborhood. The police are too careless."[35] Another owner, who happened to be a member of the Committee of Fifteen, promptly demolished his entire building when he was informed, "It was a place where white persons mixed with Negroes."[36]

For some Protestants, there were limits to such vice wars. Their primary concern was for the protection of their own neighborhoods more so than the moral purity of the entire city. William Blake, the superintendent of a relatively unknown Business Men's Morals Committee, clashed with Barnes over the extent of reform. Blake favored the re-opening of a levee district that Harrison had shut down and raised 10,000 signatures in support. He argued that in every large city, there will be a cesspool which served as "an outlet to clean up our residence districts."[37] In addition, he criticized the Committtee of Fifteen because so many of its members did not even reside in Cook County, including Barnes.

But for Barnes, there were larger issues at stake. The masses of immigrants needed the strong leadership of the native population who had been blessed with Christian principles. The criminal element that preyed upon the masses had to be stopped. Thus the war on vice became a battle for what was perceived to be truly American. Barnes had supported various Americanization projects on behalf of immigrants, but he also determined to fight "organized viciousness" with "organized righteousness."[38]

Barnes realized that police regulation could not

ultimately succeed on its own. On several occasions, he
travelled to New York and Washington for conferences on the
subject of social hygiene. A Bureau of Social Hygiene was
established funded by Rockefeller money; in early 1914, it
issued a report on vice conditions in Europe which advocated the
restoration of women involved in prostitution. Caught up in this
aura of scientific analysis, the Committee of Fifteen began to
view vice as a disease. S.P. Thrasher, the Committee's full-time
executive secretary, wrote that the main cause of commercialized
vice was "the underdeveloped mentality on the part of the
woman." He claimed that 85 per cent of the prostitutes were
"mentally subnormal." A second cause was the "overdeveloped
animalism on the part of the man."[39] To what degree these crude
observations shaped their strategy is not evident, but it seemed
to reflect a growing awareness that the "low life" element was
not about to disappear and that more long-range educational
efforts were necessary to save the city from moral decay.

In 1915, the reform element in Chicago was dealt a blow
when "Big Bill" Thompson was elected mayor. His flagrant
disregard of the clean government forces encouraged widespread
abuses and the return of vice conditions and its attendant
police corruption.[40] Though War issues diverted the energies of
reformers like Barnes, the zeal for crusading against vice and
liquor and for responsible alderman and legislators clearly
sagged after Thompson took over. By the 1920s, even the
prohibition laws were not carefully enforced and open gang

warfare had become the city's trademark.

World War I brought new opportunities for Barnes who had demonstrated superb organizational skills. He first chaired the War Recreation Board in Illinois and helped to set up club houses and entertainment for troops. Then he took a post with the American Red Cross in Greece. After the War, Barnes resumed his busy routine of managing a variety of agencies. He chaired the Chicago Community Trust, one of the largest trusts in the nation, that was begun by Club trustee, Norman W. Harris, who died in 1916. The trust distributed large sums of money to charitable organizations who could show their business-like methods of operation. Barnes was well-prepared for making these judgments for he also chaired the Association of Commerce's Subscription Investigating Committee which sorted out the honorable welfare organizations from the fraudulent ones. The list prepared by Barnes' committee became an almost essential endorsement for agencies seeking funds.

Barnes continued to be active with church-related organizations as well. In 1920, he chaired the local committee of the Interchurch World Movement, a highly ambitious ecumenical effort to raise vast sums of money for the cause of worldwide missions. Caught up in the excitement of the campaign, Barnes saw it as an opportunity to introduce "business-like methods of coordination, efficiency and economy in church activities."[41] The best advertising techniques were to be used not only to raise the funds but to mobilize churches for growth and the solution of social problems (much like Prohibition had supposedly solved the saloon problem).

In 1925, Barnes became president of the Church Federation of Chicago, a coalition of Protestant denominations whose goal was to "promote the application of the law of Christ in every relation of life."[42] Barnes' own interest continued to be with projects that stimulated moral and religious values. He saw the churches as the bulwark against spiritual decay, but they could only be effective to the degree that they cooperated with each other. Business efficiency and a spirit of good will combined to make interdenominational efforts a symbol of the modern church.

When Barnes died in 1944, he was remembered as one of those Protestant leaders whose personal religion was steeped in 19th century evangelical piety but whose public application of that faith bore all the marks of a 20th century businessman's creed.

The Club Trustees

The nature of this creed will become even more evident as one examines the Club trustees whom Barnes enlisted. The religious motivations of these individuals will be of particular interest for in them will be found glimpses of how religion and business interacted.

The original board of trustees in 1908 consisted of twenty-nine men: ten merchants, five lawyers, five manufacturers, two bankers, two publishers, a real estate

developer and an architect. Most were chief executives, senior
partners, or owners of the firms they represented. In the
ensuing years through 1920, an additional twenty-four trustees
were elected to replace those who resigned or died. The
occupational profile of these later trustees were similar to the
founders, though with a preponderance of railroad executives and
bankers. (See Appendix A for a biographical profile of the Club
trustees.)[43]

Commercial interests clearly preoccupied the attention of
the Club trustees. At least seventeen were active participants
in the Chicago Association of Commerce, a highly organized group
of business leaders who promoted the city's investment potential
and protected business interests from unfavorable government
regulation. Five trustees served terms as president of the
Association while quite a few others held committee posts. At
least eighteen of the Club trustees were members of the
Commercial Club, a private group of businessmen with grand
designs for the city's economic growth. Even more of the
trustees belonged to the Chicago Club, another men's club like
the Union League Club, which devoted itself to projects
considered beneficial to the city as a whole. In addition to
membership in these same private clubs, these trustees met each
other in the corporate board rooms of the city's banks. A
majority of them were directors for at least one bank or
financial institution. They formed an interlocking directorate
of corporate leaders who were capable of maintaining financial

stability in the city, not to mention preserving their positions of influence and power.

The vast majority of the trustees were over the age of fifty when they joined the Sunday Evening Club. The prestige and power of established wealth was theirs; the Club was only one of many avenues in which to apply their muscle for the good of Chicago. Few were directly involved in Chicago or Illinois politics, but most were very supportive of the municipal reform campaigns and lobbying efforts that people like Barnes initiated. On the national level, their administrative talents (if not their economic power) were eagerly sought after by various government bodies. Five received appointments under Taft, including two Cabinet posts (Jacob Dickinson as Secretary of War and Franklin MacVeagh as Secretary of the Treasury). Woodrow Wilson called upon a number of them to assist in the War effort. For example, Harry Wheeler and Bernard Eckhart served as federal food administrators while Thomas Donnelley held a position on the War Industries Board.

These trustees were a mixture of self-made and second-generation wealth. Men like Norman Harris, Henry Crowell, Edward Butler, Marvin Hughitt and George Reynolds were born in humble surroundings and earned their fortunes through years of hard work, loyalty to the firm, and frequently, the willingness to take calculated risks. Others inherited the wealth of their fathers and played key roles in transforming family businesses into corporate conglomerates (e.g., Cyrus McCormick, Charles

Hutchinson, Thomas Donnelley, John Farwell and A.W. Harris). Not surprisingly, all of them were Anglo-Saxons (except for two Jews who were of German origin). Eleven of them were Chicagoans by birth, thirty-one originated from the Northeast and Midwest; and six were foreign-born (Scotland, Canada and Western Europe).

Together they formed a generation of moguls for whom the creation of wealth was still an all-consuming passion. The city in which they worked so diligently, however, was also a domain for which they sensed a unique responsibility as stewards of its moral and cultural well-being. While many lived in suburban palaces, Chicago remained a prime object of their concern for in certain ways it belonged to them.

The cultural endeavors which the trustees sponsored gives evidence of this concern. The Art Institute was a favorite philanthropic project; Charles Hutchinson almost single-handedly amassed its outstanding collection of ancient and contemporary art during his 43 years as Institute president. Museums, world's fairs, libraries, hospitals, historical societies and city parks were also popular recipients of the trustees' benefaction; they gave their money and their names as directors or trustees. Most of the Club trustees were affiliated with at least several of these type of agencies.

Literary interests ran strong among the trustees, 60 per cent of whom were college-educated. About a dozen belonged to the Chicago Literary Club at which they gave speeches on occasion; another eight were part of the progressive Cliff

Dwellers where they interacted with leading Chicago authors
such as Hamlin Garland, Henry Fuller and Robert Herrick. At
least 23 were also trustees of colleges, often their alma
maters.

For most of the trustees, the moral landscape of Chicago
was as important, if not more, than the cultural one. Like
Barnes, they operated with a particular approach to the moral
uplift of Chicago: improve the individual and use religion to do
it. By religion, they often meant following the example of
Jesus. Said Barnes, "If the life of the Nazarene and his
teaching were lived today by all men, there would be no labor
and capital strife ...and less personal suffering and sorrow."[44]
Like politics, the marketplace needed good men, and good men
were those who acted like Jesus. The latter phrase was rarely
defined; the implicit assumption was that it involved such
things as caring for the individual person in need, courageously
speaking out against evil (and traditionalism within religious
circles), being honest in the face of hypocrisy, and treating
one's opponent gently or firmly as the situation required.

The tools available to harness this brand of muscular
Christianity were numerous. Such institutions as the Chicago
YMCA, the Chicago Relief and Aid Society, the Northwestern
University Settlement and United Charities benefited heavily
from the involvement of Club trustees. On the political front,
the Municipal Voters' League, the Committee of Fifteen, the
Chicago Civic Federation and the Citizens' Association

functioned as mechanisms for combatting evil (23 of the trustees worked directly with Barnes in some of these reform organizations).

Their willingness to be trustees of the Sunday Evening Club certainly indicated at least a mild religious interest. In fact, many were active laymen in their local congregations. By denominational affiliation, they were fairly typical of well-heeled white urban Protestantism. Twenty-six were Presbyterians; there were also eight Episcopalians, four Methodists, three Baptists, two Congregationalists, two Universalists and two Unitarians (One must be cautious about church membership data because it was not uncommon for the elite to belong to several churches simultaneously. In fact, some attended only sporadically; for them, it was sufficient to have rented a pew.) Several trustees belonged to independent churches like the popular Central Church that had started during the 1870s as a result of a theological battle among the Presbyterians. Two trustees were members of Sinai Temple where Emil Hirsch promulgated an extremely liberal brand of Judaism appreciated by many Protestants but few Orthodox Jews. Needless to say, there were no Catholics, no black or immigrant Protestants, no admitted agnostics nor members of any other minority sect or religion represented on the board.

Obviously, biographical data of this kind only hints at the perspectives, religious or otherwise, of the Club trustees (and it does not do justice to the unique characteristics of any

one individual in the group and the reasons he acted as he did).
To help overcome this limitation, some of the trustees should be
singled out and briefly examined as individuals with particular
points of view.

One of the most admired of all the trustees was Charles
Hutchinson, considered to be among the richest men in Chicago,
but also one of the most active elites on behalf of civic
betterment. He supported dozens of cultural organizations,
welfare agencies and educational institutions, and literally
gave away almost his entire fortune during his lifetime.

Hutchinson got his start at the Board of Trade where his
eccentric father, B.P. ("Old Hutch"), terrorized the Pit with
brazen attempts to corner the grain market. B.P. controlled
both the Corn Exchange Bank and the Chicago Packing and
Provision Company, and though he limited his son's education to
high school and started him out as an office clerk, the old man
paved the way for his son's career. By age 34, the younger
Hutchinson was president of the Board of Trade.

Undoubtedly, the Art Institute was Hutchinson's greatest
love. After the Chicago Academy of Fine Arts had been formed in
1879 and a permanent building raised in 1887, Hutchinson made
daily visits to the Museum in his role as president. He also
travelled abroad extensively greedily buying masterpieces which
he hoped would bring inspirations to the masses and prestige to
the city. (Hutchinson was one of many American millionaires who
according to one historian spent more money on art between 1880

and 1910 than had ever been spent by a similar group in Western history. Unfortunately, very little of that art was American.)[45] He also dabbled in postimpressionist and expressionist art helping to create a public stir in 1913 with an International Exposition of Modern Art. Art critics of his time were never sure if he was a man of iconoclastic tastes or of no taste at all.

Religion was no small factor in Hutchinson's career and thought. A devout Universalist, he served as a Sunday school superintendent for 25 years at St. Paul's Universalist Church. He was also president of the Universalist National Convention for four years (and served as trustee of the Universalist college in Galesburg, Illinois) often delivering major addresses on religious themes.

The key to Hutchinson's religious understanding was his rejection of creeds. "You must realize that Christianity is not a creed," he claimed. "Christianity is a life. It is a life of service and in it we cannot follow too closely the footsteps of the Master."[46] He did not deny the major tenets of Christianity but practiced a deliberate tolerance toward differing viewpoints about Christ and resented the comments of some conservative Protestants that he was not a Christian because of his Universalist ties.

Charles Holt, a lawyer and active member at Second Presbyterian Church until his death in 1918, exemplified a similar loyalty to his denomination which earned him the praise

of many in his church hierarchy. Holt pioneered the Presbyterian
Brotherhood, a loose national affiliation of Men's Societies
that had begun to emerge in Presbyterian churches in the 1880s
and 1890s.[47] The purpose of the Brotherhood was to promote a
spirit of loyal service to the church. Holt directed several
national conventions at which thousands of Presbyterian men and
clergy gathered to hear well-known speakers and engage in dialog
and mutual encouragement.

For Holt, "the church is a worthy place for the
investment of our life and influence in the service of
humanity." The church was especially a context for men because
it appealed to their "sense of the heroic" and it was a useful
"instrument for the adjustment of antagonisms." In the church,
claimed Holt, religion could be infused with the ethical and
philanthropic spirit. The ideals of righteousness could be put
into practice. Therefore, he pleaded for "individual loyalty to
the church from the inside and that we stop criticizing and go
to work."[48]

In 1911, the Brotherhood under Holt's leadership endorsed
the Men and Religion Forward Movement, an interdenominational
campaign to arouse men in urban churches to engage in evangelism
and social service. Holt noted that the dominant theme of the
Forward Movement was "More men in the Church and more efficiency
in the men."[49] Not only was this Movement a lay phenomenon; it
was a public relations campaign conducted by men who attempted
to apply the best of sales technology on behalf of the church.

What attracted Holt to "men's work" in the Presbyterian Church was the experience of belonging to a powerful movement. He likened his Brotherhood to a military campaign, the goal which was "the winning of the world, especially the men of the world, and loyalty to Jesus Christ and his Church." As he saw it, "the pathetic eagerness of men to be about something in their Church life and for Jesus Christ" could only be satisfied in a broad movement that transcended theological disputes between clergy and laity and emphasized "the great facts of eternal destiny, of sin, of forgiveness, of the love of our Elder Brother, revealing the greater love of our Father."[50]

Another layman of similar dedication was Henry Parsons Crowell, one of the founders and by 1901, president of Quaker Oats. Though a somewhat nominal church member in his earlier years, Crowell underwent a personal religious awakening at the age of 43 and became an ardent church leader.[51] He served as an elder at Fourth Presbyterian Church, strongly supported the Presbytery's Church Extension and Foreign Missions committees and added his name to a variety of evangelistic and municipal reform efforts. But he reserved the bulk of his energy and money for the Moody Bible Institute in Chicago over which he maintained a controlling influence for several decades.

Crowell's involvement with the Institute reveals a man who combined deep piety with tough business acumen. An admirer of D. L. Moody whom he never met, Crowell joined the Institute board in 1901 two years after Moody died. When he became board chairman in 1904, he engineered a change in the Institute's leadership and restructured the school along corporate lines. This involved a power struggle with some of Moody's handpicked successors but Crowell proved to be more than their match. He had long before learned how to maintain the competitive edge when he outmaneuvered opponents in the milling industry and gained control of the American Cereal Company, the holding company of Quaker Oats. Once in power, the "Godly autocrat" as his associates called him, ruled quietly but ruthlessly.

Moody's son-in-law, A. P. Fitt, became the Institute's administrator as Moody requested in his will. Fitt's ally was R. A. Torrey, another member of Moody's inner circle, who simultaneously pastored Moody's Chicago Avenue Church, functioned as Institute superintendent and conducted numerous evangelistic campaigns around the world. Both Fitt and Torrey preferred to rely upon the informal structure of the Moody subculture with its network of evangelists and pastors for support and sustenance. Their goal was quite simple: to teach lay people the Bible and equip them to be church workers.

Yet the financial pressure upon the Institute allowed Crowell to steer the school's direction. He enlarged the board from seven to fifteen trustees, almost all of them businessmen and professionals. He centralized administrative control in the hands of an executive committee composed of himself, Fitt, and the man whom he wanted to lead the Institute, James Gray. Crowell personally hired Gray at the rather astounding salary of

$5000. Torrey, more interested in evangelistic work, faded from the scene and by 1908, Fitt was gone as well.[52]

In the following years, Crowell and Gray guided the Institute's development according to a business model. Crowell's financial stewardship program brought long-term stability though he occasionally had to underwrite losses. The curriculum, though heavily Bible-centered, became more academic in its framework. Gradually, the school carved out its own constituency and geared itself to service its needs. Theological controversies were avoided as a rule and little effort was made to engage in dialog with those who were more accepting of Biblical criticism, such as Moody's own son, William.

One trustee who made a name for himself in several arenas was Edgar Bancroft. As an attorney, he won several major court battles on behalf of the railway companies he represented. He also spent thirteen years as general counsel for International Harvester. In 1919, he was asked by the governor of Illinois to chair the Chicago Commission on Race Relations established to investigate the cause of the race riots that erupted in Chicago the previous summer. The report which Bancroft and his colleagues produced in 1921 was likely the first serious analysis of the conditions of the black community in Chicago and the status of race relations. Its recommendations were directed to all the parties involved in the racial strife--whites, blacks, police, industry, newspapers--and appealed for greater cooperation and interaction between the races. While little changed after the riot, Bancroft's work on the Commission earned him the reputation as one of the more knowledgeable whites on the race question.

During the War years, Bancroft utilized his skills as an orator to stir up support for American involvement. He delivered a "Mission of America" speech at numerous patriotic affairs.[53] In it he outlined the essential elements of an American civil religion. The key to the American identity for Bancroft was "a matter of spirit and soul not a matter of a man's physical birthplace, national origin or creed."[54] By raising patriotism into a transcendent realm, he turned the Constitution into a sacred document and the naturalization ceremony into a sacrament of baptism. This glorification of the republic was not mere jingoism; Bancroft eschewed the use of force. "The animating theory of our government [is] that it embodies and expresses justice, rather than power."[55] Thus he was able to juxtapose autocracy and democracy as the two sides in the war. The spirit of America had to be preserved by winning the war. (Bancroft was not forthright about his religious affiliations; he may have nurtured a private faith or he may have simply found Americanism with its borrowed Protestant doctrines a more satisfying alternative.)

Probably the most prominent name among Chicago Protestants was McCormick. Not only was this family responsible for the presence of a major theological seminary in Chicago, but it controlled one of the largest manufacturing interests in the

Midwest, International Harvester. When the patriarch and reaper
inventor, Cyrus McCormick, died in 1884, his son, Cyrus, who was
still a college student at Princeton at the time, took over the
family firm. McCormick's wife, Nettie, who was 27 years his
junior, remained an influential figure in the family business
and personally directed the distribution of $8 million in
philanthropic gifts.[56]

Both the younger Cyrus and his mother remained loyal
Presbyterians and were somewhat sympathetic to McCormick's Old
School convictions. The seminary continued to be a major family
interest receiving sizable donations on regular occasions. The
faculty hired before the 1920s tended to be pious scholars who
showed a great willingness to assist the congregations in the
Presbytery. James G. K. McClure, who became the seminary's first
president in 1905, was one who avoided "controversial theology"
and who in the eyes of the trustees personified "the best of
modern Christianity."[57] This posture certainly pleased the
McCormicks who didn't mind a dose of "enlightened theology"
provided that the Presbyterian network stayed intact.

The McCormicks applied their wealth to a variety of
religious causes. The salaries of world travelers, John R. Mott
and Sherwood Eddy, both of whom represented the burgeoning
American missionary enterprise, were heavily underwritten by the
McCormicks. The International YMCA and Princeton University
also received large donations and the personal interest of Cyrus
and Nettie.

One Presbyterian businessman who published some of his
religious reflections was David Forgan, a Scottish-born banker,
who actually gained his reputation as a champion golfer. Forgan
grew up in a strict Scottish Presbyterian home and recalled
attending five religious services every Sunday. But he outgrew
his "child-like faith" in the simple "scheme of salvation" and
preferred a religion of inspiration that protected him from
"soul-shrivelling materialism." By 1925, he noted,

> It is years since I heard a minister in the pulpit refer to
> the fall of man, original sin, the pains of hell, a need of
> conversion in the old sense of an instantaneous change.
> What we get now are lectures and discussions in moral
> philosophy. I believe that the example and teachings of
> Jesus Christ applied to every experience of life is the best
> preaching. He taught little doctrine, except the Fatherhood
> of God and the brotherhood of man.58

True religion for Forgan combined reverence for God with
human determination, what he called "matters of Grip and
Grit."[59] He elevated the "bulldog traits of human nature" which
had served him well in his business career; human will power
brought into some kind of relationship with the "will of God"
was the key to success. Forgan's hero, Theodore Roosevelt, stood
"right with God" because he stood right with his home, his
community, his country and his world.

Forgan credited businessmen for the quality of urban life
observing that "any good work, whether it is charitable, civic,
religious, or anything else that is well done ... contains a few
successful business men who are not only supplying the funds but
have their hands on the management."[60] He was gratified that
the press and the pulpit were showing more respect for the

honorably successful businessman.

Another business family with firm religious convictions was the Farwells, a clan of New Englanders who became part of Chicago's early elite. John V. Farwell, Sr. established himself in the dry goods business and was a close associate of Moody, the shoe salesman-turned evangelist. The firm was eventually absorbed into the Sears, Roebuck Company though John Farwell, Jr. formed his own company. The younger Farwell was a major figure in the Chicago YMCA as his father had been.

The most notable member of the family was Farwell's cousin, Arthur Burrage Farwell, who helped launch both the Hyde Park Protective Association and the Law and Order League.[61] The initial impetus of these pressure groups was to campaign for local option laws turning certain residential sections of the city into prohibition districts and at the same time, to ensure the enforcement of existing regulations upon saloons. However, they were soon drawn into battles against corrupt aldermen, fraudulent voting practices, houses of prostitution, the "white slave traffic" and the intrusion of Negro populations into traditionally white neighborhoods. Arthur Farwell became a crusader for righteousness speaking in public schools "to impress upon the mind of children everything that makes for purity, industry and integrity."[62]

Like David Forgan, Andrew MacLeish grew up in Scotland in a sturdy religious environment; his family expected him to enter the ministry but he preferred business. He eventually became a partner in the dry goods firm of Carson, Pirie, Scott & Company handling its first retail store in Chicago. Before migrating to Chicago, MacLeish came under the influence of the famed preacher, Charles Spurgeon, and the early founders of the YMCA movement. These experiences nurtured his personal religious devotion and equipped him for the disciplined life of a church worker. He faithfully taught Bible classes in the several Baptist churches to which he belonged during his lifetime; he also served as president of the Chicago Baptist Social Union and vice-president of the American Baptist Foreign Missionary Society.[63]

Another giant in the corporate world of Chicago was Norman Wait Harris; he like many other Club trustees combined driving dedication to his work with deep piety. He was also a bold innovator, launching the sale of municipal bonds in Chicago in the 1880s that led to the formation of Harris Trust & Savings Bank, a powerful institution by the turn of the century. Harris' use of "missionary" representatives who acted as traveling salesmen for the bonds purchased by the firm was no small factor in his rise to prominence. When he died in 1916, he left his enormous wealth as a community trust to be distributed to approved philanthropies. (Barnes was one of the administrators of this trust.) Apparently, financial success did not diminish Harris' devotion to his Methodist church nor to the private spiritual life which he nurtured. His contributions were the lifeblood of the Methodist agencies in Chicago.[64]

Harris' son, A. W., continued in his father's footsteps, not only at the bank but also in the support of numerous organizations including the Sunday Evening Club. A.W. became a leader in the banking community in his own right when he established one of the first profit-sharing funds and also participated in the development of the Federal Reserve System.[65]

One other trustee deserves mention. Howard Van Doren Shaw, a leading architect whose clients included major business figures, articulated through his work a religious orientation that suited his clients admirably. An active member of the upper-crust Second Presbyterian Church, Shaw redesigned the church nave after a fire in 1900. He introduced free-standing angels and exquisite stained glass windows that reflected the European tastes of many Chicago elites.[66] He also designed the ornate chapel of Fourth Presbyterian Church and numerous homes of the newer aristocrats, like Adolphus Bartlett and Thomas Donnelley. His residential designs offered conservative appearances with gracious living space and elaborate gardens that usually required hired workers to maintain. Quite unlike his contemporary, Frank Lloyd Wright, who despised Eastern establishment standards and tried to create a Midwest prairie school of architecture, Shaw attempted no overt ideological statement through his work nor did he try to challenge the establishment in any way.[67] Shaw gave his clients what they wanted; he was a superb craftsman, but not a self-conscious intellectual. Shaw and Wright were friendly but didn't seem to understand one another. Shaw's religious inclinations moved along similar lines; a devout family man, he viewed his faith in terms of performing duties and holding positions within the corporate structure of the church.

Isolating a coherent set of beliefs peculiar to these men of the business and professional community may not be possible, but one can detect certain tendencies in their religious perspectives. As this study will attempt to show, these tendencies proved to be critical in the formation of the self-styled modern Christianity.

One emphasis was their preference for the practical in religion rather than the esoteric. Religion of any significance had to relate to the ordinary concerns of these laymen; this usually implied the ethical dimensions of Christianity, but it also suggested a religion that worked, that produced tangible results. Speaking at a R. E. A. convention in 1904, Nolan Best, editor of the Chicago-based Presbyterian journal, Interior (later named the Continent), pleaded, "Let us advocate practical things in our papers rather than retail much theory."[68] He deplored "the preponderance of the scholastic element" in the religious education field and called for "a great popular brotherhood of people loyal to the Bible and determined to exalt it as the law of mankind." He urged his fellow journalists to concentrate on reporting illustrations of how religion works.

Woodrow Wilson, who spoke on several occasions to Chicago business leaders and who was a close friend of the McCormick

family, gave frequent expression to a this-worldly faith rooted
in the moral actions of individuals. "Our Christian religion is
the most independent and robust of all religions," Wilson
claimed, "because it puts every man upon his own initiative and
responsibility."[69] In Christianity, men discovered the
underlying principles of moral action and a vision of a society
that could be achieved by selfless Christian leaders. Wilson
often depicted himself as orthodox in his faith, though
unorthodox in his understanding of the traditional doctrines of
the Christian faith. He was able, like many other laymen, to
distinguish between two modes of Christian thought, one that
operated within the walls of the church (and seminary) and one
that functioned outside the walls. Of course, his sympathies
were with the latter.

One obvious product of this pragmatic bias was the keen
desire to apply notions of business efficiency to religious
activity. Best described a "Gospel of Efficiency" which
attempted to employ the insights of scientific management to
the church. He warned that running a church on business
principles was not as easy as it sounded, but it could be done
if a church determined to "increase decidedly the average output
from each individual worker."[70] This would require studying each
man's individual fitness, deciding what constituted a fair
product to expect and enforcing any rules and policies that
would be developed. Though some churches took up this challenge,
the agencies of the churches dominated as they were by laymen

were even more inclined to apply efficiency standards. Local
chapters of the Sunday School Association, the Christian
Endeavor Society and the Presbyterian Brotherhood did so with
great vigor. Typically, these efficiency campaigns led to
statistical analyses of an agency's work and to streamlined
administrative structures that centralized control in the hands
of a few individuals with professional credentials.

If the laymen gravitated toward those aspects of
Christian action that resembled their vocational experience,
they also selected elements more suited to their identity as
"men on the make" (a phrase popularized by Wilson). In other
words, they tended to describe modern Christian faith as
masculine rather than feminine. Ann Douglas in her The
Feminization of American Culture argues that through the 19th
century, Protestantism became associated with a feminine image,
particularly within more liberal churches. Like their women
parishioners, liberal clergy became purveyors of a
sentimentalized culture. They attempted "to achieve religious
ends through literary means."[71] Douglas further suggests that
the old virile religion, especially of the frontier variety,
gave way to dignified unassertive sentimentality that rendered
ministers, if not the church itself, irrelevant to many people.

By the early 20th century, this feminine image of
religion was clearly under attack. Active laymen portrayed vital
Christianity as distinctively masculine and inherently appealing
to successful men. Such a vision was the foundation of the

numerous male-oriented religious movements, such as the
Brotherhoods (by 1909, a dozen denominations had such
associations), the Laymen's Missionary Movement, the Laymen's
Evangelistic Council, the Men and Religion Forward Movement, and
the increasingly popular Men's Bible classes (that often doubled
as church baseball teams).[72] The concept of masculinity
utilized by these groups was rarely defined; usually, it was
linked with modern business practices, with hard work by
dedicated men, and with militant crusading on behalf of a
glorious cause.

The Chicago Presbyterian Brotherhood published its own
journal, Men At Work, for a period of years, and extolled the
masculine, virile qualities of the Christian religion. The
periodical beckoned Presbyterian men to respond to their "common
ancestry whose heroism in service to Christ" was their glory,
and with their masculine powers, to "get to work."[73] To further
inspire its readers, the editor included reviews of "masculine
religious books" especially written for "the life of a
red-blooded, hard-headed, all-around Christian man." [74]

Evangelistic work whether overseas or locally became a
domain of male lay leadership. "There is something heroic about
the task of missions," wrote William Ellis. "It is a job for
strong men. Missions thrill men, not only because of its innate
heroism and chivalry, but also because they are a mighty
enterprise on a sound reasonable basis." Promoting the Gospel
required the same skills as merchandising a product. Argued

Ellis, "The essential masculinity of missionary propoganda is
certain to impress every man who makes a first-hand study of it
in operation."[75]

Revival campaigns such as the ones led by Wilbur Chapman
and Billy Sunday were labelled as "businessmen's campaigns"
because of the direct involvement of prominent figures like
Crowell and the use of "businesslike methods" including
precisely-timed sermons and efficiently-conducted altar calls.[76]
Sunday himself did not hesitate to invoke a business image in
his revivals. "I am not only a preacher but a businessman," he
said. "I endeavor to bring system and organization, business
principles (and) common sense into revival work."[77]

These men hardly supplanted the hosts of women who filled
the ranks of loyal church workers, but they controlled the key
leadership positions of the religious agencies. While they did
not all oppose women's suffrage, they continued to relegate
women to other spheres of activity. "There is a womanly
instinct," opined the Continent in 1918, "which ordinarily makes
it impossible for a woman to think of property interest before a
human interest."[78] Any woman who might have possessed such a
property interest certainly would have found it difficult to
penetrate the exclusive men's clubs where business deals were
often made.

The thrust of this emphasis on masculine Christianity
tended to diminish the stature of the clergy. Though ministers
participated actively in the men's organizations, they did so

partly because they were men. Charles Holt viewed the
Brotherhood as transcending lay-clergy distinctions. Within the
church itself, ministers maintained a priestly status but they
were less able to transfer its authority into other realms.
Woodrow Wilson even went so far as to say that the ministry was
"the only profession which consists in being something" as
opposed to doing something.[79] Like Levites, ministers could
serve in their tabernacles but laymen carried the burden of
religion into the real world.

A third tendency in this businessmen's version of
religion was to be inclusive rather than narrow. Both in their
occupational pursuits and their civic affairs, they cooperated
with laymen from other denominations and developed close working
relationships; thus, they were less inclined to press
denominational distinctives. Club trustee Hutchinson was rather
typical in his distaste for religious quarrels and factionalism.
"We have assembled as the children of God and followers of the
Lord," he told the Universalist Convention. "It is not a time
for retrospection. It is not a time for useless discussion of
creed. It is the time for action."[80]

For most active laymen in this period, such ecumenism
rested on a commitment to Jesus Christ as the focal point of
their faith. In their minds, he was still the supernatural Son
of God as well as the teacher of the world's finest system of
morals and the exemplar of self-sacrificing service. Some, like
Holt and Crowell, spoke of maintaining personal communication

with Christ; others like Forgan, stressed the example of Jesus, even in such matters as church attendance.

The Club Speakers

These tendencies need to be explored within the larger framework of American Protestantism to be evaluated accurately. One way to accomplish this task is to examine the type of people these trustees invited to speak at the Club services and the religious outlook these speakers represented.

During the period from 1908 to 1920, a total of 209 persons were invited to address the crowds that met in Orchestra Hall (See Appendix B). More significantly, 101 of these speakers were asked to return; fourteen of them spoke more than ten times. Among these Club favorites were Baptist preacher Harry Emerson Fosdick, who by the 1920s was a national symbol of modernism in Protestant thought, Methodist bishops Francis McConnell and William McDowell, and Charles R. Brown, a Hebrew scholar from Newton Theological Seminary. Oratorical skill was clearly one of the major criteria by which these speakers were chosen. Not surprisingly, many of the nation's premier preachers appeared on the stage.[81]

A profile of the Club speakers shows them to be not only a representative cross-section of Anglo-American Protestantism but also a roster of notable opinion-makers in that community. About 55 per cent were ordained clergymen though only 65 speakers were church pastors at the time they spoke to the Club.

These clergy belonged to the five major denominations (22 Congregationalists, 21.Presbyterians, 19 Baptists, 13 Episcopalians, and 11 Methodists). There were also two leading figures of Reformed Judaism, Stephen Wise and Emil Hirsch, four Unitarians, two Universalists and three Salvation Army leaders. No Catholics were invited to speak during this period.

In addition to the clergy, many of whom were associated with leading theological seminaries and various religious agencies, there were many college presidents and professors. Politicians were also popular with the Club trustees; during this period, ten governors, several senators and congressmen, and various Cabinet officials made appearances. President William Howard Taft spoke in 1911. (Interestingly, neither Theodore Roosevelt nor Woodrow Wilson, both of whom were held in high esteem by the trustees, ever spoke to the Club.) Journalists, reformers and social welfare workers formed another contingent of speakers (e.g., Jacob Riis, Jane Addams, Sherwood Eddy).

Twenty-one speakers came from other countries, primarily the British Isles and Canada. About 20 per cent were Chicagoans, while the vast majority came from the northeastern United States. Only four women spoke, two of whom were connected with the Salvation Army; the only blacks invited were Booker T. Washington and his successor, R. R. Moton.

Typically, the brief homilies given by the Club speakers were filled with "state of the union" musings, inspirational

appeals to seek the greater welfare of American society, and
religious references that suggested the need for divine help.
During the earliest years, these messages were printed in their
entirety in Monday editions of the Tribune. Gradually, this
coverage gave way to brief news items on the more well-known
speakers until by 1920, only announcements of upcoming speakers
appeared on the religion pages of the leading news organs.
Interestingly, the Association of Commerce's weekly publication
often carried reviews of the Sunday evening messages throughout
this period.

While it would be difficult to construct the elements of
their ideology from the speakers' addresses (since most of them
were not preserved), one can sketch the parameters of a
religious and social vision that propelled these individuals.
Obviously, the trustees who approved the invitation of the
speakers did not agree with everything that was said on the
Orchestra Hall platform, but they did give tacit endorsement to
the legitimacy of the speakers' views and activities. One can
therefore assume at least a general convergence of views. The
speakers, in effect, served as articulate spokesmen for the type
of religious impact the trustees wished to make.

The predominant orientation of the speakers was toward
moral and social change in the urban environment of Chicago;
such change was aimed at the human condition in a fast-paced
industrialized world. Virtually all of them acknowledged that
religion could, indeed must, be a part of that change. The most

obvious example of this ameliorist brand of religion was the social gospel which had emerged during the latter part of the 19th century stressing an ethic of love and social justice. Some of the leading figures in the social gospel movement appeared at the Club including Walter Rauschenbush, Charles Sheldon (whose social gospel novel, In His Steps, was a national bestseller) and University of Chicago theologian, Shailer Mathews. Other speakers were directly related to current applications of social gospel doctrine, such as the Men and Religion Movement and the popular "institutional church."

Linked with the Protestant activists were speakers whose reputations were earned on the cutting edges of the social work field. Some had made names for themselves in the treatment of juvenile delinquents (e.g., Judge Ben Lindsey) and the education of inmates in state prisons (e.g., Chicagoan John L. Whitman). Several were pioneers of the settlement house approach to improving the conditions of immigrant neighborhoods (including the most famous, Jane Addams). Journalists with sensitive social consciences were also welcomed by the Club: people such as Jacob Riis, Henry George, Jr. (who carried on his father's crusade for a more equitable tax system) and Outlook editor, Hamilton Mabie.

More than half a dozen speakers had connections to various national and local movements on behalf of children. The National Child Labor Committee (Owen Lovejoy, Alexander McKelway), the kindergarten crusade and the Playground Association were the agents for this widespread concern to protect the welfare of children (in the case of immigrant children, this often translated into protection from their parents).

The religious convictions of these reformers varied from explicit theological reasons for social engagement (e.g., Labor Temple's Charles Steltzle) to social work as a type of personal religious quest (e.g., Addams).[82] None were hesitant to call upon the resources of religious communities to support them in their efforts. Many perceived themselves or were perceived by others as prophets awakening a lethargic church to a grand task of redeeming the world -- and potentially within their lifetimes.

If many of the speakers espoused a religion relevant to the urban masses, they also expressed a commitment to a modern, contemporary faith. They wanted their religion streamlined for 20th century man. This was certainly true of theologians and preachers identified with the so-called "modernism" in American Protestantism. Men like Harry Fosdick, Cornelius Woelfkin, Lyman Abbott, W. H. P. Faunce, Herbert Willett and Bishop William Lawrence were known for their liberal interpretations of the traditional Christian doctrines but also for their efforts to recreate a faith more suitable to skeptical, empiricist minds.[83] The Unitarians and Reformed rabbis who spoke moved along similar lines though they had less theological baggage to unload. While these modernists disturbed more conservative constituencies of Protestants, they rarely upset business leaders like the trustees who had already de-emphasized theological orthodoxy and taken their own steps to modernize the faith.

Only a handful of speakers represented the emerging Fundamentalist wing of Protestantism (Moody Church pastor, A. C. Dixon, Moody Bible Institute's James Gray and William Evans, Seattle pastor Mark Matthews, none of whom spoke more than once) but even they applied modern promotional techniques to evangelism and church work.[84] Though they clung to the historic interpretations, reinforced by a notion of biblical inerrancy, these Fundamentalists presented religion as a necessary ingredient for modern living. Perhaps the only speaker with Fundamentalist leanings who did not advocate modern dress for Protestant faith was William Jennings Bryan.[85]

Not surprisingly, the speakers that were drawn from the political arena were usually participants in Progressive projects, whether Republican or Democratic. Allies and friends of Roosevelt and Wilson were especially numerous: conservation advocates Gifford Pinchot and James Garfield, Progressive Party leaders Albert Beveridge and Henry Allen, and numerous League of Nations supporters. Almost all the governors who spoke were from the Middle West and were actively pressing their state legislatures for reform in such areas as railroad regulation, food processing, local option laws, and civil service reform. Several other speakers were operating on the municipal level and were able to inspire the Club trustees who had similar concerns (e.g., Brand Whitlock, Marion Shutter).

The intimate connections between religion and progressivism will be explored in more detail later, but as David Johnson notes, "it is difficult to discern when progressives were using religion or when they were guided by it."[86] For some, the traditional view that until an individual became a professing Christian, he or she could not be expected to sacrifice their own interests for the societal good, continued to be a strong conviction. Others were content with preserving a Christian influence and general acceptance of Christian moral standards.

Recent studies of the Progressive era have shown the prominent role of business in various reform movements.[87] Their interests were not so much to extend democracy and overthrow vested interests which the rhetoric of the period might suggest, but rather to extend their control over the urban, industrial environment and continue to shape it according to their values. Those who provided the rhetoric of the Progressive movements, such as the Club speakers, were by no means unwitting dupes of the business class but were in most cases willing partners. They looked to the muscle of their business friends to accomplish their goals and they believed that the superior intelligence of successful businessmen could only aid in resolving many social problems. Obviously, such an assertion must be made cautiously but the portrait of the Club speakers and trustees that follows will tend to support this conclusion.

The compatibility of the speakers with the trustees who

paid them to speak can be illustrated by the speakers' attitudes toward business. At least a dozen speakers were openly sympathetic to large-scale corporations. For example, two speakers worked directly for the Rockefeller Foundation and its General Education Board (Raymond Fosdick, George Vincent); Harry Garfield and Charles Thwing, both college presidents, were involved in the formation of the Cleveland Trust Company. Two academics, Jeremiah Jenks and Ernest Hopkins, were noted authorities on trusts and industrial management. Perhaps most notable of this group of speakers were Episcopalian bishop, William Lawrence, known as the "banker-bishop" (because of his good connections to corporate wealth in the Boston area) and Baptist preacher, Russell Conwell, whose famous "Acres of Diamonds" speech extolled the virtues of pursuing wealth.

On the other end of the spectrum, only a handful of speakers could be labelled in any way as critics of industry. Henry George, Jr. and Louis Post were advocates of sweeping land and tax reform that would have impacted business activities significantly, though not necessarily adversely. Both of them gained public respectability through their government positions but their ideas were never taken very seriously. As governor of Kansas, Henry Allen established a Court of Industrial Relations to arbitrate labor disputes. Only Charles Stelzle could boast that he had the respect of union leaders (no actual union representative was ever invited to aid in healing the divisions between capital and labor); several ministers who had converted

their churches into effective social service centers that
catered to the needs of the working class were welcomed by the
trustees.

If there was one interest that the speakers and trustees
shared in common, it was the desire for efficiency. Whether it
was the church, the corporation or the social environment, these
individuals were enamored with managerial effectiveness and the
maximum utililization of human resources. The speakers admired
the trustees as men who "got things done" while the trustees
supported speakers who articulated an efficient religion that
also "got things done."

The First World War expanded the agenda of concerns for
the trustees. The national debate over American entry into the
War between 1914 and 1917 was carried to the stage of Orchestra
Hall. Leading peace activists like Hamilton Holt, Theodore
Marburg and Jenkin Lloyd Jones were given the platform to plead
for neutrality (and later for Wilson's League), while pro-War
enthusiasts like Newell Hillis, Lyman Abbott and Carl Milliken
were invited to argue the cause of militant democracy. In the
final analysis, the majority of Protestants lined up in
patriotic support of the War effort, but for a time even the
Club trustees acknowledged that the international peace movement
did operate with some Christian principles. In fact, several of
the speakers journeyed with Henry Ford on his ill-fated peace
mission in 1915.

The most common response of Club speakers to the War was

to participate in International YMCA and Red Cross activities.
At least 20 of the speakers spent time in Europe during the War
with these two agencies. Some held administrative posts (like
Barnes), some preached to the troops, some worked in hospitals
and canteens and others assisted the devastated communities of
Belgium and France. Painful questions about the morality of the
War could be set aside by such altruistic action; the War was
simply a tragic reality that could not be stopped. The Christian
community had the opportunity and the obligation to relieve
human suffering and offer hope for better days ahead.

Ironically, the War itself was perceived by many speakers
as a vehicle for establishing civic righteousness on a
world-wide scale; winning the War was synonymous with ushering
in a new age of international cooperation where men would treat
each other with greater respect and dignity. It was only after
the War ended that these optimistic Protestants awoke to a far
less pleasant reality. The Kingdom of God on earth was still a
great distance away. All the societal ills that disturbed the
speakers and trustees were still around, often with greater
intensity. The grim persistance of these problems caused many of
them to sag with weariness and quietly leave the scene of
battle.

Finally, the speakers, like the trustees, were on the
front lines of educational change, particularly in the
bureaucratization of public school systems and the tailoring of
educational services to distinct segments of the population.

Several speakers were members of the Chicago Board of Education
which during this period attempted to centralize its
administrative apparatus and increase its control over school
curriculum and teacher appointments.

Many of the speakers were active in the R. E. A. where
they probably met Barnes and some of the trustees; the R. E. A.
like the Sunday Evening Club was a suitable forum for them to
articulate visions for injecting religious and moral values into
the public arena, including the public schools. Similarly,
numerous Club speakers travelled the Chautauqua circuit where
the Sunday school movement and the emerging field of adult
education made common cause. Even as late as 1920, it was not
uncommon for college presidents to circulate among the broader
constituency of educators, acting as benevolent overseers of the
religious and vocational training of the adult population. Quite
a few of the presidents who appeared at the Club were
responsible for expanding their colleges into universities and
extending the resources of their institutions to the community
at large (Stanford's David Starr Jordan, Brown's W. H. P.
Faunce, Vanderbilt's James Kirkland, Cornell's Jacob Schurman
and Western Reserve's Charles Thwing were a few of the more
notable ones).

Education, for the speakers and trustees, served
instrumental purposes. It was not an end in itself, nor was it
meant to be the same for everyone. Rather, educational agencies
of all types were to serve the public good. The public schools

trained future American citizens. Bible institutes trained
Christian workers. Seminaries trained the clergy. Colleges
trained the elite. Lay religious organizations trained laymen to
be more efficient.

Taken as a whole, the sentiments of the Club speakers
harmonized well with the interests of the trustees. While there
was certainly room for a diversity of viewpoints on the part of
the speakers, their fundamental religious orientation hardly
threatened the trustees; if anything, it helped to illumine and
reinforce the instincts of the trustees.

This overview of the different parties involved in the
Orchestra Hall meetings raises fascinating questions, not the
least of which is how an ideology, or a set of propositions,
which governs social behavior, is formed, articulated and
sustained. A more careful analysis of this process will follow
in a later chapter.

What can be said already is that in Chicago during the
early decades of this century, laymen were setting the terms for
the church's dialog with the world. They were determining the
aspects of the faith that were to be emphasized. They were in
fact leading their ministers in applying an updated religion to
a modern society.

NOTES

1. Steven P. Vitrano, An Hour of Good News (Chicago: Chicago Sunday Evening Club, 1974), p.10.

2. Biographical details of Clifford Barnes' life are found in his unpublished and unfinished Personal Reminiscences located in the Chicago Historical Society.

3. Chicago Tribune, 13 October 1930.

4. The founding trustees in 1908 included John G. Shedd, Charles L. Bartlett, Bernard A. Eckhart, J. Lewis Cochran, William C. Boyden, Charles L. Hutchinson, John T. Pirie, Jr., George E. Cole, Philip L. James, Eugene Buffington, A. C. Bartlett, Frank H. Armstrong, Richard C. Hall, Henry Parsons Crowell, Thomas E. Donnelley, William F. Hypes, John B. Lord, Howard Van Doren Shaw, Towner K. Webster, Abel Davis, Charles Alling, Lloyd Bowers, James H. Douglas, Norman W. Harris, Franklin MacVeagh, William P. Sidley and Norman Williams.

5. Vitrano, An Hour of Good News, p.14.

6. Home Herald, 18 November 1908. Another reporter added: "A number of businessmen have frequently admitted they consider support of the Club a good business investment producing in return a betterment of conditions and morals among their employees." The Saturday Times, 2 October 1909.

7. Barnes participated in the Hull House-sponsored Citizens' Club in the 19th Ward that unsuccessfully attempted to oust the notorious alderman, Johnny Powers.

8. Among these businessmen who served as trustees of Illinois College were A. C. Bartlett, Howard Van Doren Shaw, David Forgan and Henry Crowell. When he left in 1904, Barnes endowed a chair of Biblical literature with the sum of $25,000. See Charles H. Rammelkamp, Pioneer's Progress: Illinois College, 1829-1979 (Carbondale: Southern Illinois Press, 1979).

9. Stephen A. Schmidt, A History of the Religious

Education Association (Birmingham, Ala.: Religious Education Press, 1983), p.33.

10. Theodore Soares, "A History of the Religious Education Association," Religious Education 23 (1928), p.622.

11. Chicago Tribune, 3 January 1905.

12. Ibid.

13. See Peter A. Sola, "Plutocrats, Pedagogues and Plebes: Business Influences on Vocational and Extracurricular Activities in Chicago High Schools, 1889-1925" (Ph.D. dissertation, University of Illinois, 1972).

14. Chicago Tribune, 3 January 1905.

15. Clifford Barnes, Personal Reminiscences (unpublished). Clifford Barnes Papers, Chicago Historical Society.

16. Clifford Barnes, "The Public Schools as an Agency of Moral Training," (Unpublished speech delivered in 1907). Clifford Barnes Papers, Chicago Historical Society.

17. George A. Coe, A Social Theory of Religious Education (New York: Charles Scribner's Sons, 1917); George A. Coe, The Psychology of Religion (Chicago: University of Chicago Press, 1916).

18. Undated newspaper clipping announcing Barnes' appointment as general secretary of the Religious Education Association. Clifford Barnes Papers, Chicago Historical Society.

19. Chicago Daily News, 15 December 1906.

20. Chicago Tribune, 7 December 1910.

21. Quoted in Bruce Grant, Fight for a City: The Story of the Union League Club (Chicago: Rand McNally, 1955), p.145. See also Hoyt King's sympathetic but candid biography of Cole, Citizen Cole of Chicago (Chicago: Horders' Inc., 1931). For related studies of Cole and the Municipal Voters' League, see Joan S. Miller, "The Politics of Municipal Reform in Chicago during the Progressive Era: The Municipal Voters' League as a Test Case, 1896-1920" (M.A. thesis, Roosevelt University, 1966); Nick A. Komons, "Chicago 1893-1907: The Politics of Reform" (Ph.D. dissertation, George Washington University, 1961); Sydney I. Roberts, "The Municipal Voters' League and Chicago Boodlers," Journal of the Illinois State Historical Society 53:2 (Summer, 1960), pp.118-147.

22. Joel Tarr, "The Expulsion of Chicago's `Blond Boss' from the U.S. Senate" _Chicago History_ 2 (Fall 1972).

23. _Chicago Tribune_, 8 September 1910.

24. Ibid.

25. _Chicago Tribune_, 4 December 1913.

26. _Chicago Tribune_, 1 March 1911.

27. _Chicago Tribune_, 14 August 1912.

28. _Chicago Tribune_, 13 October 1930.

29. _Social Hygiene_, Volume 4 (1918).

30. Committee of Fifteen members included John G. Shedd, Henry P. Crowell, A. C. Bartlett, Julius Rosenwald and Jane Addams. For a biting critique of these vice wars by a contemporary observer, see Walter Lippman, _A Preface to Politics_ (Ann Arbor: University of Michigan Press, 1914), pp.97-123.

31. _Chicago Tribune_, 3 January 1913.

32. Mark Haller, "Civic Reformers and Police Leadership: Chicago, 1905-1935," in _Police in Urban Society_, ed. Harlan Hahn (Beverly Hills: Sage Publications, 1970), pp.39-55.

33. Carter Harrison, _Stormy Years_ (Indianapolis: Bobbs-Merrill, 1935), p.273.

34. _Chicago Tribune_, 29 July 1914.

35. _Chicago Record-Herald_, 14 June 1913.

36. _Chicago Tribune_, 23 February 1914.

37. Ibid.

38. S. P. Thrasher, "A Big City's War on Vice" (Article published in 1915 in local Kiwanis magazine). Clifford Barnes Papers, Chicago Historical Society.

39. Ibid.

40. Haller, "Civic Reformers," p.44.

41. _Chicago Tribune_, 17 April 1920.

42. _Church Federation Bulletin_ (Chicago), December, 1925.

43. Biographical data on the Club trustees is drawn primarily from the A. N. Marquis directories, The Book of Chicagoans, in its 1905, 1911, 1917, 1926 and 1936 editions. Several other studies of Chicago elites include data on some of the Club trustees. See for one example, Richard Jensen, "Metropolitan Elites in the Midwest, 1907-1929: A Study in Multivariate Collective Biography" in The Rich, the Well Born and the Powerful: Elites and Upper Classes in History , ed. Frederic C. Jaher (Urbana: University of Illinois Press, 1973), pp.285-303.

44. Chicago Tribune, 17 April 1920.

45. Thomas C. Cochran and William Miller, The Age of Enterprise: A Social History of Industrial America (New York: Harper & Row, 1961), p.257.

46. Unpublished collection of speeches by Charles L. Hutchinson, Charles L. Hutchinson Papers, Newberry Library, Chicago, Illinois. See also Thomas W. Goodspeed, University of Chicago Biographies, Volume 2 (Chicago: University of Chicago Press, 1924), pp.27-53; Ernest Cassara, Universalism in America: A Documentary History (Boston: Beacon Press, 1971), pp.5-6; Anne Felicia Cierpik, "History of the Art Institute of Chicago from its Incorporation on May 24, 1879 to the Death of Charles L. Hutchinson" (M. A. thesis, DePaul University, 1951); Vera L. Zolberg, "The Art Institute of Chicago: The Sociology of a Cultural Organization" (Ph.D. dissertation, University of Chicago, 1974).

47. Daniel W. Martin, "The United Presbyterian Church Policy on the Men's Movement - an Historical Survey" Journal of Presbyterian History 59:3 (Fall, 1981).

48. Charles S. Holt, "The Church and the Man" in Presbyterian Brotherhood: 1906 Convention Proceedings (Chicago: Presbyterian Brotherhood, 1907), pp.71-82.

49. Men at Work (Chicago), October, 1911. Published by the Chicago Presbytery.

50. Charles S. Holt, "The Scope and Significance of the Brotherhood Movement" in Men's National Missionary Congress (New York: Laymen's Missionary Movement, 1910), pp.562-565.

51. Richard E. Day, Breakfast Table Autocrat (Chicago: Moody Press, 1946), p.155. See also Arthur Marquette, Brands, Trademarks and Good Will: The Story of the Quaker Oats Company (New York: McGraw-Hill, 1967).

52. James A. Mathison, "The Moody Bible Institute: A Case Study in the Dilemmas of Institutionalization" (Ph.D.

dissertation, Northwestern University, 1979).

53. Edgar A. Bancroft, The Mission of America and other War-Time Speeches (Washington: n.p., 1927).

54. Ibid., p.11.

55. Ibid., p.16.

56. Charles O. Burgess, Nettie Fowler McCormick: Profile of an American Philanthropist (Madison: State Historical Society of Wisconsin, 1962); Stella V. Roderick, Nettie Fowler McCormick 1853-1923 (Rindge, N.J.: Richard R. Smith Publishing, 1956); Kathleen D. McCarthy, Noblesse Oblige: Charity and Cultural Philanthropy in Chicago, 1849-1929 (Chicago: University of Chicago Press, 1982).

57. James Gore King McClure, 1848-1932 (Chicago: McCormick Theological Seminary, 1932). Author unknown.

58. David R. Forgan, Sketches and Speeches (Chicago, n.p., 1925), p.24.

59. Ibid., p.99.

60. Commerce (Chicago), 28 May 1909.

61. John Clayton, "The Scourge of Sinners: Arthur Burrage Farwell," Chicago History 3:2 (Fall 1974). The Farwells were leading figures in the Chicago temperance movement. For helpful background to this phenomenon, see Perry Duis, The Saloon and the Public City: Chicago and Boston, 1880-1920 (Chicago: University of Chicago Press, 1975); Peter H. Odegaard, Pressure Politics: The Story of the Anti-Saloon League (New York: Columbia University Press, 1928); James H. Timberlake, Prohibition and the Progressive Movement, 1900-1920 (Cambridge: Harvard University Press, 1963).

62. Chicago Law and Order League, "Report of August 28, 1919." Chicago Historical Society.

63. Goodspeed, University of Chicago Biographies, Volume 2, pp. 55-76. See also Paul Gilbert and Charles Lee Bryson, Chicago and Its Makers (Chicago: Felix Mendelssohn Publishing, 1929), p.740.

64. Goodspeed, University of Chicago Biographies, Volume 2, pp. 125-154; A. W. Harris, Forty Years of Investment Banking 1882-1922 (Chicago: Harris Trust & Savings Bank, 1922), p.22.

65. A. W. Harris, The First Seventy-Five Years of the Harris Organization 1882-1957 (Chicago: Harris Trust & Savings

Bank, 1957).

66. Eine R. and Florence Fureh, The Second Presbyterian Church of Chicago: Art and Architecture (Chicago: Second Presbyterian Church, 1978).

67. Leonard Eaton, Two Chicago Architects and Their Clients (Boston: MIT Press, 1969).

68. Nolan Best,."The Relation of the Religious Press to Religious Education" in Proceedings of the Second Convention of the Religious Education Association, 1904 (Chicago: Religious Education Association, 1904), pp. 427.

69. Quoted in John Mulder, Woodrow Wilson: The Years of Preparation (Princeton: Princeton University Press, 1978), p.148.

70. Continent (Chicago), 6 July 1911.

71. Ann Douglas, The Feminization of American Culture (New York: Alfred A. Knopf, 1977), p.94.

72. William B. Patterson, Modern Church Brotherhoods (New York: Fleming Revell, 1911). See also George A. Salstrand, The Story of Stewardship (Grand Rapids: Baker Book House, 1956), pp.47-52; Robert Speer, The Stuff of Manhood (New York: Fleming Revell, 1917).

73. Men At Work (Chicago), May 1912.

74. Men At Work (Chicago), October 1912.

75. William T. Ellis, Men and Missions (Philadelphia: Westminster Press, 1910), pp.41, 43. See also James A. Patterson, "Robert E. Speer and the Crisis of the American Protestant Missionary Movement, 1920-1937" (Ph.D. dissertation, Princeton University, 1980).

76. Chicago Tribune, 17 October 1910.

77. Quoted in William McLoughlin, Modern Revivalism from Charles G. Finney to Billy Graham (New York: Ronald Press, 1959), p. 420.

78. Continent (Chicago), 7 March 1918.

79. Woodrow Wilson, The Minister and the Community (New York: Association Press, 1912). See also John Milton Cooper, Jr. The Warrior and the Poet (Cambridge: Belknap Press, 1983); Elwyn A. Smith, The Presbyterian Ministry in American Culture: A Study in Changing Concepts (Philadelphia: Westminster Press, 1967).

80. Charles L. Hutchinson, "Opening Address" delivered at the Universalist Convention in Buffalo, New York, 1901, Charles L. Hutchinson Papers, Newberry Library, Chicago, Illinois.

81. A Christian Century poll of Protestant clergy in 1924 listed the 25 outstanding preachers in America: Charles R. Brown, Henry Sloane Coffin, S. Parkes Cadman, Russell H. Conwell, Harry Emerson Fosdick, George A. Gordon, Charles W. Gilkey, Lynn A. Hough, Newell D. Hillis, Edwin H. Hughes, Charles E. Jefferson, Francis J. McConnell, William F. McDowell, William P. Merrill, G. Campbell Morgan, Mark A. Matthews, Joseph F. Newton, Merton S. Rice, Frederick F. Shannon, John T. Stone, William Sunday, Robert E. Speer, George W. Truett, Ernest F. Tittle, James I. Vance. Twenty of the 25 addressed the Sunday Evening Club.

82. Jane Addams, Twenty Years at Hull House (New York: Macmillan, 1935), pp. 113-128. For an excellent discussion of Addams' personal struggles, see Paul Violas, "Jane Addams and the New Liberalism," in Roots of Crisis, ed. Joel Spring (Chicago: Rand McNally, 1973).

83. By the 1920s, Fosdick was to become a national symbol of modernism in Protestant thought. See Robert Moat Miller, Harry Emerson Fosdick: Preacher, Pastor, Prophet (New York: Oxford University Press, 1985).

84. Helen C. Dixon, A. C. Dixon: A Romance of Preaching (New York: G. P. Putnam's Sons, 1931); William Runyon, ed., Dr. Gray at Moody Bible Institute (New York: Oxford University Press, 1935).

85. Lawrence W. Levine, Defender of the Faith, William Jennings Bryan: The Last Decade 1915-1925 (New York: Oxford University Press, 1965).

86. David W. Johnson, "The Social Significance of Religion in the Progressive Period" (Ph.D. dissertation, University of Kansas, 1972), p.3.

87. Michael McCarthy, "Businessmen and Professionals in Municipal Reform: The Chicago Experiment" (Ph.D. dissertation, Northwestern University, 1970) is a fine study of Chicago businessmen involved in reform efforts, many of whom were Club trustees. Stephen Diner in his A City and Its Universities (Chapel Hill: University of North Carolina Press, 1980) examines 181 men and women reformers in Chicago during the period of 1892-1919 (17 of whom were Club trustees) and notes that 33 per cent (53) were businessmen, 21 per cent (34) were lawyers, 14 per cent (23) were university professors, and 4 per cent (6) were clergymen. This predominance of business leaders also

appeared on the boards of trustees of both the University of Chicago and Northwestern University (44 per cent and 36 per cent respectively).

CHAPTER 2

MEN ON THE MAKE: DOING BUSINESS IN CHICAGO

Since one of the purposes of this study is to examine
the interaction between economic practice and religious faith, a
more thorough historical treatment of each of these factors is
essential before causal connections can be made. Having
introduced the trustees briefly in the previous chapter,
attention will now shift to the socio-economic context in which
they operated. Specifically, the industrial and political
conditions in Chicago during the first two decades of this
century need to be explored in order to locate the Club trustees
within the milieu which shaped them and which to some degree
they helped to shape.

One of the most obvious signs of growth in Chicago was
the continuing influx of new residents, both foreign immigrants
and native Americans moving to the city from farms and towns. By
1900, Chicago was the second largest city in the nation with 1.6
million inhabitants.[1] Even though the rate of population
increase had peaked in 1890, the city was still expanding by 25
per cent every decade (by 1920, the census showed 2.7 million

residents).

The native white population had been in the minority numerically almost since the city was founded though by the turn of the century, their ranks were growing with the addition of second and third generation immigrants. In 1910, 20 per cent of the Chicago population was native white with another 30 per cent who were native born with one or both parents of foreign extraction. Of course, this still left half the population foreign born. The black community in Chicago represented only two per cent of the population in 1910, but it was to double in size in each of the next two decades as southern blacks migrated to northern cities.[2]

There was an important change in the origin of foreign immigrants around the turn of the century. While the Germans, Irish, British and Scandanavians remained dominant among the city's ethnic groups by virtue of size and the benefit of several generations of assimilation, their numbers had stabilized with less of their own moving from the homelands and their deaths keeping pace with births. A noticeable increase developed in the flow of immigrants from East European territories, especially Russia, Lithuania, Yugoslavia, Austria, Hungary and Italy (the flow subsided dramatically in the 1920s with the passage of federal laws restricting immigration to quotas based upon 1890 ethnic percentages). These latter immigrants, unlike most from western Europe, tended to be impoverished, unaccustomed to urban, industrial life, devoutly

religious but adherents of Orthodox Judaism, Greek or Russian
Orthodoxy, 'Old World' forms of Catholicism rather than Western
forms of Protestantism or Catholicism. Steeped in more
traditional folkways and unfamiliar with the English language,
these immigrants retreated into neighborhood enclaves and
resisted efforts by native white leaders to "Americanize" them.[3]
The sheer numbers of this "foreign element" unnerved upper and
middle class Protestants who felt that their turf had been
invaded once again.

Paralleling Chicago's population growth during this
period were the collar counties, DuPage, Will and Lake, that
were beginning to evolve into suburban areas. In 1910, these
counties together were only one-twelfth the size of Chicago but
they too were growing at least 25 per cent per decade. With
urban rail systems and improved roads, it became more feasible
for well-to-do Chicagoans to work in the city and retreat to
quiet estates away from the congestion and squalor. A number of
Club trustees did not actually live in Chicago. The physical
distance of their homes from the city also tended to reduce the
concern of these individuals for the moral well-being of
Chicago.

What drew the immigrants to Chicago was among other
things the opportunity for work. The city's factories and shops
seemed to have an insatiable hunger for cheap foreign or black
labor, while the offices and stores offered plenty of jobs at
meager salaries for native white men and women. In 1920, 40 per

cent of the working population was employed in industry and manufacturing; clerical occupations were next with 17 per cent followed by trade and merchandising at 16 per cent. In that same year, in all the industries combined, 82 per cent of the persons involved were wage earners; another 16 per cent were salaried employees, and only two per cent were proprietors or firm members.[4]

Manufacturing

During the first two decades of the century, Chicago reached the zenith of its growth as an industrial center. Already well-established as the nation's transportation hub, grain and meat-packing capital and major money market (second only to New York), the city by the 1890s began to attain preeminence in numerous manufacturing sectors. Farm equipment, meat-packing, furniture, railroad cars, men's and women's clothing, shoes and other leather goods, foundry and machine-shop products, lumber products, electrical machinery and printing were the major industries in which Chicago ranked either first or second in total production among the nation's cities.[5] These were also the industries that employed the largest segment of Chicago's working force.

For example, in 1909, the leading employers were in these areas:

Industry	Establishments	Persons Employed
Men's Clothing	678	38,370
Foundry/machine shop	669	36,868

Printing/publishing	1395	33,439
Slaughtering/packing	67	27,147
Lumber/timber	195	11,680
Cars/general shop	22	11,562
Furniture/refrigerators	202	11,097
Steam-railroad cars	18	9,226
Bread/bakery products	1177	8,842
Iron/steel works	6	7,689

The total number of industrial establishments was roughly the same ten years later though the number of persons employed in industry grew only about 15 per cent. By comparison, the total number of persons employed in clerical occupations almost doubled during this same period from 120,000 to 210,000.[6]

Several patterns can be observed in this process of industrialization that occurred in Chicago. First, there was some consolidation of control among the larger corporations. Generally, these firms were owned by families with a patriarchal figure at the helm. For example, the McCormicks and the Deerings dominated the manufacture of agricultural implements for several decades after the Civil War, eventually merging into the International Harvester Company in 1902. The formation of the giant conglomerate, U.S. Steel, in 1901, included several Chicago iron and steel companies. Similarly, the so-called "Big Five" families (Armour, Swift, Morris, Cudahy, Schwartzchild & Sulzberger) controlled the meat-packing industry.

By the turn of the century, many of the patriarchs who had started the businesses were passing from the scene. In most cases, their children assumed control but the huge size and complexity of the corporations forced them to rely upon other executives to manage day-to-day affairs. Increasingly, these companies developed streamlined bureaucratic structures with separate departments handling specific functions (e.g., production, purchasing, accounting, marketing). This encouraged the creation of middle-level management positions, usually assigned to "bright young men" with good connections and leadership potential.

At the same time, these firms extended their control over the raw materials they needed for production and over the marketplace for the eventual sale of their products. Thus, on the one hand, they insured a reliable source of raw material (e.g., Illinois Steel's purchase of ore fields in northern Minnesota) and on the other, the effective distribution of their goods (e.g., McCormick's use of salaried sales representatives to provide "full service" to his customers).[7] More significantly, marketing departments gained greater prestige in the corporate structure as these firms found it necessary to "create" markets for their products and develop "customer loyalty" to sustain the business.[8]

While espousing the advantages of free enterprise, the individuals who headed these industrial firms left little to chance. They maintained a more than competitive edge by serving as bank directors (which guaranteed the large injections of capital for plant expansion) and directors of railroad companies (which often led to reduced rates for the transportation of raw materials or finished goods). Furthermore, these men invested much of their wealth into real estate holdings within the city limits and in other prime locations, thus paving the way for future expansion while enriching the value of their capital.

Several Club trustees were eminent figures in Chicago's industrial growth. Thomas Donnelley took over the printing firm started by his father upon the latter's death in 1889 while at the same time, continuing to serve as president of Lakeside Press. He also assisted his brother in the management of Reuben H. Donnelley Corporation which published the annual city directory. This local conglomerate under Donnelley's management established itself as one of the leading printers (and publishers) in the Midwest. Donnelley's unique contributions to the family business was his current knowledge of printing technology that propelled him to obtain 'state of the art' equipment, a dedication to efficiency schemes of management, the successful removal of union members from his company and the development of an apprentice school to train boys as future craftsmen.[9]

Eugene Buffington and John O'Leary were both established figures in Chicago's iron and steel industry. Buffington was president of Illinois Steel during the 1890s, then the largest steel-making corporation in the West. He participated in

engineering several mergers of steel companies with the likes
of John "Bet-a-Million" Gates, Judge Elbert Gary and J. Pierpont
Morgan that finally resulted in the formation of U.S. Steel.
Despite the efforts of executives like Buffington to convince
the public that U.S. Steel was not monopolizing the iron and
steel market, the corporation controlled two-thirds of the trade
among Steel Rail Association members. It also produced 60 per
cent of all structural steel products, 85 per cent of the
bridges, 60 per cent of wire and wire rods and 95 per cent of
wire nails. Buffington never made it into the public limelight
but he was assigned the task of developing Gary, Indiana, as the
major site of the new U.S. Steel plants.[10]

O'Leary, on the other hand, remained a local iron works
manufacturer (and banker) but functioned as a business statesman
of sorts. He was invited to represent industry in a national
conference called by Woodrow Wilson in 1919 to help settle the
nationwide steel strike. O'Leary's sentiments were undisguised;
speaking to a gathering of Chicago businessmen, he said,

> We must recognize that the steel strike is not an issue
> between Mr. Gary and Mr. Fitzpatrick; that the steel strike
> is not an issue between the Federation of Labor and the open
> shop, but is a clear-cut issue between democracy and
> syndicalism; a clear challenge ·to the government of which we
> are so proud, to give to the independent workmen the
> protection and support which he must have to overcome the
> self-styled militant minority.[11]

In the end, the steelmakers more than overwhelmed
organized labor adding to the widespread condition of "open
shop" in large-scale manufacturing.[12]

As president of Quaker Oats and the American Cereal

Company, Henry Crowell was an opportunist with all the instincts of a promoter. Like other entrepeneurs, he latched upon a promising technological innovation (in his case, steel-cut oats), packaged it in an attractive, consumer-oriented way (he chose the name "Quaker" because of its virtuous connotations), and vigorously advertised his product through innovative sales techniques (e.g., leaving free oatmeal samples at every doorstep in a city-wide campaign and conducting cooking schools in large grocery stores).[13]

Another Chicago industrialist, Bernard Eckhart, typified this breed of capitalists. He was simultaneously president of his own milling company and a Midwestern railroad company. He was also a director of the Harris Trust & Savings and the Chicago Title & Trust Company. Eckhart managed to find time for a variety of political involvements including a post on the Illinois State Railroad and Warehouse Commission (from 1907-1913). Though he was known by his associates as an unselfish, civic-minded individual, it is rather obvious that he was well-positioned to guard his business interests.

The success of these industrialists was due largely to the conditions for growth existing in the Midwest during the late 19th century; yet, certain individuals emerged into prominent roles because of their aggressiveness and diligence in finding better ways to satisfy their customers. The traditional description of entrepeneurship as the "doing of new things" has some validity. Men like Crowell, Donnelley and McCormick (who

introduced mass production techniques into his father's reaper
manufacturing firm) were looking for ways to expand their share
of the market, at least, during a certain period in their
careers. The pressure to hold down costs and preserve the
stability of the firm, not to mention the usual inertia of
bureaucratic operations, kept sweeping changes in check; but
even so, the dint of personality remained an important factor in
the growth of industry.

Merchandising

While sizable fortunes could be made in large-scale
manufacturing, there were other avenues that were equally
inviting. Merchandising was certainly one of them and Chicago
had its share of innovative merchants. Men like Potter Palmer,
John V. Farwell, Marshall Field, John Shedd, Julius Rosenwald
and Levi Leiter all acquired national reputations as retailers
of dry goods.[14] Each of them contributed in some way to the
cultivation of modern merchandising techniques: extravagant
display windows, mail-order catalogs, travelling salesmen, easy
credit, refunds, bargain basements, fashion clothing imported
from Europe, luxurious department stores that catered to
well-to-do women.

Retail sales were only part of the business for these
Chicago merchants; wholesale was equally profitable as the
stores bought and sold goods from New York and Europe and
distributed them to small country stores in the hinterlands.
Thus, it was not surprising to find these merchants investing

and overseeing railroads and banks. John Shedd, for example, was a director of the Illinois Central Railroad and the Illinois Trust & Savings (Shedd's predecessor, Marshall Field, had maintained a close personal friendship with George Pullman, who purchased all his interior decorating materials from Field). John Farwell, Jr. held positions with the Chicago Northwestern Railroad and the Chicago Trust Company. A. C. Bartlett, president of one of the larger wholesale hardware houses in the Midwest, had interests with several major banks and the Chicago & Alton Railroad. These affiliations were far from perfunctory for these men were directly involved in managing the affairs of these diverse corporations.

Transportation

By 1900, almost all of the national rail systems crisscrossing the nation had been built though peak mileage was not reached until 1916. By then, the glamorous era of corruption made famous by flamboyant railroad barons was long over. Moguls such as James Hill, Cornelius Vanderbilt, Edward Harriman and George Pullman had passed from the scene. In their wake, they left a cluster of bruised but still solidly entrenched railroad companies.[15] While financial control of the roads remained in New York, several major lines operated out of Chicago. The Chicago Northwestern was the largest and headed by two Club trustees, Marvin Hughitt (considered by his peers to be the dean of Chicago railroad men) and for a shorter time, William Gardner.[16] Two other trustees, Chauncey Keep and John Farwell,

were long-time directors of the Chicago Northwestern, while
Lloyd Bowers was general counsel for the road before being
appointed solicitor-general by William Taft. Club trustees were
also involved with the Atchison, Topeka & Sante Fe line, the
Illinois Central, the Wabash, the Chicago, Terre Haute &
Southeastern line and the Pennsylvania road.

Railroading was still the prime method of intercity
transportation for freight and passengers. Automobiles were far
from offering any serious competition; inadequate roads and
mechanical flaws kept them from being anything more than rich
men's toys. But the roads were almost constantly under attack
well before 1900 but even more so, after the turn of the
century. Labor unions butted their heads against the companies
to little avail. Numerous legislative efforts attempted to curb
rate increases and discriminatory treatment. Public resentment
toward them had been nourished by the none-too-rare scandals
involving stock manipulations, rebates to favored companies and
the perceived exploitation of public land donated to them by the
government for their own gain. (In fact, by the 1880s, railroads
had received title to more than 131 million acres of government
land; Illinois had more miles of track than any other state.)[17]

Yet they proved to be hardened combatants. The agency
established in 1887 to regulate the roads, the Interstate
Commerce Commission, was unable to compel them to comply with
its standards. Between 1887 and 1905, fifteen of the sixteen
litigation cases that reached the Supreme Court were decided in

favor of the roads. The Hepburn Act of 1906 and the Mann-Elkins
Act of 1910 gave the ICC more power but by then the roads were
already feeling the pinch of increased labor and fuel costs.
Profits were harder to come by; in 1916, several major lines
were in receivership. Their period of growth was coming to an
end.

However, urban transit systems were still a lucrative
business for the ambitious, but not too scrupulous, capitalist.
In Chicago, the construction of street car lines and the
elevated rail system unleashed a notorious effluence of
corruption involving discredited tycoons like Charles Yerkes and
Samuel Insull and hosts of aldermen and political bosses anxious
to benefit from the boodle. Since the City Council issued the
contracts to street car companies and financed the construction,
it was not surprising that bribes, pay-offs and even phony
companies to bid against the legitimate ones were regular
occurrences. Some of the Club trustees, usually bankers,
invested in these companies but did not take an active role with
them. Men like Shedd, Bartlett, Keep, Hutchinson and McCormick
were generally too conservative and morally sensitive to be
closely linked with the traction crowd.[18]

Banking

Undergirding the industrial and commercial power of the
Chicago elite were their financial institutions. The tie between
business and the banks was so intimate that they almost appeared
to be extensions of one another. Manufacturers, grain merchants

and meat packers owned large amounts of stock in various banks
(and in many instances, even serving as bank officers) and
helped stabilize the banks' credit during difficult times. The
same pattern held nationally. Of one hundred railroad
capitalists around the turn of the century, 69 were officers of
New England banks; these 69 individuals held 104 bank
directorships and 50 bank presidencies.[19] Bankers, on the other
hand, applied their financial resources to promising business
ventures and municipal projects, not to mention managing huge
estates on behalf of the wealthy.

Banking was a precarious business even in the best of
times. Disasters occurred almost regularly and bank failures
were not an uncommon event. Those institutions that survived
were usually led by conservative, unbending and sober bankers,
like George Reynolds of Continental and Commercial, David Forgan
of National City Bank and Solomon Smith of the Northern Trust.[20]
These Chicago bankers were never really in control of their own
destinies for Chicago's money market depended upon the New York
banks. Financiers like J. Pierpont Morgan controlled financial
reserves of such magnitude that he singlehandedly bailed out the
Federal Government on more than one occasion (critics at the
time were suspicious that Morgan had enriched himself at the
expense of aiding the Treasury department).[21] Brokerage firms
such as the one begun by Norman Harris were largely confined to
extending credit and selling bonds for municipal projects,
street railway construction and farm mortgages. Rarely during

this period prior to World War I did any institutions bring out a major securities issue. Corporate finance on the national scale continued to be based in New York.

Yet Chicago financiers exerted considerable influence not only on the local level but nationally as well. This influence became evident in the formation of the Federal Reserve System in 1913. The need for a more elastic currency and credit was generally acknowledged as a solution to the periodic panics that occurred during business downturns. Both Wall Street firms and local clearing house associations had served as stabilizers but both businessmen and bankers were anxious to have the power to expand their credit when the conditions warranted. A National Monetary Commission attempted to coordinate the flow of bank resources but its power was limited.[22]

Several Club trustees participated in the revamping of this loose structure into a bona fide national banking system. When Chicago was designated as one of the twelve Federal Reserve Bank locations, several of these same trustees joined its board of directors. Frederic Delano, a railroad executive, eventually became one of the Federal Reserve's Governors. One of the most vigorous supporters of the Federal Reserve was George Reynolds whose Continental and Commercial Bank was the largest in the city after its formation in 1910. He led other Chicago bankers in surrendering his bank's gold to the Federal Reserve. Reynolds' concept of banking was to service business endeavors, an attitude that propelled many others who helped form the

Federal Reserve. Interestingly, one of the first services that the System actually provided was to facilitate the funding of the War effort.

Like other products of the so-called Progressive era in American politics, the Federal Reserve System was viewed by many as a victory for the nation as a whole insuring people against financial collapse while bringing order to the complex world of high finance (and serving as a buffer against reckless speculators who gambled vast sums on the stock market). Yet at the same time, it was clearly a victory for the class of businessmen and bankers who profited from the backing of the Federal government.

Legal Profession

Just as the bankers greased the wheels of business, so the legal profession functioned as an important cog in the corporate apparatus. Attorneys provided business firms with several services: drafting legal documents for corporation ventures, analyzing impending municipal and state legislation for its impact on the firm and defending the company in court against suits. Often lawyers were in the employ of the company (particularly railroad companies and major manufacturers) rather than in private practice.

At the turn of the century, lawyers were still struggling to establish the credibility of their profession. Law school degrees from Harvard, Columbia and Northwestern had become commonplace among Chicago attorneys, but there were still many amateurs practicing as well. The Chicago Bar Association came into existence partly to weed out lawyers without the right credentials.[23] Club trustee Edgar Bancroft during his term as Association president in 1905 was responsible for stricter admissions standards and public exposure of "bogus attorneys." Eventually the Association was successful in obtaining legislation to forbid the "illegal" practice of law, a determination that was largely made by Association membership.

The Association also wrestled with the judiciary. Numerous judges were merely political appointees, often subject to the authority of ward bosses. Wanting to cultivate a more appropriate image befitting the judicial process, the lawyers in the Association entered the political arena on behalf of their preferred candidates. This usually meant doing battle with the local Republican and Democratic party machines.

Bancroft, who prosecuted the injunction suits against Eugene Debs' American Railway Union strikers in 1895 on behalf of the Sante Fe, observed that "the forces of industry and trade had made many lawyers" into "administrators and counselors" rather than what he termed "forensic fighters."[24]

Business Associations

One common concern shared by all of these businessmen, bankers and lawyers was to enhance the city's commercial potential. A primary means to accomplish this goal was the business association or club. The Chicago Association of

Commerce (CAC) was a prime example of this economic organization, one which the Club trustees actively supported. Built upon the vestiges of several predecessors, the Association was organized by some 90 merchants and manufacturers in 1904. In addition to its most obvious purpose of promoting and protecting their business interests, the founders vowed to work for "the enforcement of the constitutional guarantee of property rights and individual liberty" as well as to implement their "supreme respect for law and order."[25] The first president, John Shedd, may have had in mind some of the local teamsters' unions which were threatening to strike against firms like Marshall Field's. David Forgan, the second president, believed that "civic patriotism" was the driving force behind the Association, while another president, Richard Hall, claimed that business would prosper as the businessmen took upon themselves the responsibility to "promote good government, encourage education and art, improve sanitation, transportation and in general the various safeguards of life and property."[26] A. C. Bartlett stated, "This Association stands not only for the increase of commercial prosperity but for the moral and social uplift of the community."[27]

These statements by Association leaders (and Club leaders as well) point to a kind of "business ideology" in which the notions of public welfare merged with those of business welfare. "Whatever is right for Chicago is right for us," said Hall, probably meaning exactly the opposite.[28] Furthermore, the public good was not only defined in essentially capitalistic terms but it was viewed as the particular stewardship of business leaders. "It is one of the minor advantages of our association that we are discovering who the really able men of Chicago are," said Forgan. He added that in the Association there were "brains enough to make a cabinet."[29] Apparently, someone in Washington heard him because at least three Association members of this period ended up in the Cabinet.

Some of the clergy who addressed Association dinners reinforced this ideology. The Episcopal bishop of Chicago, Charles Anderson, claimed that "it would seem America's contribution (to humanity) must develop along the lines of commerce."[30] What was needed, however, was a "sound ethical basis" for commerce which could be attained by "personal integrity and enforced obedience to the law." University of Chicago religion professor, Herbert Willett, assured Association members that they were bringing to economic life "those higher moral impressions with reference not simply to the making of money, but to the making of citizenship, the making of civilization, for that is the very work your business men's organization can so admirably accomplish."[31]

The weekly gatherings of the Association allowed its several thousand members to hear speakers like these clergymen. The Association also encouraged public welfare projects, such as relief work for earthquake victims in San Francisco. Americanization classes were a special interest to Association

members who provided language instruction in their plants and
factories and pressured the school board to be more aggressive
about vocational training for immigrant children. Perhaps its
most far-reaching contribution was its evaluation of local
philanthropies through its Subscription Investigating Committee
led by Clifford Barnes for some years. The result was that
charitable giving by wealthy Protestants became subject to
expectations rooted in business values, not necessarily
religious or humane ones.

The standards set by the Subscription Investigating
Committee required a charitable institution to have a board of
managers, show an "efficient" use of its funds, cooperate with
other institutions not duplicating the work of others, and have
an annual audit. Implicit within these guidelines was an
assumption that philanthropic work could best be done
scientifically by trained experts through legally incorporated
organizations that utilized current management methodology.
Needless to say, the Committee's endorsements became essential
to the success of most philanthropies in ensuing years.[32]

The promotion of business, however, was still the primary
concern. The Association assigned its members to committees
(e.g., Banking and Finance, Metal Trades, Foods, Chemicals and
Drugs) for the purpose of assessing conditions, determining
possible courses of action, especially on the legislative front.
Though not a lobbying group per se, the Association in more
discrete ways made sure that its interests were protected. At

the same time, the Association sent delegations to other cities
and countries to encourage investment and trade with Chicago
firms. It was also an instrument in steering a large share of
"War business" into the Midwest.

Chicago businessmen did not organize only to promote
business and the "civic spirit." They also banded together to
resist the efforts of their workers to gain greater control of
the workplace. Past events in Chicago had convinced many
employers that unions were led by dangerous radicals who were a
grave threat to the social well-being and progress of the city.
The Haymarket riot in 1886 had shaken the elite as did the
Pullman strike seven years later; strikes in one industry or
another were common events in Chicago right up to World War I.[33]
As already indicated, many of the Club trustees had particularly
strong antagonisms toward all forms of unionism, refusing to
even negotiate with union leaders, and willing to resort to
strong-arm tactics to maintain control of their plants and
factories. Several of the cases warrant further examination.

As the vice-president of Marshall Field & Company (and
president after Field's death in 1906), John Shedd fought
several battles with teamster unions, most of which he won.[34]
Like Field, Shedd had a strong distaste for the closed shop and
helped form both the Illinois Manufacturers' Association in 1897
and the Chicago Employers' Association in 1902 to oppose it.
Both employer groups did little to hide their belligerent
attitude toward unions, hiring armed guards to protect plants,

importing Negro strike-breakers and employing their own private
police. The IMA eventually became a powerful lobby in
Springfield opposing minimum hours, factory safety and workmen's
compensation legislation.[35] At times, the anti-union sentiment
of IMA members (Club trustees Bernard Eckhart and John Wilder
served terms as presidents) bordered on paranoia; its full-time
director, John Glenn, adopted an "IMA--Right or Wrong" stance
and at one congressional hearing noted, "I don't see how labor
unions and the church can exist together. Anyone who thinks they
can doesn't know who Christ threw out of the Temple."[36]

The closed shop was in fact anathema to most Chicago
businessmen. Beyond simply wanting their workers to have the
choice of joining a union or not, these employers were convinced
that the majority of their workers had no real desire to join.
At least two Club trustees, John O'Leary and Thomas Donnelley,
were active in the Citizen's Committee to Enforce the Landis
Award, named after a legal decision favorable to the open shop.
The committee assumed the task of protecting men working under
open shop agreements. Several of the trustees, including
Donnelley, were powerful enough to eliminate closed shop
arrangements in their own companies. Between 1903 and 1907,
Donnelley successfully broke the bindery union, the compositors'
union and the pressmen's union, in each case continuing to keep
his plants in operation while strikes occurred, and hiring
workers back on an individual basis only. Some employers
resorted to "welfare unionism" whereby benefits of various kinds

(e.g., recreational facilities, Americanization classes, special
events for workers and their families, pensions, accident
benefits, and on occasion, profit sharing) were offered to the
workers, in this way hoping to compete with the unions.
McCormick was hailed for hiring a full-time female social
workers to do "betterment work" among the International
Harvestor employees (the woman, Gertrude Beeks, lasted less than
a year unable to persuade the company managers with whom she
worked that welfarism was necessary or helpful).[37] In the final
analysis, these industrialists abandoned these schemes and chose
to snub the unions while giving wage increases whenever the
pressure became too intense.

Chicago's Labor Movement

The labor movement in Chicago, though plagued by
countless failures due to internal bickering and ruthless
suppression by management, was nevertheless more indigenous to
the working class than most other institutions. The story of its
development helps to explain why it failed to undermine the
power of men like the Club trustees.

The older patterns of craft unionism which had catered to
skilled artisans became increasingly inadequate after the Civil
War, because the new face of industrialism had fundamentally
altered the nature of the workplace and created a permanent
wage-earning class. An early response to the disintegration of
communal work conditions was the Knights of Labor, which grew
dramatically in the early 1880s and declined just as rapidly in

the early 1890s. The Knights drew members from almost every part
of the work force (including women and blacks). In Illinois in
1884, the Knights had 52,000 members (together with the 61,000
trade union members, organized labor comprised 54 per cent of
the total state work force).[38] The thrust of the Knights'
activity was anti-monopolistic and anti-wage system; in reality,
it was a native American (with British emigrants providing
significant leadership) lower middle-class effort to. redirect
the nation toward a cooperative society in which workers exerted
a share of control.[39] Whether the upper classes realized it or
not, the Knights posed a direct challenge to the economic
arrangements and the class structure of American society. Its
liberal orientation was rooted in a Jeffersonian notion of a
small producer economy; in failing to appreciate the way in
which the class structure of industrial society had already
become embedded in public dialog, its reformist character was
never translated into concrete political strategy. However,
Knights president Terrence Powderly's lack of enthusiasm for
strike action undermined the Knights' strength at critical
moments; when the backlash of the Haymarket Affair set in, the
Order crumbled.[40]

At the same time as the reform unionism of the Knights
was prospering, a "pure-and-simple" unionism was developing with
the formation of the American Federation of Labor. Often called
business unionism, this pattern came to dominate the labor scene
by the end of the century giving each trade full autonomy to

pursue its own goals and fight for better wages, an eight-hour
day and other employee benefits. Implicit in this course of
action was an acceptance of the wage-labor system and an
unwillingness to organize among the unskilled, minorities and
any immigrant groups that threatened the status of a particular
trade. This was buttressed by a refusal to act politically. In
simple terms, the mainstream of American labor focused on narrow
job interests and never developed a political
self-consciousness.[41]

The Socialist movement was a constant feature of
organized labor but both the Knights and the AFL systematically
excluded political radicals from positions of influence.
Usually, this was done to give the unions a more respectable
image in the eyes of the upper classes. By the early 1900s, AFL
leaders like Samuel Gompers were active members of the National
Civic Federation together with leading industrialists; their
accomodation obtained material benefits for their members but
did little for the unorganized masses.

In Chicago, Thomas Morgan led the Chicago Trades and
Labor Assembly from 1875 until 1890 when he was toppled by more
self-serving unionists like William Pomeroy, who became
notorious for padding his pockets and acting as a dictator over
the city's labor force. Pure-and-simple unionism seemed to have
an affinity for corruption. John Fitzpatrick managed to gain
control of the organization in 1905, by then the Chicago
Federation of Labor, and successfully achieved workable

compromises among the unions, extended recognition to more of
the unorganized and tepidly supported a political involvement by
labor in city politics. The Building Trades unions were a
dominant force in the CFL; they were described as "wage earners
who accept industrial society as it is, who have personal and
community interests separated from those of a wage-earning class
as a class, who are opportunistic in their outlook and regard
organization as a device to improve wages and conditions here
and now."[42]

A decisive factor in shaping Chicago's labor movement
was the ethnic character of American working people.[43]
Ethnicity determined the choice of occupations (most trades were
dominated by a particular ethnic group), the degree of union
radicalism (some ethnics like German and East European Jews
brought socialist commitments with them and often formed
Socialist unions in which they conducted business in their
native tongues), and the relations between working people (the
prejudices of various immigrant groups always hampered
cooperative efforts and was one reason that AFL organizers
concentrated on bread-and-butter issues). Racism and sexism also
characterized much of organized labor's leadership; only when
recruiting blacks and women was necessary for survival did AFL
unions actively seek their membership. Many of the Socialist
parties were also guilty of discrimination against blacks, women
and unskilled workers. Only the International Workers of the
World practiced a policy of open membership to all workers.[44]

One byproduct of management's efforts to control labor in Chicago was the Fort Sheridan military base on the city's North Side. Following the Haymarket incident, members of the Commercial Club determined to provide property for a permanent garrison of Federal troops. Two Club trustees, A. C. Bartlett and Charles Hutchinson, and one other individual donated 600 acres of land on which Fort Sheridan was built.[45] The facilities were used to house the troops sent in by Grover Cleveland to crush the Pullman strikers.

Two decades later Fort Sheridan became the site of a "preparedness camp" for training businessmen and professionals in essential military skills. Called the Plattsburg idea or plan, this program was initiated on a national scale by General Leonard Wood and supervised by the American Legion organizations which he launched in 1916. Wood, who later commanded the National Guard troops that put an end to the 1919 steel strike in Gary and Chicago (and who was a Sunday Evening Club speaker during those events), had resigned from his military post partly in frustration over Woodrow Wilson's resistance to an enlarged peacetime army. With the active support of his intimate friend, Theodore Roosevelt, Wood gained War Department approval to establish several camps for "overage" volunteers who were required to pay their own expenses to attend. These camps, like Fort Sheridan, proved to be immensely popular among wealthy Republicans who shared Wood and Roosevelt's desire for an aggressive, even imperialistic, foreign policy, not to mention a

strong distaste for the peace movement; these men who grunted
and groaned through the "boot camp" experience may have also
nurtured "Rough Rider" dreams that were so fulfilling to Wood
and Roosevelt when they led a half-cocked civilian force into
Cuba in 1898.[46]

When the War finally came, Fort Sheridan was used
primarily as a hospital. Many of the "veterans" of the
preparedness camp also formed a military fraternity to raise
funds and obtain supplies for the troops overseas.

The Illinois National Guard was another type of alliance
between businessmen and the military establishment. Originally
formed in response to labor unrest in the decades after the
Civil War, National Guard units were eventually erected in every
state. Club trustee Abel Davis, a banker and state legislator,
was a general in the National Guard. In his report to the
Association of Commerce at its 20th anniversary, Davis noted
that the "Illinois National Guard has often been called upon to
prove its training, discipline and mettle, not on the
battlefield, but in sustaining and supporting civil law,
protecting life and safeguarding property."[47] The Association
showed a particular interest in the National Guard unit sta-
tioned in Chicago.

Black Community in Chicago

One segment of the Chicago working class was largely
ignored by elite Chicagoans until a race riot exploded bringing
the conditions of the "black belt" to the public attention. The

black community in Chicago had been generally neglected even by progressives, social gospellers and most politicians. Unlike many ethnic groups in Chicago, blacks were compelled to live in an entirely "separate world" produced primarily by white hostility.[48]

This discrimination and the rapid population growth during the War era combined to create a black ghetto on the South Side in which blacks established their own institutions and culture. Prior to the War, the black population had been relatively small. It had been fairly easy for white Chicagoans to treat the disenfranchisement and deplorable living conditions of blacks as a southern problem and ignore the 45,000 blacks in the city. However, between 1916 and 1920, 50,000 black migrants settled in Chicago as part of a mass exodus of southern blacks to northern cities. The Negro work force in Chicago climbed from 27,000 in 1910 to 70,000 by 1920.[49]

One of the immediate responses of whites to this sudden increase in the black population was to attempt to restrict blacks to certain neighborhoods. The Chicago Real Estate Board aided in this effort by trying to persuade black realtors not to sell in white neighborhoods and by attempting to get the City Council to block any further black immigration. An even more active group was the Hyde Park-Kenwood Property Owners' Association which vigorously protested any movement of blacks into their neighborhoods (some of the Club trustees had connections to this Association when its main agenda was anti-saloon campaigns).[50]

Racial tensions increased enormously and finally broke
loose in the summer of 1919. Clashes between whites and blacks
developed on several fronts. The event that triggered the five
days of violence (resulting in the deaths of 15 whites and 23
blacks) was the entrance of several young black teens on a beach
considered to be segregated for whites. But resentment had been
growing in the stockyards where blacks comprised 32 per cent of
the work force. Particularly galling to the white laborers was
the unwillingness of blacks to join the unions (which continued
to require segregated locals) thus giving employers significant
leverage against them. Blacks, on the other hand, confined to
severely overcrowded sections of the city, grew increasingly
restless about their housing conditions and inadequate schools.
Also, many Chicago blacks had fought in the War (including the
heroic, entirely black 8th Illinois regiment) and returned with
a distinct inclination to fight back against white aggression.
All of these factors converged to produce an environment of
suspicion and hostility; little was needed for bloodletting to
occur.

When the rioting subsided, members of the Association of
Commerce initiated a study of the causes of the riot. Its
ability to draw the significant leaders of the city together for
such a project was shown by the governor's appointment of a
Commission on Race Relations. Club trustee Edgar Bancroft became
the chairman of the interracial committee.[51] Association

members provided the financial backing for the Commission's work. The Commission's report did not appear until 1922 but it turned out to be a thorough study of all the issues with input from blacks and whites. Its recommendations boldly called for further integration, increased dialog among blacks and whites and a greater sense of responsibility for positive race relations to be shown by the police, the press, business leaders, school officials and the public at large. In the following years, little meaningful integration occurred. The pattern of segregated neighborhoods was permanently entrenched.

The formation of an institutional ghetto had proceeded through several phases. Before 1900, blacks interacted more directly with whites even though from a position of inferiority. Many blacks worked for whites, often in downtown businesses, or were professionals with some credentials; the leaders of the black community had regular contacts with white leaders. Men like John Jones, Daniel Hale Williams, Charles Bentley and James Madden had roots in the free Negro population of the North and endorsed the Reconstruction agenda of pressing for equal rights. This older elite were often critical of Booker T. Washington's accomodationist Tuskegee ideology and supported W. E. B. DuBois' Niagara convention in 1905. Locally, they resisted the establishment of separate black institutions, such as kindergartens or a YMCA center, considering any all-black organization as a compromise of political rights and the ideal of integration.

Between 1900 and 1915, increased pressure developed to
establish black institutions that would serve the black
community exclusively. Much of the pressure came from a younger
breed of black businessmen and professionals who saw more to
gain through separate black development. Jesse Binga, a black
realtor, opened his own bank and built tenement houses. The
Wabash Avenue YMCA was finally erected in 1913 to serve a black
clientele.

While some of these individuals were attracted to
Washington's emphasis on self-help and black economic
development, it would be a mistake to read the Washington-DuBois
debate into this shift.[52] Much of Washington's support rested
on his personal ties with key black leaders and clergy around
the nation, including many in Chicago, as well as his national
prestige and connection with the Federal government. The Chicago
black businessmen were more concerned about local growth. Issues
of racial solidarity and self-help were not critical to them as
political strategies. Not all of them were even altruistic and
concerned for the welfare of the black community; they were
often more interested in what they could get from the system for
themselves.[53]

Faced with a wide array of obstacles, the black community
tended to ally itself with whites on some occasions and to
withdraw from contact in others. In spite of strong suspicions
of organized labor among blacks, unionization of the black work
force made steady progress. By 1920, 12,000 blacks in Chicago

were union members   (about 18 per cent of the total number of
working persons).[54] The Jim Crowism entrenched in most of the
unions had been a constant obstacle and the AFL leadership had
done little to eradicate it; this worked to the favor of
employers who frequently hired black strikebreakers. The fact
that some Socialist unions, the I. W. W. in particular, were
deliberately integrated only served to alienate them from the
conservative mainstream of unionism.

Social service organizations also appeared within the
black community to deal with problems; some of these involved
cooperation with white liberals and philanthropists in the city.
The first civic institution created by blacks was Provident
Hospital in 1891; under black physician Daniel Williams'
leadership, it maintained an interracial medical staff and an
open door policy until World War I. When the Wabash Avenue YMCA
was built, the earlier resistance from integrationists like
Williams had subsided and the South Side Association building
received substantial gifts from white donors, especially from
Sears Roebuck's Julius Rosenwald. The white press hailed Wabash
Avenue as a model of self-help.[55] What it failed to perceive
was that the rise of self-help was directly linked to the rise
of discrimination.

The activity of the Colored Women's Clubs of Chicago
illustrates this same process. Operating with a similar program
as their white counterpart, these clubs sponsored educational
and welfare activities for children, working mothers, single

black girls who were recent migrants, the infirm elderly and dependent children. In many of these cases, black children were simply not accepted at state institutions and the women's organizations were compelled to fill in the gap.

Several settlement houses were begun after 1900. The Frederick Douglass Center, founded by Celia Woolley, a white woman, and her husband, a Unitarian minister, attempted to be an experiment in interracial unity. Complaints were frequently lodged against the center for neglecting pressing needs in the slum areas and for patronizing attitudes displayed by whites. In 1911, the Wendell Phillips Settlement was launched with Rosenwald money and utilized black social workers only. Institutional church work was also evident led by such ministers as Reverdy Ransom and Archibald Carey.[56]

Probably the most prominent social work agency during this period was the Chicago Urban League. Spawned by a successful New York operation, the Chicago branch began in 1915. The primary thrust of the coalition was to help black workers, male and female, find employment, to promote vocational training, to help improve housing conditions and to aid the crowds of migrants entering the city almost every day.[57] Social work experts from the University of Chicago, like Robert Park, Sophonisba Breckenridge and Edith Abbott, were in the forefront of League activities at the start, though they found it difficult to maintain the support of black leaders. Park, who was the first president, tended to look down on other black

welfare agencies as primitive and not scientific as the Urban
League was attempting to be with its departments of records and
urban research. The League oriented itself to the labor
requirements of the city believing that lack of skills was the
greatest hindrance to job opportunities and mobility for blacks.
After the War and the 1919 riot, the League gained increasing
support as it supplied workers for employers anxious to fight
unions and as it provided "sane" leadership in the black
community. As in the case of the NAACP chapter, the original
white leadership of the Urban League gave way to black control
and a decline in white financial support followed.[58]

Politically, Chicago's blacks had little control over the
public decisions that affected their lives. However, as their
numbers grew they became a voting bloc to be considered by
aldermen in South and West Side wards (all of whom were white
until Oscar DePriest was elected to the City Council in 1915).
Blacks traditionally voted heavily for Republican party
candidates and often in Chicago, gave their votes to
notoriously corrupt politicians, such as "Big Bill" Thompson,
much to the irritation of municipal reformers. What these
reformers failed to grasp was that from the black voters'
perspective, they stood to gain far more through favors from
party bosses than the benign neglect of white voters with a fe-
tish about clean government and honest politicians.

Municipal Reform

While the scions of business and industry in Chicago were

able to utilize their economic muscle against labor, they were
less able to control the city's political life. As already seen
in the activities of Clifford Barnes, victories were hard won
and easily lost again. Men like the Club trustees were able to
entertain Presidents but yet could be foiled by mayors or the
City Council.

Several factors about Chicago politics during this period
help to explain this relative lack of influence. First, Chicago
was governed by a patchwork of councils and boards that were
accountable to different authorities. For example, the mayor
appointed the Board of Education and Public Library board
members while the governor appointed persons to the three Park
boards. City, county and state governments overlapped each other
as well. Such municipal feudalism hindered the development of an
extensive power base by any one individual person or group.
Numerous efforts by both political and civic leaders to obtain
home rule powers for Chicago and streamline some of the
excessive structure always floundered in Springfield (if for no
other reason than that Downstate legislators were unwilling to
grant Chicago any power).

Charles Merriam, who pioneered the field of political
science at the University of Chicago and who was an active
municipal reformer, noted that behind this visible government
was an invisible one of reform groups, business associations,
special interest bodies and civic organizations through which
many citizens, especially the well-to-do, pursued their

political goals. The Union League Club, for example, where the Sunday Evening Club got its start, was a collection of reform-minded businessmen.[59] Both the Civic Federation and the Municipal Voters' League were launched by members of the Union League; later, in the 20s, Union Leaguers headed the Chicago Crime Commission and attempted to deal with the likes of Al Capone and the city's gang warfare.

Secondly, both the local Democratic and Republican parties were divided into several factions, all of them headed by power-hungry bosses without any particular political orientation other than to control a certain portion of the political booty. Native middle and upper class whites tended to find this kind of party politics distasteful. Merriam, who had many close friends among the business class, was also critical of them, noting:

> In Chicago, the Association of Commerce, the Commercial Club, the Commonwealth Club, the Chicago and Cook County Real Estate Boards, the Department Stores, the manufacturers, the bankers, the Industrial Club are strong factors. These groups are extremely powerful, but as a rule do not fully control and rarely assume complete responsibility for the conduct of the government. The business group dominates when it will, but it does not will to rule continually as a responsible class might commonly be presumed to do. The government is at its beck and call, but this class has not thus far been willing to assume unquestioned responsibility for the conduct of public affairs in the municipality. Commonly, it shifts direct responsibility to the "politicians," whom business men are always ready to denounce, but who are usually at their service when summoned. At the heart of the city problem, therefore, we have this anamolous situation, that the most powerful group does not govern. Power and responsibility are divided. Those who can rule, will not. Those who would rule, cannot.60

Third, the city's mayors tended to be individuals who could put together the right combination of party factions and appeal to enough ethnic groups to get into office. This usually required a pragmatic style of leadership. One mayor who mastered this technique was Carter Harrison II (who succeeded his father who had been assasinated in 1897; both father and son were elected to five terms), an opponent of both Merriam and Barnes. Harrison's attitude toward the vice problem ("I have never been afflicted with Puritan leanings, I have always recognized the apparent necessity of prostitution in such social organizations as have been so far perfected in this world of men") reflected a political realism that proved to be far more successful than the moralistic agenda of the Protestant reformers.[61] Even Merriam acknowledged in later years that Harrison was closer to the "spirit" of Chicago. In a somewhat less than empiricist tone, he observed,"The spirit of a city is made of traditions and aspirations, of interests and experiences, to which symbols and attitudes and types of behavior are adapted and incarnated in personalities."[62]

However, this did not mean that a personality who fell short of that "spirit" could not get elected. William Thompson, elected in 1915 and several terms after, was generally recognized as an unprincipled political boss. He ran on a 'wet' platform and allowed free reign to the vice districts which Barnes and the Committee of Fifteen had tried so hard to eliminate. He appointed incompetent individuals to major

positions on strictly political grounds. During the War, he
engaged in an ugly anti-British tirade (labelled "America First"
but which helped him gain the large German vote) even to the
point of censuring school textbooks that contained sympathetic
statements about Britain. For reformers like Barnes and Merriam,
Thompson was an embarrassment and a disgrace. But for many
blacks and ethnics, who voted for him overwhelmingly, Thompson
represented the real purpose of engaging in politics: to obtain
some share of the spoils.[63] Ironically, the reformers did not
recognize that they too operated by the same criteria, though
they cloaked their desires in the rhetoric of the "public good."

Urban reformers and the businessmen who supported them
also failed to appreciate the value of ward politics. They
viewed ward committeemen as greedy, corrupt politicians ruling
their tiny fiefdoms through graft and patronage. The selection
of candidates for office by ward bosses struck the reformers as
blatantly undemocratic and in violation of the will of the
majority. But ward bosses were more than politicians; they were
also agents of government who were able to obtain the necessary
city services (e.g., police protection, sanitation, water, gas,
coal) for loyal voters. They were in a position to "take care of
their own" providing jobs in the ward, protecting the ethnic
identity of the schools in the ward, permitting a workable
coexistence of necessary evils with close-knit family
neighborhoods. Not that ward bosses were such altruistic souls
but neither were they the preying wolves that reformers made

them out to be.

The story of municipal reform in Chicago is too complex to explore fully but some brief description of it will help to provide background. One fairly representative figure was Graham Taylor. As a recent arrival in Chicago just as the 1893 World's Columbian Exposition was going on display, Taylor soon discovered the underworld of squalor, poverty and unrest beneath the glamor and pageantry. Newly appointed to teach Christian sociology at Chicago Theological Seminary (the first such department at any institution), Taylor left the comforts of a New England Congregational pastorate to embark upon a pioneering work "devoted to the social interpretation and application of religion."[64] Like his colleague, Albion Small, hired to launch a sociology department at the University of Chicago, Taylor intended to combine careful analysis of social and industrial conditions based on a wealth of collected data and a moral commitment to the improvement of living conditions of the masses. Already inspired by the settlement movement in England, Taylor soon met Jane Addams and one year later, began his own settlement house, Chicago Commons.[65] Taylor became a prominent figure in Chicago reform circles; he was a prime mover in such groups as the Chicago Civic Federation, the Municipal Voters' League, the School of Civics and Philanthropy and the National Federation of Settlements.

Taylor abhorred class antagonisms. To him the class-conscious spirit was opposed to the democratic spirit. He

visualized himself as a neutral mediator between conflicting
segments of society. He felt keenly "the obligation to
understand, and make understood by others, the reasons and
issues causing industrial antagonisms" and respond to "the
trumpet call to refuse to be classified and to stand in between,
in order to keep in personal touch with some on both sides."[66]

In late 1893, Taylor participated in an extraordinary
gathering of Chicago citizens at Central Music Hall. Sponsored
by several trade unions, the meeting brought together people
from all strata ostensibly to face the social evils and effects
of the depression in the early 1890s. The special guest at this
event was William T. Stead, a British muckraking journalist and
Christian Socialist, who had come to Chicago to report the Fair
but remained to harangue the citizens of Chicago for their
tolerance of vice, corruption and poverty. Taylor considered
Stead a "Hebrew prophet" and welcomed his attack.[67] So did the
socialist Thomas Morgan who spoke after Stead and aroused the
audience when he blasted the upper classes for their oppression
of the working people and hinted that dynamite might be an
appropriate form of judgment. The recent, highly unpopular,
pardon of several Haymarket anarchists by the governor (one of
them was in fact present at the meeting) had revived memories of
the 1886 riot; Morgan's rhetoric touched some raw nerves. Taylor
spoke next and only with great difficulty was able to calm the
crowd, claiming that Morgan had said the right thing but in the
wrong way. The meeting concluded with a resolution to form a

civic federation. Notably, the mayor and members of the City
Council were not included.

Taylor was named to the executive of the new Chicago
Civic Federation and with several businessmen and reformers,
helped to create the wide range of services it adopted,
including charity relief, arbitration of labor strife, vigilante
constables to raid gambling houses, summer programs for children
and sanitation workers to clean up the streets. Several years
later, the Federation spawned the Municipal Voters' League, in
which Taylor and Club trustees Franklin MacVeagh and Edward
Butler were active, to specifically drive out the corrupt
politicians from city government (the League identified 57 of
the 68 aldermen as thieves). Composed of business and
professional men, this new political machine determined to fight
the ward bosses in the name of non-partisan civic-mindedness.[68]

The Pullman strike in 1894 was another influence on
Taylor. Not overly impressed with Pullman's paternalistic
control of his model town in which the workers were required to
live, Taylor was discouraged by the intensity of class-conscious
feeling. He resolved to "stand in-between, representing only the
public" and "keep in touch with both sides" in any social
dispute.[69] His settlement house was intended to be a community
center in which the bonds of social democracy would prevail over
inter-group conflicts, a place where different subcommunities
could make common cause for their welfare. This ideal carried
distinct religious overtones for Taylor; civic consciousness for

him was in effect, the Christian way of life.

Yet Taylor in his settlement work was not operating at
the cutting edge of municipal reform in Chicago. In many ways,
he represented a more liberal wing of urban progressives whose
primary concerns were humanizing an impersonal environment,
creating a sense of community in place of class divisions,
extending citizen participation in city affairs and aiding the
working classes. They were somewhat different from the group of
municipal reformers that Melvin Holli described as "structural
reformers" who consisted of the business elite dedicated to
rebuilding the machinery of city government along the lines of a
corporate management system.[70] Promoting city commissions and
city managers to bring efficiency to municipal structures, these
advocates of centralized bureaucratic power dominated the reform
organizations.[71]

The later history of the Civic Federation confirms this
argument. People like Jane Addams quit the Federation within
several years as did the few labor representatives. The leaders
of the Federation were clearly more interested in administrative
reforms rather than focussing on the social conditions of the
working class. By 1900, the primary activities of the Federation
were the city charter conventions, tax reform, changes in the
election laws (though it opposed the "initiative and referendum"
campaign which would have allowed direct participation by the
public in the legislative process) and the promotion of
efficiency in municipal government.[72] Through capitalist Julius

Rosenwald, the Federation was drawn into supporting the Chicago
Bureau of Public Efficiency which published reports on a wide
range of government matters and developed amendments and
proposals for both the city and state government.

The wide diversity of individuals and agencies operating
in Chicago to cure urban ills was nevertheless impressive.
Taylor's network of associates included other settlement
workers, like Addams, Julia Lathrop and Mary McDowell; Merriam,
Mayor William Dever, Chicago Daily News publisher Victor Lawson
and manufacturer Charles Crane were also part of his circle. The
Chicago Women's Club led by hotel owner Potter Palmer's wife
took an active role in educational and recreational programs for
children and working girls. They sponsored such popular causes
as tutoring juvenile offenders, the kindergarten movement,
manual training in schools, the compulsory education law,
women's suffrage and child labor restrictions. The settlement
workers were rather effective in persuading upper class women of
Chicago to become active in social welfare programs; Addams and
the Abbott sisters took on the role of mediators between the
upper class and the working class.[73]

One would have to also include conservative Protestants
who operated rescue missions and various forms of welfare work.
The Salvation Army had made a noticeable impact by the 1890s.
Thieves, gamblers, drunkards and prostitutes were also "saved"
by such groups as the Volunteers of America, Pacific Garden
Mission and various homes for "fallen" women.[74] The city mission

movement was extensive enough to form a national association in 1906 and hold conventions.

Another innovation of reform-minded Protestants was the institutional church - a transformation of a city church into a social service center complete with recreational facilities, counseling services and educational programs. In Chicago by 1906, there were almost 25 institutional churches in the white denominations and several more in the black community. These did not differ much from the YMCA and the YWCA which by 1900 had downplayed their original evangelistic purpose and concentrated on the more earthly concerns of men and women.

Nor can the untiring efforts of the temperance societies be forgotten. The Anti-Saloon League had the support of 20,000 churches nationwide in 1905; the women's suffrage movement clearly benefitted from its association with the prohibition cause. In Chicago, the prohibition issue divided native Americans from the ethnics who formed their own pressure group in 1906 to keep the "drys" at bay. The prohibition movement gained the participation of a wide spectrum of progressives, not simply the religiously-inclined. As Paul Boyer argues, "the prohibition and anti-prostitution crusades touched countless Americans at a deep emotional level - a level where flourished profound apprehensions about the long-range implications of massive, unremitting urban growth."[75]

In his work, Boyer divides urban reformers along a continuum of negative to positive environmentalism. Holding a common commitment to developing a morally uplifting urban environment, and accepting the task of social control of the masses that seemed necessary to achieve this goal, these hosts of reform-minded people either adopted a coercive, moralistic approach (e.g., prohibitionists) or a strategy of benevolent social control through environmental change (e.g., creation of parks and playgrounds). The coercive strategy took a variety of shapes but it always assumed moral deficiencies and character flaws in those who were to be helped. Therefore, personal uplift of degraded persons could be attained by discriminate charity, proselytizing into the Protestant faith, "friendly visits" to immigrant families with helpful suggestions for child care, or a direct war on the perpetrators of urban evils - vice peddlars and "white slavers" (one settlement worker in 1910 called for the lynching of 1000 men in Chicago guilty of operating prostitution rings). When voluntary efforts of individuals and pressure groups could not achieve adequate results, many of these reformers turned to civic power and control of the political apparatus to gain dominance over the inferior classes.

The more subtle environmental approach assumed that better living conditions and a more aesthetically-pleasing cityscape would produce more responsible citizens. The bold new architecture of the World's Columbian Exposition site sparked an interest in architecture and city planning producing such grandiose schemes as the Chicago Plan. Pageantry and festivals were held to boost civic pride; professionals in city administration, if given the chance, would create a responsive, efficient government that would solve the problems of transportation, utilities and schools. Among other things, this notion implied an organic concept of human society in which individuality, at least for the common citizen, gave way to corporate planning by experts whose public devotion was taken for granted.[76]

The businessmen, bankers and lawyers who supported such groups as the Sunday Evening Club, however, cannot be easily located on such a spectrum. Some were more inclined to focus on the redemption of individuals, others gravitated toward improving the environment. The particulars of their religious faith may have been a factor in determining which way they leaned.

As pivotal figures in municipal reform, the settlement workers provided the statistics that gave social legislation its scientific hue; they also modeled the communal ideal in the midst of the city's lowliest slum dwellers and preserved the glow of moral fervor and reformist zeal.[77] Their youthful radicalism tended to distinguish them from other progressives. William Bliss' Encyclopedia of Social Reform in 1905 described over 300 of the most prominent settlement workers in the nation. The vast majority had strong religious affiliations. Over 90 per cent had attended college. Most were single, in their 20s, raised in native American and well-to-do homes. Many were anxious to do something useful with their lives that would benefit the wider society.[78]

Academics as Reformers

Another dimension of urban reform was the rise of academic interest in social life and improvement. Sociology as a discipline in American universities came into existence largely because of social reform activity, especially in relation to the settlements, city planning and the social gospel movement. Albion Small and Graham Taylor pioneered a "scientific" study of society at the University of Chicago. The city itself became the subject of this study and the reputation and influence of the Chicago School of sociology took root. Concern for the moral condition of urban life was a controlling feature of this discipline.[79] Small viewed sociology as moral philosophy conscious of its task; Taylor's early outlines on "Biblical sociology" reveal his hard work in carving out a new field of study.

None of this was incompatible with empirical research of which they, like the settlement workers, did a great deal. They were groping for the levers to run the urban organism efficiently and properly. It was a later generation of social workers that lost this sense of personal involvement and approached their science in a more or less professional manner.[80]

Economics also underwent a major transformation at the hands of reform-minded progressives. The classical interpretation of economic theory based on Adam Smith, Ricardo and Mill was challenged by a young breed of German-trained scholars led by Richard Ely. These rebels rejected the rigidity of natural laws and the laissez-faire approach to government involvement in regulating and stimulating the economy. They disavowed the atomistic and self-interest foundation of classical theory and urged the development of an industrial society that was communal in nature and which relied on participation in public affairs by both civil servants and the citizen at large.[81] This anti-monopolistic stance was a distinct feature of the new school of economic thought.

When Ely coordinated the formation of the American Economic Association in 1885, almost half of the original members were clergymen. Eventually, reform zeal waned (including that of Ely's) and more neutral scholarship prevailed. Ely himself contributed significantly to the collection of statistics for land and public utility economics, much of it under the aegis of Robert LaFollette, then governor of Wisconsin. Ely's students at Johns Hopkins and Wisconsin were perhaps even more illustrious as progressives: Edward A. Ross, John Commons, Woodrow Wilson and Frederick C. Howe.

Like other liberal progressives, Ely's conservative colors showed when his position was seriously challenged. His 1885 work, Recent American Socialism, was fairly sympathetic to working class concerns and advocated nationalization of natural resources. He also associated with a Christian Socialist group during the late 1880s. However, when his position at Wisconsin was threatened in 1894 by a state board of education member who considered Ely a dangerous radical, Ely retreated and loudly proclaimed his moderate stance. He won the celebrated case mainly because his less-than-radical ideas were all too obvious. In 1889, he had written, "I am a conservative rather than a radical, an aristocrat rather than a democrat. I believe in a natural aristocracy, which lives for the fulfillment of special service," and in 1894, "The eighteenth century doctrine of essential equality among men is, in my opinion, pernicious."[82] Following his victory, he became a bureaucratic progressive collecting data and giving counsel at the state and national levels for rationalizing government· (Ely ended his career at Northwestern University and throughout his life, participated actively in the Episcopal Church·)

Ely's withdrawal revealed a more fundamental weakness in the urban reform camp. For all their apparent concern for the masses, they had little personal contact with them and little inclination to meet immigrants, blacks, unionists and socialists as equals in any sense. The intellectuals, in particular, were genteel reformers and paternalistic in their social service. Ely once wrote:

> Consider a case like this: a man spends $1500 on an evening's entertainment to gratify vanity. What could have been done with the money? It could have been used to endow a permanent scholarship in the Hampton Normal and Agricultural Institute in Virginia. This is Christian and patriotic...for our American institutions depend upon the elevation of the ignorant masses. The training of the head and hand is essential for the development of the colored race.83

Their elitism reinforced by an intense desire to be respected as professional and scholarly, created a barrier between them and much of the urban population that was learning to cope on its own. Thus, both social workers and social scientists retreated from their earlier activism. As they did so, they found themselves fitting in comfortably with the business leaders who preferred a more bureaucratic approach to civic betterment.

Business and the Chicago Schools

Education was a frontier of reform in Chicago that attracted both progressive-minded thinkers and businessmen with ideas of their own. Their efforts at refashioning the curriculum of the public schools were typical of educational reform occurring in most other cities during this period. The classical liberal ideals of educating students to exercise their reason and to act in a morally responsible manner as free citizens had slowly given way to demands for using the schools to ensure social stability and prepare a pliable work force for an industrial economy. The advent of vocationalism in public schools marked the differentiation of the school curriculum and the sorting of students by socio-economic class to fit the social hierarchy (though disguised by the rhetoric of meritocratic ideals). To accomplish these social purposes, schooling systems became bureaucratized, staffed by professionals and experts in the technology of education, and empowered by state regulations to compel attendance and act on

behalf of the students' interests as defined by the new science
of educational psychology.

Much of this educational reform effort revolved around
the centralization of control over urban schools.[84] The
progressives who led the battles in the 1890s and the following
decades were university presidents (such as Charles Eliot,
William Rainey Harper, Andrew Draper, David Starr Jordan and
Nicholas Butler), a new breed of school superintendents with
managerial philosophies of school administration, and numerous
businessmen, professionals and social workers. Their agenda was
to abolish ward school boards, which in their judgment were
hopelessly inefficient, ill-equipped to determine educational
policy and mired in local politics. Their preference was for a
single city-wide school board, small in membership and
professional, not partisan, elected by the population at large
or appointed by the mayor. This streamlined board was to hire a
superintendent who could manage the entire system along the
lines of a chief executive officer. In Chicago, Harper chaired
an Educational Commission in 1899 that made many of these
recommendations. However, it was not until 1917 that the Chicago
school board was reduced to eleven members all appointed by the
mayor.

The opposition to these attempts to restructure the power
base of the schools came from several sources. Local ward
politicians and neighborhood leaders active in school affairs
responded to the direct challenge of the city's elite. For them,

decentralized system enabled them to control the hiring of
teachers and preserve the ethnic character of their schools;
many local board members, though not sophisticated in their
educational thinking, honestly believed in the primacy of
keeping the control of the schools close to the parents and the
local community. Union officials resisted the reformers as well
primarily because of the strong involvement of powerful business
people. The image of "non-partisanship" and "expertise" which
the reformers tried to portray did not deceive those who were
accustomed to doing battle with managers and executives.

The school teachers themselves were strongly opposed to
centralization of power. In Chicago, a powerful teachers' union
led by Margaret Haley represented a self-conscious body of
teachers motivated by a desire to be treated as professionals.
The Chicago Teachers' Federation proved to be a serious obstacle
to those anxious to reform the administrative structure of the
school system. The CTF gained national attention when it sued
several large corporations for failing to pay their school
taxes. This case only added to the public suspicion of
industrialists who were calling for school reform. The CTF also
joined the Chicago Federation of Labor in 1902 which provided
them with significant strength in negotiating for better
salaries and benefits, job security and participation in
decision-making processes. However, this association with
organized labor eventually became the focal point of bitter
battles with the school board during the War.[85]

Professionalization was a common response of teachers whose formal training in the state's normal schools and colleges of education was matched with more difficult teaching conditions, especially in urban schools. The classrooms in Chicago were seriously overcrowded and the majority of students were from foreign-born families (over 70 per cent in 1900). The Americanization impulse, in both its nativist and more humane forms, leaned heavily on these teachers to help immigrant children adopt a new language and culture. In choosing to press for more material rewards and respect for their status, the teachers abandoned the higher cause of questioning the validity of using schools to solve social problems. In effect, they accepted the same business model of schooling which the reformers and industrialists had. Even the rival Catholic parochial system absorbed much of the bureaucratic, instrumental philosophy of education.

However, a type of native pedagogy did emerge in Chicago during the late 19th century.[86] Francis Parker and John Dewey in particular, produced some innovative directions for education especially suited to the American urban environment.

Parker had acquired a national reputation as superintendent of schools in Quincy, Massachusetts, where he revamped the curriculum radically to accord with the "laws of the mind" which he derived from the knowledge of a child's development. Parker became the principal of the Cook County Normal School in Chicago in the mid-1880s where he refined his principles in a practice school for teacher trainees. Though an overbearing and patronizing administrator, Parker exhibited a genuine commitment to a child-centered curriculum and an ability to inspire teachers to the nobility of their mission.

Dewey and his wife, Evelyn, conducted a laboratory school as an adjunct to his department of philosophy, pedagogy and psychology at the University of Chicago. From 1896 to 1904, the Deweys developed a scientific analysis of human learning and articulated an educational theory appropriate for the schools. Dewey's Schools and Society talks in 1899 gave expression to his view of the school as an embryonic community, one in which a child learns to fit in and take responsibility for change of the larger society. For Dewey, the school would do for the child of the industrial age what the home and small town life had done for the child of the agrarian age.[87]

Numerous educators in the public school system and in private endeavors took Parker's and Dewey's ideas and experimented with them.

While these academics articulated their child-centered educational philosophies, the business leaders promoted their own "advances" in educational innovation. Vocational and commercial education experiments were by far the most popular. Manufacturers, like Donnelley and McCormick, created training schools within their factories. Others, like industrialist Richard Crane who summarized his own sentiments about schooling by stating, "Academic learning beyond the essentials of the grammar grades in public school is a waste of time and waste of money for the boy who is to enter commercial life," established a manual training high school that was eventually taken over by the school board (Crane was not representative of most capitalists in his hatred for higher education and his one-man campaign against any financial support of colleges and universities).[88] One Club trustee, Bernard Eckhart, was sent as a delegate by Taft to an International Congress on Commercial Education.

More direct influence upon the Chicago schools was always an option. A. C. Bartlett and Franklin MacVeagh served terms on the school board. The Association of Commerce also became an avenue for businessmen to exert pressure upon the school board to establish vocational and commercial education programs. John Shedd called for "the expansion of schools as academies of commerce" and to a degree, the Chicago school board responded to that challenge.[89] With Association funds, it created a vocational guidance office, a Commercial Club for high school students, Civic Industrial Clubs for students and teachers to meet personally with businessmen, and press clubs for student newspapers. All this was in addition to classes in commercial and vocational subjects; by 1914, the Association claimed success because one-third of all Chicago high school students were enrolled in day or evening commercial classes.

From the business point of view, vocational training was not only fair for the students who had no academic futures but

was also in the best interests of the city. Said one Illinois
Steel executive, "The menace of Socialism (which was imported by
immigrants) can be minimized by vocational training which will
increase intelligence and future earning power of our
children."[90]

Compared to Dewey and Parker, the businessmen may have
been more successful in achieving their agenda. As one
Association member put it, "Business is beginning to be taught
in the classroom."[91]

Conclusion

The preceding survey of Chicago's economic and political
life has revealed the extensive participation of Club trustees
in virtually every aspect of the city's development. They were
anything but isolated from the centers of power and
decision-making which affected the city's economic well-being
and cultural life. Residing comfortably in plush offices and
luxurious homes, these men feared few personal threats. They
were free to apply their power to the entire range of civic
problems, confident that they could make a difference. Their
occupational success, which they tended to think was the result
of hard work and self-discipline on their part, spurred them on
to fulfill public obligations (and religious ones as well) which
they felt belonged to them as the city's elite. Their
limitations were certainly not material; rather it was in their
perception of the world and in the religious explanations they
incorporated into that perception where they proved to be less

than adequate to the task.

NOTES

1. Thirteenth Census of the United States (1910): Abstract of the Census (Supplement for Illinois) (Washington: Government Printing Office, 1913), pp. 614, 619, 733-736.

2. Chicago Plan Commission, Population Facts for Planning Chicago (Chicago: Chicago Plan Commission, 1942).

3. Barbara Solomon, Ancestors and Immigrants: A Changing New England Tradition (Cambridge: Harvard University Press, 1956).

4. Ernest W. Burgess and Charles Newcomb, Census Data of the City of Chicago, 1920 (Chicago: University of Chicago Press, 1931).

5. Victor S. Clark, History of the Manufactures in the United States: 1893-1928, Volume 3 (New York: Peter Smith, 1949). See also Frederic C. Jaher, The Urban Establishment: Upper Strata in Boston, New York, Charleston, Chicago and Los Angeles (Urbana: University of Illinois Press, 1982), pp.454-539).

6. Burgess and Newcomb, Census Data, p.43.

7. David A. Hounshell, From the American System to Mass Production 1800-1932: The Development of Manufacturing Technology in the United States (Baltimore: Johns Hopkins Press, 1984), pp.153-187. For a more critical analysis, Harry Braverman, Labor and Monopoly Capital: The Degradation of Work in the Twentieth Century (New York: Monthly Review Press, 1974) and David F. Noble, Forces of Production: A Social History of Industrial Automation (New York: Alfred A. Knopf, 1984).

8. The larger impact of scientific management and the formation of large corporations will not be explored in this essay though it deserves at least a notation. See Richard J. Barber, The American Corporation (New York: E. P. Dutton Company, 1970); Reinhard Bendix, Work and Authority in Industry

(New York: Harper & Row, 1956); Thomas C. Cochran, Business in American Life A History (New York: McGraw-Hill, 1972).

9. Gaylord Donnelley, "Donnelley History 1864-1933," The Donnelley Printer (Winter, 1965), pp.29-32.

10. The Chicago Visitor 1:3 (March 1930), pp.14-15.

11. Commerce (Chicago), 4 October 1919.

12. See David Brody, Labor in Crisis: The Steel Strike of 1919 (Philadelphia: J. B. Lippincott, 1965) for a full account of the strike.

13. Arthur Marquette, Brands, Trademarks and Good Will: The Story of the Quaker Oats Company (New York: McGraw-Hill, 1967).

14. Lloyd Wendt, Give the Lady What She Wants (Chicago: Rand McNally, 1952) regales the exploits of Marshall Field, and his successor, John Shedd. See also Gordon Weil, Sears, Roebuck, U.S.A.: The Great American Catalog Store and How It Grew (Briarcliff Manor, N.Y.: Stein & Day, 1978).

15. John F. Stover, The Life and Decline of the American Railroad (New York: Oxford University Press, 1970), pp.57-88; Keith L. Bryant, History of the Atchison, Topeka & Sante Fe Railway (New York: Macmillan, 1974); John F. Stover, History of Illinois Central Railroad (New York: Macmillan, 1975).

16. Robert J. Casey and W. A. S. Douglas, Pioneer Railroad: The Story of the Chicago & Northwestern System (New York: McGraw-Hill, 1945), pp. 215-249.

17. Stover, American Railroad, p.60.

18. Forest McDonald, Insull (Chicago: University of Chicago Press, 1962) portrays the life of one of the traction barons in Chicago; Theodore Dreiser's The Titan (New York: John Lane Company, 1914) and The Financier (New York: A. L. Burt Company, 1916) offer a fictionalized biography (two of a three-part series) of the much despised Charles Yerkes.

19. Paul B. Trescott, Financing American Enterprise: The Story of Commercial Banking (New York: Harper & Row, 1963), p.128.

20. Andrew Russell, ed. Financing an Empire: History of Banking in Illinois, Volume 2 (Chicago: S. J. Clarke Publishing, 1926), pp.5-20; Arthur D. Welton, The Making of a Modern Bank (Chicago: Continental and Commercial Bank, 1923); Industrial Chicago: The Commercial Interests, Volume 4 (Chicago: Goodspeed

Publishing, 1894).

21. Morgan deserves more careful analysis than this essay
can afford. He has either been neglected or reified. George
Wheeler, Pierpont Morgan & Friends: The Anatomy of a Myth (New
York: Prentice-Hall, 1973) gives the most balanced treatment of
the New York banker. See also Jonathan Hughes, The Vital Few:
American Economic Progress and Its Protaganists (New York:
Oxford University Press, 1965), pp.399-439.

22. Benjamin Klebener, Commercial Banking in the United
States: A History (Hinsdale, Ill.: Dryden ˉˉ˞ess, 1974),
pp.103-110; Benjamin H. Beckhart, The Federal Reserve System
(New York: Columbia University Press, 1972); Andrew Russell, ed.
Financing an Empire: History of Banking in Illinois, Volume 1
(Chicago: S. J. Clarke Publishing, 1926), p.388; Ben B.
Seligman, The Potentates: Business and Businessmen in American
History (New York: Dial Press, 1971).

23. Herman Kogan, The First Century: The Chicago Bar
Association 1874-1974 (Chicago: Rand McNally, 1974); Industrial
Chicago: The Bench and the Bar, Volume 6 (Chicago: Goodspeed
Publishing, 1894).

24. Kogan, First Century, p.107.

25. Commerce (Chicago) 25:40 (December 1929), p.27. See
also J. Seymour Currey, Manufacturing and Wholesale Industries
of Chicago (Chicago: Thomas B. Poole, 1918), pp.403-408.

26. Commerce (Chicago), 5 June 1908.

27. Commerce (Chicago), 9 October 1908.

28. Commerce (Chicago), 5 June 1908.

29. Commerce (Chicago), 9 October 1908.

30. Commerce (Chicago), 11 December 1908.

31. Commerce (Chicago), 18 September 1908.

32. Chicago Association of Commerce and Industry, Survey
of Civic Development 1904-1925 (Chicago: CACI, 1925). See also
Louise Walker, "The Chicago Association of Commerce: Its History
and Policies" (Ph.D. dissertation, University of Chicago, 1941).

33. William J. Adelman, Haymarket Revisited (Chicago:
Illinois Labor History Society, 1976); Henry David, The History
of the Haymarket Affair (New York: Farrar & Rinehart, 1936);
Lewis Wheelock, "Urban Protestant Reactions to the Chicago
Haymarket Affair" (Ph.D. dissertation, University of Iowa,

1956); Stanley Buder, Pullman: An Experiment in Industrial Order and Community Planning 1880-1930 (New York: Oxford University Press, 1967); Ray Ginger, The Bending Cross: A Biography of Eugene Victor Debs (Brunswick: Rutgers University Press, 1949).

34. Robert W. Twyman, History of Marshall Field & Company (Philadelphia: University of Pennsylvania Press, 1954), p.166.

35. Alfred Kelly, "A History of the Illinois Manufacturing Association" (Ph.D. dissertation, University of Chicago, 1938).

36. Ibid., p.75.

37. Robert Ozanne, A Century of Labor-Management Relations (Madison: University of Wisconsin Press, 1972), pp.162-174. See also Richard Edwards, Contested Terrain: The Transformation of the Workplace in the 20th Century (New York: Basic Books, 1979), pp.93-105.

38. Eugene Staley, History of the Illinois State Federation of Labor (Chicago: Illinois State Federation of Labor, 1930), p.11.

39. Gerald N. Grob, Workers and Utopia: A Study of Ideational Conflict in the American Labor Movement 1865-1900 (Chicago: Northwestern University Press, 1961), p. 39.

40. Norman Ware, The Labor Movement in the U.S. 1860-1895 (New York: Appleton, 1929).

41. Barbara Newell, Chicago and the Labor Movement: Metropolitan Unionism in the 1930's (Urbana: University of Illinois Press, 1961); Thomas R. Brooks, Toil and Trouble: A History of American Labor (New York: Dial Press, 1964); Philip S. Foner, History of the Labor Movement in the U.S., Volume 2 (New York: International Publishing, 1955); David Brody, Workers in Industrial America: Essays on the Twentieth Century Struggle (New York: Oxford University Press, 1980).

42. Royal Montgomery, Industrial Relations in the Chicago Building Trades (Chicago: University of Chicago Press, 1927), p.2.

43. Some labor historians have argued that the continual influx of cheap immigrant labor kept the labor market unsettled and enabled employers to thwart union activism. Workers were unable to mount an effective battle against large corporate interests because they were too divided among themselves. Ethnic cultural interests always took priority over class interests. The relationship between these two, however, was more complex. The immigrants entering the industrial work force relied on

their cultural heritage to aid them in adjusting to a new
environment; for some immigrants, it was less hostile and
strange than for others. But at the same time, they were subject
to the economic pressures of the industrial system. Eventually,
ethnic preservation tended to give way to opportunities for
economic mobility, or at least, cultural identity adapted to fit
the new status. Where mobility was denied, cultural isolation
served useful purposes in providing meaning and acceptance
beyond the workplace. This suggests that each ethnic group had
its own process of adaptation and assimilation, in effect, its
own working class culture. Nor can each of them be treated as a
whole because intra-ethnic differences became significant (e.g.,
time of arrival in the United States, region of homeland from
which a person migrated, religious affiliation, dialect spoken).
Josef Barton emphasizes the need for dealing with multiple
levels of immigrant adjustment to American life. While they
cannot be posited as the sole determinants, cultural
distinctives are necessary in explaining the process of
adaptation to the American environment. Josef Barton, Peasants
and Strangers (Cambridge: Harvard University Press, 1975). See
also David Brody's superb entry on "Labor" in Harvard
Encyclopedia of American Ethnic Groups, ed. Stephan Thernstrom
(Cambridge: Belknap Press, 1980); John Higham, ed. Ethnic
Leadership in America (Baltimore: Johns Hopkins University
Press, 1978); Peter d' A. Jones and Melvin Holli, ed. Ethnic
Chicago (Grand Rapids: Eerdmans, 1981); Randall Miller and
Thomas Marzik, ed. Immigrants and Religion in Urban America
(Philadelphia: Temple University Press, 1977); Leonard
Dinnerstein and David Reimers, Ethnic Americans: A History of
Immigration and Assimilation (New York: Dodd, Mead & Company,
1975); Stephen Steinberg, The Ethnic Myth: Race, Ethnicity and
Class in America (New York: Atheneum, 1981).

44. Paul Brissenden, The I.W.W.: A Study of American
Syndicalism (New York: Russell & Russell, 1919); Patrick
Renshaw, The Wobblies: The Story of Syndicalism in the United
States (New York: Doubleday, 1967); Donald Winters, "The Soul of
Solidarity: The Relation Between the I.W.W. and American
Religion in the Progressive Era" (Ph.D. dissertation, University
of Minnesota, 1981).

45. Robert Schall, The History of Fort Sheridan, Illinois
(unpublished document dated January 1, 1944). Chicago Historical
Society.

46. For an excellent discussion of the preparedness
camps, see Jack C. Lane, Armed Progressive (San Rafael, Calif.:
Presidio Press, 1978).

47. Chicago Association of Commerce and Industry, Survey
of Civic Development 1904-1905 (Chicago: CACI, 1925), p.30.

48. Allan H. Spear, Black Chicago: The Making of a Negro Ghetto, 1890-1920 (Chicago: University of Chicago Press, 1967), p.94.

49. William M. Tuttle, Race Riot (New York: Atheneum, 1972), p.128. See also Julius Jacobson, ed. The Negro and the American Labor Movement (New York: Doubleday, 1968); Florete Henri, Black Migration Movement North 1900-1920 (New York: Doubleday, 1975).

50. Chicago Tribune, 17 February 1912, 15 March 1912. The Hyde Park Protective Association and the Law and Order League were both headed by Arthur B. Farwell; both organizations published tracts and documents on such topics as sexual hygiene, prohibition and fraudulent voting. In one of its tracts, the Association noted that "the worst enemies of the [black] race are bad men and women of color" and the "best friends are those individual members of the race who do the best possible work of their lives by faithfulness and promptness." Negro physicians and nurses were examples of the latter. Hyde Park Protective Association Papers, Chicago Historical Society.

51. Chicago Commission on Race Relations, The Negro in Chicago: A Study of Race Relations and a Race Riot in 1919 (Chicago: University of Chicago Press, 1922). One white interviewed by Commission researchers said, "I know but two persons who might speak with authority on the race question. They are Edgar A. Bancroft and Miss Mary McDowell" (p.460).

52. Louis R. Harlan, Booker T. Washington: The Wizard of Tuskegee, 1901-1915 (New York: Oxford University Press, 1983), pp.99-101; ; Donald F. Tingley, The Structuring of a State: The History of Illinois, 1899-1928 (Urbana: University of Illinois Press, 1980).

53. There has been a temptation among urban historians to divide prominent black leaders into conservatives and radicals, or conciliators and agitators. A philosophical position is usually staked out for both sides and linked to Washington or DuBois. Such a division tends to overlook many other reasons for particular actions or statements; it also ignores the fact that most blacks, leaders or not, would have agreed to both racial solidarity and integration without necessarily seeing any contradiction. August Meier's Negro Thought in America 1880-1915: Racial Ideologies in the Age of Booker T. Washington (Ann Arbor: University of Michigan Press, 1963) is a case in point. For a critique of Meier, see James D. Anderson, "History Through a Pantheon of Famous Black Men: Meier and Rudwick on the Black Experience," in Journal of Ethnic Studies 6:4 (Winter 1978), pp. 87-97.

54. Spear, <u>Black Chicago</u>, p.165.

55. Ibid., p.101.

56. Ibid., pp. 105-106. One agency in which there was virtually no white interference and which offered a vast array of social services was the church. The Baptists and Methodists were the controlling influence with the more prestigious congregations (e.g., Olivet Baptist, Quinn Chapel A.M.E., Bethel Church) attracting the well-to-do and emulating the activities of white congregations. Generally, the ministers of these churches refrained from any political involvement or bold social commentary. With the huge migration of the War years, and the consequent appearance of a black proletariat, the church scene became increasingly diversified. The newcomers, most of whom were from rural areas in the Gulf States where their religious experience had been more communal and uninhibited and always a source of consolation from the hardships of white hostility, simply did not find the denominational churches in Chicago attractive. The storefront church pattern of tiny congregations meeting in rented quarters, often led by unsalaried clergy (who were usually workers themselves), and encouraging feverish expression of religious emotion, was largely a product of the southern migration. They proliferated rapidly throughout the black sections of the city, and by 1930, they totalled 72 per cent of all black churches in Chicago. See Seth Scheiner, "The Negro Church and the Northern City, 1890-1930" in <u>Seven on Black: Reflections on the Negro Experience in America</u>, ed. William Shade (Philadelphia: Lippincott, 1969), pp. 92-117; E. Franklin Frazier, <u>The Negro Church in America</u> (New York: Schocken Books, 1963), pp. 52-71; Carter Woodson, <u>The History of the Negro Church</u> (Washington: Associated Publishers, 1921), pp.242-260; Arthur Paris, <u>Black Pentecostalism: Southern Religion in an Urban World</u> (Amherst: University of Massachusetts Press, 1982).

57. Arvarh Strickland, <u>History of the Chicago Urban League</u> (Urbana: University of Illinois Press, 1966).

58. Ibid., p.81.

59. The Union League Club was a bastion of municipal reformers, Roosevelt enthusiasts and "law and order" advocates. It even raised funds for a monument to the policemen killed in the Haymarket Riot. See <u>The Spirit of the Union League Club of Chicago 1879-1926</u> (Chicago: Union League Club, 1926); Bruce Grant, <u>Fight for a City: The Story of the Union League Club</u> (Chicago: Rand McNally, 1955); Emmott Dedmon, <u>A History of the Chicago Club</u> (Chicago: The Chicago Club, 1960).

60. Charles Merriam, <u>The Rise of Urban America</u> (New York: Arno Press, 1929), pp.109-110. For further discussion of Merriam

and his business associates in Chicago reform, see Barry D.
Karl, <u>Charles E. Merriam and the Study of Politics</u> (Chicago:
University of Chicago Press, 1974).

61. Carter H. Harrison, <u>Stormy Years</u> (Indianapolis:
Bobbs-Merrill, 1935), p.308. See also Alex Gottfried, <u>Boss
Cermak of Chicago: A Study of Political Leadership</u> (Seattle:
University of Washington Press, 1962), pp.353-364.

62. Merriam, <u>Rise of Urban America</u>, p.265.

63. Herman Kogan and Lloyd Wendt, <u>Big Bill of Chicago</u>
(Indianapolis: Bobbs-Merrill, 1953); John Bright, <u>Hizzoner Big
Bill Thompson: An Idyll of Chicago</u> (New York: J. Cape & H.
Smith, 1930).

64. Graham Taylor, <u>Pioneering on Social Frontiers</u>
(Chicago: University of Chicago Press, 1930).

65. Graham Taylor, <u>Chicago Commons Through Forty Years</u>
(Chicago: Chicago Commons Association, 1936); Louise Wade,
<u>Graham Taylor: Pioneer for Social Justice</u> (Chicago: University
of Chicago Press, 1964).

66. Taylor, <u>Pioneering</u>, p.116.

67. Ibid., pp.27-39; William Stead's <u>If Christ Came to
America</u> (Chicago: Laird & Lee, 1894) provides an expanded
version of his Music Hall speech.

68. Ray Ginger, <u>Altgeld's America, 1890-1905</u> (Chicago:
New Viewpoints, 1958), pp. 253-256; James Weinstein's discussion
of the National Civic Federation in <u>The Corporate Ideal in the
Liberal State, 1900-1915</u> (New York: Beacon, 1968) offers some
interesting parallels to Federation activity in Chicago.

69. Taylor, <u>Chicago Commons</u>, p.117.

70. Melvin Holli, "Urban Reform in the Progressive Era"
in <u>The Progressive Era</u>, ed. Lewis L. Gould (Syracuse: Syracuse
University Press, 1974), p.147.

71. Michael McCarthy makes the same distinction as Holli
identifying the structural reformers as the "right wing" of
urban progressivism. McCarthy's analysis of the Municipal
Voters' League's leadership shows a predominance of businessmen,
merchants and realtors, all relatively young, well-educated and
impatient with the archaic, patchwork city government that was
clearly unable to provide adequate services for the rapidly
expanding population. This younger breed of businessmen and
professionals emerged at the end of the 1890s; they were less
idealistic and humanitarian than earlier reformers but far more

confident and determined to apply the techniques of business
efficiency to the chaos of municipal government.

Robert Wiebe notes a similar divergence among urban
progressives, particularly after 1905. Both groups spoke of
efficiency but the conservatives were more interested in
stability, social control, economy and rationality than in
social service and greater democracy. This coheres with Wiebe's
central thesis that the heart of progressivism was the ambition
of a new middle class to fulfill its destiny through
bureaucratic means. Blaine Brownell warns against dividing urban
reformers into two clear-cut groups but at the same time
supports the pivotal role of the local business elite. He points
out that activists like Addams clearly set the criteria for
social reformers but they also battled the big-city political
machines and sought efficient and economical government.
Conversely, many of those who wished top control and "improve"
the behavior and morals of the lower classes also often promoted
expanded social services. Michael McCarthy, "Businessmen and
Professionals in Municipal Reform: The Chicago Experience,
1887-1920" (Ph.D. dissertation, Northwestern University, 1970);
Robert Wiebe, The Search for Order, 1877-1920 (New York: Hill &
Wang, 1967); Blaine Brownell, "Twentieth Century Urban
Progressive Reform" in David Colburn and George Pozetta, Reform
and Reformers in the Progressive Era (Westport, Conn.: Greenwood
Press, 1983), pp.3-23.

72. Douglas Sutherland, Fifty Years on the Civic Front
(Chicago: Civic Federation of Chicago, 1943), pp.22-43; Daniel
Levine, Varieties of Reform Thought (Madison: State Historical
Society of Wisconsin, 1964).

73. Lela B. Costin, Two Sisters for Social Justice: A
Biography of Grace and Edith Abbott (Urbana: University of
Illinois Press, 1983)

74. Norris Magnussen, Salvation in the Slums: Evangelical
Social Action 1865-1920 (Metuchen, N.J.: Scarecrow Press, 1977),
pp.1-29.

75. Paul Boyer, Urban Masses and Moral Order in America,
1820-1920 (Cambridge: Harvard University Press, 1978), p. 205.

76. What emerges from this discussion is the recognition
that the identity of the progressives cannot be reduced to one
single segment of urban society. Progressivism was a
multi-layered phenomenon that drew into its vortex individuals
from almost every sector. The original view of a
status-threatened middle class argued by George Mowry and
Richard Hofstadter has been vigorously debated but still
contains a certain degree of plausibility. The hard distinction
between pre-1900 populism and post-1900 progressivism is
overstated and yet the younger professional elite who appeared

on the scene in the 20th century have more on their minds than
protest. The participation of an upper class elite, especially
businessmen but also professionals and academics, has been
well-documented by Samuel Hays, Gabriel Kolko and James
Weinstein. Joseph Huthmacher's attempt to show lower class and
immigrant initiative also deserves to be considered but not to
the degree that it neglects the clear attempt of nativist
progressives to impose social control on immigrant populations
and destroy the ward system that served ethnic enclaves so well.
Nor can the neglect of disenfranchised and abused blacks in the
South and later in northern cities by progressives be dismissed.
Brownell seems to find the right balance when he notes,
"progressivism and reform meant different things to different
people, and it produced, not surprisingly, a variety of
different coalitions on an array of issues in scores of
communities across the country " (Brownell, "Twentieth Century
Urban Progressive Reform," p. 20). George Mowry, Theodore
Roosevelt and the Progressive Movement (Madison: University of
Wisconsin Press, 1946); Richard Hofstadter, The Age of Reform:
from Bryan to F.D.R. (New York: Alfred A. Knopf, 1955); Gabriel
Kolko, The Triumph of Conservatism (New York: Free Press, 1963);
Samuel Hays, The Response to Industrialism (Chicago: University
of Chicago Press, 1957); Hays, "The Politics of Reform in
Municipal Government in the Progressive Era," Pacific Northwest
Quarterly 55 (October 1964); Joseph Huthmacher, "Urban
Liberalism and the Age of Reform" in Twentieth Century America:
Recent Interpretations, ed. Barton Bernstein and Allen Matusow
(New York: Harcourt, 1969), pp.23-33; Dewey Grantham, "The
Progressive Movement and the Negro" in Bernstein and Matusow,
Twentieth Century America, pp.59-73.

77. Allen Davis, Spearheads for Reform: The Social
Settlement and the Progressive Movement (New York: Oxford
University Press, 1967).

78. Christopher Lasch, The New Radicalism in America
1880-1963 (New York: Alfred A. Knopf, 1965).

79. Robert M. Crunden, Ministers of Reform: The
Progressives' Achievement in American Civilization 1889-1920
(New York: Basic Books, 1982); Roy Lubove, The Professional
Altruist: The Emergence of Social Work as a Career, 1880-1930
(Cambridge: Harvard University Press, 1965); Robert E. L. Faris,
Chicago Sociology 1920-1932 (Chicago: University of Chicago
Press, 1967). See also Dorothy Ross, "The Development of the
Social Sciences" in The Organization of Knowledge in Modern
America 1860-1920, ed. Alexandria Oleson and John Voss
(Baltimore: Johns Hopkins University Press, 1979), pp.107-138,
for background to the emergence of social science research by
such individuals as Merriam and Dewey.

80. Morton White and Lucia White, The Intellectual Versus

the City (New York: Oxford University Press, 1962), pp. 155-168.

81. Benjamin Rader, The Academic Mind and Reform: The Influence of Richard T. Ely in American Life (Lexington: University of Kentucky Press, 1966); David F. Noble, The Paradox of Progressive Thought (Minneapolis: University of Minnesota Press, 1958), pp.157-173; Paul Violas, "Progressive Social Philosophy: Charles Horton Cooley and Edward Alsworth Ross" in Roots of Crisis, ed. Joel Spring (Chicago: Rand McNally, 1973).

82. Robert Handy, ed. The Social Gospel in America, 1870-1920 (New York: Oxford University Press, 1966), p. 220.

83. Ibid., p.201.

84. David B. Tyack, "City Schools: Centralization of Control at the Turn of the Century" in Power and Ideology in Education, ed. Jerome Karabel and A. H. Halsey (New York: Oxford University Press, 1977), pp.379-411; Robert L. Church, Education in the United States: An Interpretative History (New York: Free Press, 1976); David Tyack, One Best System (Cambridge: Harvard University Press, 1974); Clarence J. Karier, Shaping the American Educational State, 1900 to the Present (New York: Free Press, 1975).

85. Robert L. Reid, "The Professionalization of Public School Teachers: The Chicago Experience 1895-1920 (Ph.D. dissertation, Northwestern University, 1968). See also Joan K. Smith, "Ella Flagg Young: Portrait of a Leader" (Ph.D. dissertation, Iowa State University, 1976) and Margaret Haley, Battleground: The Autobiography of Margaret A. Haley, ed. Robert L. Reid, (Urbana: University of Illinois Press, 1982).

86. Robert Tostberg, "Educational Ferment in Chicago 1883-1904" (Ph.D. dissertation, University of Wisconsin, 1960).

87. John Dewey, Schools and Society (Chicago: University of Chicago Press, 1900); Dewey, The Child and the Curriculum (Chicago: University of Chicago Press, 1902); George S. Counts, School and Society in Chicago (New York: Harcourt, Brace & Company, 1928).

88. Chicago Tribune, 9 June 1907. See also Abigail Loomis and Franklin E. Court, "Richard Teller Crane's War with the Colleges," Chicago History 11:3 (Fall/Winter, 1982), pp.205-213.

89. Quoted in Peter Andre Sola, "Plutocrats, Pedagogues and Plebes: Business Influences on Vocational Education and Extracurricular Activities in the Chicago High Schools 1899-1925" (Ph.D. dissertation, University of Illinois, 1972), p.27. See also Paul Violas, The Training of the Urban Working Class (Chicago: Rand McNally, 1978); Robert A. Carlson,

"Americanization as an Early Twentieth-Century Adult Education Movement," History of Education Quarterly (Winter 1970), pp.440-464; John M. Brewer, History of Vocational Guidance (New York: Harper & Brothers, 1942).

90. Sola, "Plutocrats, Pedagogues and Plebes," p.83.

91. Quoted in Chicago Faces and Places: Seventy-Five Years of Chicago Association of Commerce and Industry (Chicago: CACI, 1979), p.15.

CHAPTER 3

GETTING CHICAGO RELIGIOUSLY RIGHT

If the group of businessmen in this study were subject to the economic and political currents operating in Chicago, they were also influenced by the religious developments of the period. Their faith was a combination of self-initiated theologizing and environmentally-produced beliefs which to a sizable degree guided their activities both in the marketplace and in the religious world. To better appreciate these activities and the religious sources that stimulated them, one must examine the religious life of Chicago after the turn of the century.

It may be an exercise in hyperbole to call Chicago a "religious town" in the early 20th century. Only about half the population attended a church or synagogue on a regular basis (in 1902, there was one church for every 2400 inhabitants and one Sunday school for every 785 persons under the age of 21).[1] Nor was church membership growth keeping pace with the population growth. Protestants, Catholics and Jews were all struggling to preserve religious vitality in their communities, frequently losing their young to other religious bodies or to the ranks of the secular, agnostic public.

Yet at the same time, there was such extensive religious activity that even the non-religious segment of the population could not escape its pervasive influence. Even though religion was becoming an increasingly private affair for many persons, it was still a matter to be pursued aggressively, whether that meant saving souls, fighting immorality or raising funds for a noble cause. The sheer earnestness with which so many expressed their religious visions gave added weight to their numbers.

Undoubtedly, the Protestants in Chicago held the prominent position and were able to direct their energies into maintaining their empire. The Catholics, on the other hand, were still constructing theirs (not until Cardinal Mundelein arrived in 1917 did the Church become a major force in the public arena).[2] Numerically, the Catholics outnumbered all the Protestant bodies during these decades but they were unable to operate as monolithically as the Protestants given the language and cultural barriers separating their ethnic parishes (in some cases, several Catholic churches were located on the same block, each serving a different ethnic group and having little to do with the others). The Protestants, though divided denominationally, had far more in common with one another and were able to harness their energies and resources for large-scale religious projects.

Urban revivals were one example of these highly-organized

spiritual ventures. These city evangelistic campaigns utilized modern techniques of promotion and salesmanship while maintaining the theological vocabulary (and its meanings) of 19th century rural revivalism. Chicago witnessed several of these massive campaigns "to win Chicago for Christ."

One occurred in October, 1910, led by Presbyterian evangelist, J. Wilbur Chapman, who pronounced, "Chicago is sin sick, weary of filth and vileness. The city wants to be good. It wants to come up out of the slough."[3] Chapman had pioneered a method of urban evangelism that relied on the leadership and expertise of Protestant businessmen. This particular crusade was billed as a "businessman's campaign" and involved simultaneous meetings at such locations as the Chicago Opera House, the old World's Exposition grounds and churches all over the city. The meetings were noted for their precise timing, relatively brief sermons and well-coordinated altar calls. Chapman brought a team of preachers with him who invaded the prisons, saloons and factories with the Gospel message. An army of lay volunteers canvassed the entire city with promotional literature. Chicago newspapers gave the meetings front-page coverage and took note of the moral uplift generated by the religious awakening. Attendance at the Chapman meetings averaged about 5000 nightly with thousands more participating in neighborhood church gatherings. Yet Chapman and his associates later concluded that the results of the campaign had fallen short of their expectations. Several years later, Chapman abandoned this method of organized urban revivalism, though his protege, Billy Sunday, continued to carry the torch.[4]

Sunday did not get to Chicago until 1918 but by then he was a national figure symbolizing both war-time patriotism and old-fashioned religion. Later estimating that it cost him $395 to save a soul in Chicago, Sunday drew massive crowds to hear him blend the Gospel with anti-German rhetoric. At one meeting, Sunday prayed, "Thank God the Huns will never see Heaven," though that petition was mild compared to his prayer before the House of Representatives a few months earlier.[5] Said Sunday, "Thou knowest, O Lord, that we are in a life-and-death struggle with one of the most infamous, vile, greedy, avaricious, bloodthirsty, sensual, and vicious nations that has ever disgraced the pages of history."[6]

Sunday cultivated the support of businessmen even more vigorously than Chapman. He addressed both the Association of Commerce and the Chicago Club (sitting at a head table with almost a dozen of the Sunday Evening Club trustees). His advance man told the business leaders that Sunday received hundreds of letters from employees thanking him for the "increased efficiency which has resulted among operatives and employees generally from changed habits of life."[7] Sunday even held noonday meetings in factories and department stores for the benefit of workers. Though the Chicago clergy swallowed hard at Sunday's frequent crudities on stage and his occasional unorthodoxies in Protestant doctrine, they chose to support his revivals. One Chicago minister, W. E. Barton, indicated that "what Sunday stands for, I stand for" even though Sunday by his own admission "knows no more about theology than a kangaroo knows about ping pong."[8] The business community was only too happy to have an entertaining religious speaker admonish their workers.

Protestants in Chicago did not wait upon travelling evangelists to spread the Gospel. They had numerous agencies of their own that sent volunteers into the streets armed with tracts, Bibles and an invitation to accept Christ. The Chicago Tract Society, for example, adapted the traditional use of tracts as tools of frontier evangelism in order to reach the immigrant population; publishing tracts in numerous foreign languages, the Society relied upon volunteers and part-time workers initially, and later full-time ordained colporteurs, to distribute the tracts throughout the city.[9] The Society's most important leader, Luther Mills, had been one of the attorneys prosecuting the anarchists in the Haymarket trial, and through that experience, acquired a deep concern about the burgeoning immigrant population. Thus, distributing tracts was viewed as more than simple evangelism; it was also a means of assimilation for ethnic groups. Converting immigrants was "something that is worthwhile--something that is telling mightily for the future of Christ's kingdom in America."[10]

Similarly, institutions like the Moody Bible Institute sent its students out into the streets to do evangelistic work, emphasizing that such activity was to be expected for every devout Christian.

The Salvation Army combined this dedication to street evangelism with a social welfare program that earned it high marks. The Army's uniformed brass bands, parades and "open air" meetings had become common sights in Chicago by the late 1880s.[11] It took some time for the Protestant churches to accept these "soldiers for Christ" who aimed to convert the "dregs" of society. But the Booth family members who visited Chicago proved to be compelling and attractive personalities (even though one son broke ranks from the Army and began his own Volunteers of America in Chicago). By 1914, the Army in Chicago had 120 officers and 22 corps halls, nine of them large enough to seat more than 3000 persons. Its welfare work concentrated on soup kitchens, housing for the homeless and second-hand clothing depots.

While some of these religious organizations concentrated on winning souls to the faith, others emphasized commitment to a Christian lifestyle. The Christian Endeavor societies were a prominent instigator of activist Protestantism. Part of a national movement that began in New England in the 1880s, Christian Endeavor groups invited young adults to weekly prayer meetings and required a pledge to follow a disciplined routine of daily Bible reading, prayer and service to others.[12] Society members were expected to hold each other accountable. National and local conventions of "Endeavorers" were held to inspire and instruct these religious youth.

The Christian Endeavor idea spread quickly to other countries so that within a few years, the organization had evolved into an international network of zealous members numbering over a million (by 1912, there were four million members worldwide and more than 75,000 societies).[13] The success of this movement prompted the Protestant denominations to either establish societies within their churches or launch similar organizations for their youth. It also became common practice to hold a Christian Endeavor Sunday once a year, primarily to recruit membership.

In 1915, the quadrennial World's Convention of Christian Endeavor was held in Chicago with some 10,000 delegates attending. Even the Board of Trade hoisted the Christian Endeavor flag.[14] The convention publicly identified itself on the side of international peace, prohibition, the enlightenment of Negroes, and the Golden Rule as the best way to resolve labor unrest. However, the convention chose to be silent on women's suffrage arguing that "many Endeavorers in the South were not yet converted" to that way of thinking.[15]

Another youth-oriented organization that was shedding its earlier religious fervor was the YMCA, and its sister agency, the YWCA. Formed in Britain in the 1840s to promote Christian piety among young males, the YMCA spread rapidly through the U.S. under the aegis of Protestant evangelists like Dwight Moody. The movement became more institutionalized as recreation centers were built in major cities to provide physical activity, employment information and fellowship for young adults moving to urban areas. By the early 1900s, explicit proselytizing had been discontinued in most places. The YMCA buildings became community centers that served the immediate needs of men and women, later expanding into boys' and girls' clubs and railway "Y" centers. The Chicago YMCA, like most others, was heavily financed by the businessmen of the city. Several Club trustees made huge donations, including John Farwell, John Shedd, Cyrus McCormick and Norman Harris. One of the largest contributors was Julius Rosenwald, a Jew, whose money helped build the YMCA building in the black belt in 1913. Clearly, by this time, the Chicago YMCA was using the term "Christian" rather loosely.[16]

However, the YMCA operated on an international level as well and here it remained more religious in tone for a longer period of time. In 1907, the International YMCA convention in Washington reaffirmed its commitment to the historic Christian faith. The leadership of John R. Mott, a frequent Club speaker, was partly responsible for this emphasis.[17] Together with other zealous spokesmen, Mott used the YMCA network overseas as a structure for promoting foreign missions. YMCA centers in other nations offered native young men the opportunity to adopt both Christianity and the Western way of life. Mott himself became a well-respected statesman meeting Third World leaders as an unofficial emissary of the U.S.

During the War, the International YMCA actively supported

Allied troops in Western Europe providing a full range of services to uniformed men including canteens, hospital visitation, transferring mail and recreation. YMCA staff also functioned as chaplains for the Army. Chicagoans like Clifford Barnes were instrumental in raising incredible sums of financial support for the YMCA work in France and Belgium.

Fund-raising for overseas Christian missions (and to a lesser degree, "home" missions) was a Protestant activity that allowed many laymen to exercise their business skills for a religious purpose. Churches and parachurch organizations constantly conducted services and special programs to support the work of missionaries. One organization that was based in Chicago was the Laymen's Missionary Movement launched in 1906 by a New York businessman zealous for "the evangelization of the world in this generation."[18] Both Mott and Robert Speer, a Presbyterian missions leader, actively supported the organization which took as its agenda the development of systematic methods in securing missionary offerings. This included a call for committed men to earmark a specific portion of their income for missions and a nationwide canvass to place weekly offering envelopes in church pews. Annual missionary conferences in large cities functioned as forums for expanding missions awareness among church laymen.

Many religiously-motivated laymen were convinced that they could do a better job of financing world missions than the clergy. No other phenomenon illustrates this better than the abortive 1919 Interchurch World Movement, a grandiose scheme to raise several hundred million dollars on behalf of major Protestant denominational foreign missions boards. This astronomical sum of money was to be applied to both evangelistic and social service work in such a way that the churches would be united in a common cause of meeting needs in a post-war society. Denominational agencies were to implement the projects but the IWM was to collect the funds.[19]

The impetus for this ecumenical undertaking was the success of the YMCA-sponsored United War Work Campaign which under Mott's leadership raised over $200 million to minister to servicemen in Europe waiting to be shipped home. Mott was partly responsible for the IWM idea but drew in his friend, John D. Rockefeller, Jr., who took the project on as a personal mission. Rockefeller also established a fund of over $50 million to subsidize the fund-raising campaign, money which he obtained from his aging father, telling him,

> I do not think we can overestimate the importance of this Movement. As I see it, it is capable of having a much more far-reaching influence than the League of Nations in bringing about peace, contentment, goodwill and prosperity among the people of the earth.20

Executives from the Federal Council of Churches, including Barnes who was active in the Chicago chapter, jumped on Rockefeller's bandwagon, determining to raise a generous portion.

Rockefeller's dream cost him dearly, for the campaign fizzled in less than a year. Several denominations were suspicious of the scheme right from the start unwilling to see their funds drained elsewhere. Some of the same denominations were experiencing internal tensions between fundamentalists and liberals; from the conservative point of view, the IWM was a liberal, ecumenical extravaganza, sponsored by a Rockefeller whose religious views were somewhat suspect. Besides all this, the IWM was an example of "going to the well" once too many times. Church members had given repeatedly to War-related projects and appeared to be weary of giving.

Barnes had little to say about this fiasco. However, he remained an ardent supporter of "interdenominational activities which tend to the moral and religious betterment of our city" such as those sponsored by the Chicago Church Federation.[21] By minimizing non-essentials and emphasizing essentials on which all denominations could unite, he was convinced that Protestants could put their wealth to work for the benefit of Chicago.

Chicago was the scene of another religious campaign, the Men and Religion Forward Movement, a national campaign during 1911 and 1912 designed to arouse church laymen to greater involvement in social problems. The Movement led by Protestant figures associated with the social gospel consisted of eight-day city campaigns in which special speakers such as Charles Stelzle and Raymond Robins sought to focus the attention of the male population upon various social injustices. All the finest techniques of advertising were to be used to promote "the program of Jesus."[22] Walter Rauschenbusch endorsed the Movement as one of the best ways to indoctrinate the Church into the social gospel.

The result of this media blitz (which ultimately reached 1.4 million persons in 60 cities with a total of 7062 meetings) was to be the formation of social service groups in local churches with ministers speaking out on social issues and even supporting organized labor. The organizers hoped to attract a wide spectrum of men to this broad religious thrust; thus they incorporated Bible study and missions with boys' work and community service trying to appeal to both employees and working men. Unfortunately, in Chicago other media events captured the headlines instead of the Movement. Planners for the Chicago campaign in April, 1912, were obviously unable to predict the sinking of the Titanic that occurred that same week.

Abundant activity was not the only sign of religious vitality in Chicago in this period. The status of church leaders in the community indicated that religion was still an important contributor to public opinion. Local clergy such as M. P. Boynton of Woodlawn Baptist, Charles Cheney of Christ Church, Johnston Myers of Immanuel Baptist, Frederick Shannon of Central Church, Emil Hirsch from Sinai Temple, Jenkin L. Jones of All Souls' Church and John Timothy Stone of Fourth Presbyterian all mingled comfortably with the city's elite and enjoyed warm relationships with the business community. While their zeal for religious matters exceeded that of their laymen, these ministers could be counted upon to make religion relevant and suitable.

For example, Shannon, who pastored the famous Central Church begun by free-thinking Presbyterian David Swing in the 1870s, said of his most prominent parishioner, Edward Butler: "He belongs in the noble galaxy of men (Field, Shedd, Burnham)." Shannon added that "Religion is the utterance in life of great truths in a worthy manner. Mr. Butler asserted by word and deed his faith in the Immortal Hope."[23] Jones, though an ardent pacifist whose theology was so liberal that even Unitarianism was restrictive to him ("being a Christian is believing we are part of an infinite Order and children of a tender Providence," Jones wrote in one of his tracts. "It does not mean belief in a supernatural Christ, vicarious atonement, an infallible Bible or the dual division of humanity at death")[24] nevertheless articulated an American civil religion that endeared him to many Chicagoans. Through his Unity magazine and his regular G. A. R. lectures on Civil War heroes, Jones promoted a vision for democracy that struck responsive chords.[25]

Chicago's Denominational Scene

A further indication of Protestant strength was the success of the city's denominations in keeping laypersons involved in their local congregations and increasing their number of churches. Most businessmen with religious inclinations belonged to one of the major denominations. To a large degree, these religious bodies provided the environment in which these men were nurtured in their faith.

Perhaps not surprisingly, the Presbyterians possessed a

disproportionate share of city's business class (and as
mentioned earlier, dominated the Sunday Evening Club trustees).
Presbyterians had been active in Chicago since the city's
earliest days, and though never the largest religious body, they
were always influential (Andrew Stevenson, a railroad executive
and founder of Young Men's Presbyterian Union, boasted that
Chicago was "preeminently a Presbyterian city" citing the hosts
of major businessmen, lawyers and doctors sitting in
Presbyterian pews as prime evidence).[26] In 1900, there were
over 80 congregations in Chicago and in the surrounding area of
northeastern Illinois representing over 20,000 members; more
than a dozen of these churches had memberships of over 500. By
World War I, that number had climbed to 106 churches with over
35,000 members. The increase in part reflected the vigorous
church extension program of the Presbytery among the numerous
immigrant communities of Chicago. Through settlement houses,
missions, and foreign-language Sunday schools, the Presbytery
eventually established congregations among Bohemians, Poles,
Italians, Mexicans, Czechs, Persians and Asians. Several black
congregations also emerged during this period.[27]

The Presbytery made gallant efforts to respond to the
host of urban ills spawned by tumultuous population growth.
Presbyterians were in the forefront of local temperance
campaigns, anti-vice crusades, public school battles and
community welfare efforts. The Presbyterian Hospital was a
favored charity of the Social Register set.[28] By the end of the

War, the Presbytery had established its own Social Service
Commission to deal with "social questions in the light of
Christianity."[29] One of the Commission's first studies was the
1919 race riot.

Spiritual concerns remained at the top of the
Presbytery's agenda, however. The salvation of an individual
soul continued to be the only lasting solution to any social
problem. Thus, traditional evangelistic approaches were rarely
questioned. In fact, Presbyterian ministers were intimately
involved with the Gipsey Smith campaign in 1909 as well as the
Chapman and Sunday crusades. Those within the fold required
continual spiritual nurture; to this end, the educational
agencies of the Presbytery poured their energies into more
effective Bible instruction. A Presbyterian Training School was
launched in 1908 to prepare church workers. Christian Endeavor
societies, Young Men's and Young Women's Bible classes and
Presbyterian Brotherhood chapters all received strong support
from the clergy.

One might ask what difference it made that so many of the
Club trustees were Presbyterians. The fact that many were
officers in their local congregations likely strengthened
aristocratic impulses, given the fact that Presbyterianism
reflected a republican form of church government by qualified
leaders (theoretically, to be determined by spiritual criteria
but more easily chosen by external standards of success).
Majoritarian democracy was kept in check by Presbyterian

structures, a condition that would have pleased these Presbyterian men if it were also true in Chicago politics.

Yet another factor about these Presbyterians was their Anglo-Saxonism. Rooted in the Scotch-Irish immigrations of the 18th century, the main stream of Presbyterianism had produced its share of sturdy patriots who conceived of American culture as a distinctively Christian civilization, to be cherished, protected and expanded. "I believe that the destinies of mankind, the salvation of civilization, and the hope of permanent peace are by God's providence largely in the hands of English-speaking people," claimed David Forgan, calling for the ideas of Napoleon and the Kaisers to be discarded and the teachings of Jesus Christ to be adopted.[30] Woodrow Wilson shared a similar view when he said, "The Anglo-Saxon people have undertaken to reconstruct the affairs of the world and it would be a shame upon them to withdraw their hand."[31] Presbyterian ministers conveyed the same message in their occasional attacks upon "German ideas and influences." Evanston minister David Hugh Jones even suggested that attending Sunday afternoon concerts was in effect to "promote German Kultur and help the German invasion of our land."[32]

Anglo-Saxonism displayed its racist edge when these Presbyterians viewed both the East European and the black populations of Chicago. Individuals from these inferior races could only achieve success by adopting the ethics of hard-working, white Protestants. That great model of manhood,

Jesus Christ, was available to them, according to the Continent in 1911:

> ...the negro is already beginning to recognize that color separates absolutely the two races [and] that between white and black, peace and harmony is to depend on their living together in separation but each recognizing the other's rights. In a negro decently dressed, industrious, sober, provident, law abiding and courteous, the white man will find no cause for offense.33

A few years later, the journal urged whites to call blacks "mister" and "mistress" but recognized that "racial aspiration and personal self-esteem alike conspire to make him (the progressive black man) prefer the companionship of his own people."[34] On several occasions, the Presbyterian organ protested the rash of Negro lynchings across the nation, even scoring Protestant churches in a Pennsylvania town for not intervening on behalf of a victim. Yet at the same time, there was little evidence that Presbyterians in Chicago had much familiarity with any black Protestants in Chicago.

The clergy in the Chicago Presbytery were generally a conservative group; only 19 per cent signed the theologically liberal Auburn Affirmation in 1924 indicating a majority were reluctant to question the fundamental doctrines of Christianity.[35] Some of the McCormick Seminary faculty had obtained advanced degrees in German theological schools and were exploring the implications of the higher criticism of the Bible yet without calling for any wholesale rejection of traditional beliefs. Theologian Andrew Zenos in his The Elements of Higher Criticism claimed that it was a useful weapon to employ in Bible

study, but not necessary to authenticate the Bible; "the Bible
commends itself, apart from criticism or authority of the
Church, as a source of religious information and inspiration."[36]
Nolan Best sounded the same reassuring note when he wrote that
the "true proof of inspiration is that it is profitable." He
claimed, "Men obey the Bible because it imperiously calls to
what is deepest in the consciousness of their souls."[37] The
efficacy of the Bible did not require acceptance of an
error-free text because its spiritual power lay elsewhere, in
fact, in the sympathetic, but informed reading of its contents.
Best urged church workers to teach with an unhostile attitude:
"Teach it, teach it, whatever you believe, and just as much as
you can believe."[38] This balancing of an acceptance of Biblical
authority with a skepticism of the Bible's veracity became
increasingly difficult; by 1920, McCormick professor Arthur Hays
assigned the individual conscience the authority to determine
which books of the Bible were God's revelation.[39]

If these ministers were willing to concede some of the
Bible's authority in areas of scientific and historical
knowledge, they continued to campaign for its moral authority.
Periodically, the Presbytery called for legislation to require a
portion of the Bible to be read daily in the public schools.
Princeton Seminary professor, Charles Erdman, told a gathering
of the Presbyterian Brotherhood, "the Bible is the very
foundation of our free institutions, the palladium of our
national life."[40] The study of the Bible would result in new

efficiency and power for any organization. Apparently, many took
the idea seriously for the support of Bible distribution
agencies, like the Gideons and the Pocket Testament League,
flourished among Presbyterians.

If there was an enemy for the Presbyterians, it was still
the Catholics who appeared to be monopolizing the public
schools, detention homes and health stations to the chagrin of
the Presbytery.[41] This "false religion" simply did not fit into
their amalgam of Protestantism, patriotism and modern business
values. Interestingly, one of the problems Presbyterians had
with Catholics was what they perceived as the supposed
dictatorship of priests over Catholic laymen. A Continent
editorial wondered whether a Catholic should run for national
office because he couldn't be counted upon to refuse the orders
of his priest and "go beyond his own church with perfect
patriotic fellowship."[42]

There was little hint of any trouble within the fold.
Zenos spoke of "exclusionists" within the church, "well-meaning
though misguided champions of the old faith."[43] He remained
confident that these traditionalists would come to appreciate
the modernizing that was incumbent upon the church; at the same
time, he maintained close ties with those who espoused the old
faith, including Billy Sunday.[44]

If the Presbyterian churches were outposts of rugged
Christianity, the Episcopal churches were semi-private clubs for
upper-crust persons with refined religious tastes. The once

maligned, and even persecuted, denomination had by the end of the 19th century become the bastion of high society. Their membership among the well-to-do climbed steadily during these years. By 1900, four Episcopal churches in Chicago numbered over a thousand members each. Nationwide, the Episcopalians were the only Protestant denomination growing faster than the population growth.[45] The Diocese of Chicago was quite representative of the entire denomination (though only about 10 per cent of all Episcopalians lived in the Midwest) containing within its borders the diverse elements of this ritualistic brand of Protestantism.[46]

From its colonial days, American Episcopalianism had always wrestled with a tension between its "high church" and "low church" tendencies, whether to be more Catholic or more Protestant. The high church contingent usually predominated, especially among the bishops; this led to elaborate liturgy, vestments for the clergy, strict adherence to the Book of Common Prayer, ornate church architecture and interior design, music sung by trained voices and greater authority for the bishops. Low church Episcopalians minimized the ceremonial features of worship and the authority of church tradition and rather stressed the preaching of Biblical doctrines and a willingness to cooperate with other Protestant bodies.

During the 1830s and 1840s, the high church leanings of the denomination were given an added boost by an Anglo-Catholic movement within the Anglican Church that spread into its

American counterpart. Known as Tractarianism, because of a
lengthy series of tracts written by several high church
Anglicans (some of whom like Cardinal Newman eventually
gravitated into the Roman Catholic Church) arguing for the
adoption of specific Catholic doctrines and an increased
spiritual authority for the church heirarchy (i.e. apostolic
succession), this Anglo-Catholicism found fertile ground among
young Episcopalian clergy. They were unusually sympathetic to
this effort at de-Protestantizing the Church.[47]

By the 1860s, this younger breed of high churchmen were
able to create enough of a shift in the denomination that low
church evangelicals became increasingly uncomfortable. The
inevitable split came over the issues of baptismal regeneration
(i.e. the idea that an infant becomes a Christian in the act of
baptism) and the freedom of Episcopal clergy to preach in other
denominational churches. A group of rectors and at least one
bishop were deposed when they refused to submit to the high
church positions on these issues. Led by Chicago clergyman,
Charles Cheney, they formed a splinter denomination called the
Reformed Episcopal Church.[48] Because it was concerned with
doctrinal purity rather than with ritual, this new denomination
remained small and relatively unknown, though Cheney himself was
highly-regarded by many people in Chicago. Unhindered by this
evangelical resistance, the high church emphasis flourished. By
the end of the century, the Church was building cathedrals, and
in some churches, celebrating the Eucharist in a manner

indistinguishable from the Catholics.

About the same time another movement appeared among the Episcopalians that was responsive to current liberal theological thought and the social gospel. Clergymen like Phillips Brooks, E. A. Washburn and W. R. Huntington found that orthodox doctrine could not be easily squared with the discoveries of Biblical criticism.[49] They were also sensitive to the need for a religion that spoke meaningfully to the urban, industrial scene. This "Broad church" emphasis did not prove to be acceptable to either the high or low church wings and drew reactions from much of the church heirarchy. But this thrust gained support, even from the well-to-do; in some unusual cases, rectors were preaching prophetic social gospel messages to wealthy capitalists sitting in the pews.[50]

In Chicago, high churchmen controlled the scene especially after Cheney departed. Bishop Charles Anderson laid the groundwork for a cathedral to be built in Chicago though it was never built; decades later, his St. James Church was converted to cathedral status. By then, it was a popular place for Chicago's elite to make occasional appearances, even if they weren't members. At least five of the Club trustees attended St. James.[51]

This attraction for Episcopal worship among the elite was more than high class snobbery. There was, in fact, a type of religious aestheticism propelling the ritual and art which adorned the houses of worship and the Sunday High Communions.

What many Episcopalians were seeking was the restoration of
mystery and awe in their religion, something which had been lost
by the mainstream of Protestantism. Those with Anglo-Catholic
sentiments found Protestant church life to be banal, overly
rationalistic, and devoid of any real sense of the supernatural.
Artistic splendor and elaborate worship served as religious
surrogates for these people. Even the other Protestant
denominations showed evidences of this impulse, especially in
the architecture and interior design of their church buildings
and in the increasing formality of their corporate worship.
Beyond this there may have been a psychological need for
expiation felt by some of the wealthy, which the Eucharist
sacrament was designed to provide (what Weber called "the very
Catholic cycle of sin, repentance, atonement, release, followed
by renewed sin").[52]

One contribution of Chicago Episcopalians at St. James
was the national Brotherhood of St. Andrew, a men's organization
begun in the 1880s by Club trustee James L. Houghteling. Like
the Presbyterian Brotherhood, this fellowship of Episcopal men
was dedicated to "pray daily for the spread of Christ's Kingdom
among men (or boys) and to make an earnest effort each week to
bring some man (or boy) nearer to Christ through His Church."[53]
Several hundred chapters were in operation by the early 1900s
with national conventions held annually. A regular feature of
these conventions was the celebration of a mass.

The Methodist and Baptist churches in Chicago represented

two large constituencies of Protestants, not only among whites
but blacks as well. Both of these denominations had evolved from
frontier faiths marked by intense piety and zealous evangelism
into cosmopolitan bodies with large urban congregations where
religion had become less fervent and more respectable.
Conservative rural and small town churches still predominated in
both denominations but they were unable to stem the tide of
materialism and spiritual laxity. As one Chicago Baptist mourned
in 1897, "The growth of worldliness in our churches is
appalling." He cited the "pleasure loving spirit, greed for
gain, desecration of the Sabbath, neglect of the Lord's table,
the spirit of restlessness, self-indulgence, and poor attendance
as unmistakeable evidence of declining spirituality."[54] The
Methodists were more equivocal: "The rigid and minute Church
discipline of former years is relaxed: is this a sign of
pastoral unfaithfulness, or is it a sign of growing respect for
individual liberty and a better conception of the function of
the Church?" asked a group of bishops in 1900. "The plainness of
the early Methodist congregations has disappeared: is this
simply vanity and worldliness, or is it, in part, the natural
and justifiable development of the aesthetic faculty under more
prosperous external conditions?"[55]

Clearly both groups were in transition. The Baptists in
Chicago had within their ranks clergy with strong liberal
leanings and others who clung tenaciously to the traditional
doctrines. The Divinity School at the University of Chicago

sponsored by the Northern Baptist Convention, had acquired a
national reputation for its theological innovations. Claiming to
have adopted a scientific approach to religion, theologians such
as Shailer Mathews, George B. Foster and Shirley Case explored
the implications of critical Biblical scholarship emanating from
Germany and articulated an American brand of social
Christianity.[56] By 1913, conservative ministers in Chicago
launched their own seminary in reaction to the Divinity School's
liberal bias. This turned out to be only the opening salvo in a
long battle within the Northern Baptist camp over liberalism.[57]

Similarly, the Methodists found themselves struggling
with new forms of Christian thought. Their historic doctrine of
"holiness" (Wesley's emphasis on living a disciplined Christian
life which included the possibility of achieving some degree of
"perfection") had always mitigated against theological polemics
and encouraged the priority of activism as the mark of
spirituality. By the turn of the century, many Methodists were
channeling their activism into social service. In fact,
Methodists like Chicago's Harry F. Ward and favorite Club
speaker Bishop Francis McConnell were proclaiming a "Social
Creed in Methodism" that was not far removed from Christian
socialism. Five Methodist ministers, including Ward, formed the
Methodist Federation for Social Service in 1907 which pioneered
social reform dialog among the major denominations. The First
Methodist Church in Evanston was a center of controversy in this
dialog since its minister, Ernest Fremont Tittle, was a close

ally of Ward.[58]

While these struggles occupied the minds of the more thoughtful clergy, Baptist and Methodist congregations continued to develop their religious programs. Both were successful in establishing new churches in various immigrant neighborhoods. Both established church-run training schools for future missionaries and church workers. Both experimented with institutional churches as one method of serving the community while proclaiming the faith. Johnston Myer's Immanuel Baptist Church provided hot meals daily for the poor; the Methodists sponsored a German deaconess group that conducted a wide range of services for the needy. Baptist ministers Ernest Bell and Melbourne Boynton became well-known in Chicago for their Midnight Mission in the vice districts. In response to the popularity of Christian Endeavor, the Methodists started Epworth Leagues and the Baptists Young People's Unions to rally their youth to engage in Bible study, prayer and church work. Finally, like other denominations, the Baptists and Methodists were forced to cope with changing neighborhoods. Several large Baptist congregations sold their buildings to black Baptist churches after most of their membership had already moved away. The most notable was First Church, which in 1918 became Olivet Baptist (then the largest black church in Chicago); William Main, First's pastor, noted, "No eloquent preaching, no social service, could save a church in a community that was nearly 100 per cent Negro."[59] A 1912 editorial in the Chicago-based

Northwestern Christian Advocate opined that "behind the Negro
question lies the whole worth of our religion and our
civilization. We must pull him up or he will pull us down."[60]

Among the Sunday Evening Club trustees were very active
Baptist and Methodist laymen. Andrew MacLeish, John Nuveen and
Thomas Donnelley all served with Baptist denominational agencies
in Chicago and at the national level as well; Norman Harris, his
son, A. W., John O'Leary and Harry Wheeler were devout
Methodists who contributed large sums of money and considerable
personal time to such Methodist agencies as Garrett Biblical
Institute, Wesley Memorial Hospital and Northwestern University
(still nominally Methodist).[61]

The black Methodist and Baptist denominations in Chicago
had also made their own adjustments to the urban environment.
They were, as many sociologists have noted, social centers that
served a diverse set of functions; in particular, the heirarchy
of leadership roles afforded church members a measure of social
status unavailable in most other life experiences. W. E. B.
DuBois noted in 1900 that

> ...one can see in the Negro church today, reproduced in
> microcosm, all that great world from which the Negro is cut
> off by color prejudice and social condition. In the great
> city churches the same tendency is noticeable and in many
> respects emphasized.62

By the turn of the century, these churches were
comfortably entrenched in the black community drawing upon more
prosperous blacks. In 1910, the National Baptists in Chicago
numbered over 12,000 while the African Methodist Episcopal

Church had reached 9000 members.[63] The theological formulations
of these black Protestants were generally in line with orthodox
Christianity, though stated in experiential, not abstract,
propositional terms.

Yet a pattern of secularization was beginning to appear
among these groups. The rigid legalism so acceptable in the
South became modified in the urban churches as community
concerns, political involvements and business pursuits occupied
the attention of clergy and lay leaders. The urban environment
itself offered alternative avenues for the attainment of some
prestige and power; for many blacks, the church was becoming
less than relevant. For example, after the race riot in 1919,
thirteen black leaders were interviewed by the Commission on
Race Relations. When asked about the role of religion as a
solvent of racial strife, half of them dismissed it as
hopelessly unable to contribute anything; the remainder felt
that religion could help if it was actually practiced.
Apparently, in their minds, neither black nor white churches
were expressions of true religion.[64]

Since the mid 19th century, a number of northern blacks
had been drawn into the large white denominations. Usually,
these black congregations consisted of blacks whose economic
status was more secure and who were anxious to maintain prestige
among blacks and whites. Frequently, the pastors were college
graduates with some seminary training. The style of the church
life resembled that of white Protestant congregations and

represented a distinct rejection of emotionalism, Negro forms of
music and the use of the black dialect.[65]

Segregationist patterns hardened, however, as the white
denominations made overtures to their southern counterparts in
the decades after Reconstruction. For example, the Presbyterians
in reuniting with the Cumberland Presbyterians in 1905,
abandoned integrated presbyteries as a policy and permitted the
southern judicatories to divide along color lines. At the same
time, some black church leaders supported segregation believing
they could help their own people more effectively on their own.

By World War I, the massive influx of migrants from the
Deep South into cities like Chicago produced a rather different
pattern of black Protestant religion. Catering to lower class
blacks primarily, these new churches were in effect small
collections of recent migrants meeting in rented buildings; they
gave expression to their religious vision in more esoteric and
ecstatic terms. A variety of Spiritualist and Holiness cults
took root among these newcomers, all stressing intense
spirituality, a strict code of behavior, charismatic leadership
and otherworldly attitudes that looked beyond the grave for
rewards denied them here on earth.[66] This highly subjective
form of religion was also evident in white Protestantism among
Holiness groups that stressed additional encounters with the
divine beyond conversion. Pentecostal groups after 1900 also
gave primary importance to a divine infusion needed for
Christian living. The latter stemmed from the Azusa Street

revival in San Francisco in 1906 that was led by Charles Parham, a white, and William Seymour, a black. For several decades, a number of Pentecostal groups were interracial and often divided primarily over minute theological or lifestyle differences.[67] On the fringes of both white and black Pentecostalism were cases of more bizarre religious behavior, often involving tyrannical, self-serving individuals claiming to have unique powers or to be divine themselves.[68]

Denominational accounts, however, portray only a segment of the story. There were larger currents sweeping through the entire Protestant establishment crossing all denominational lines. These changes involved more than theological squabbles; they raised fundamental questions about how the church was to relate to the urban, industrial scene that often divided America into opposing camps. Protestants in Chicago were deeply influenced by these developments and took part in them.

The Social Gospel Agenda

Undoubtedly, the most decisive response of Protestants to the emergence of a class society was the social gospel movement.[69] In the 1880s, Protestant clergy and some laymen, like Richard Ely, began stressing the application of the teachings of Jesus to the social problems of the cities. In so doing, they redefined the individualistic and pietistic Gospel into a message and program of social amelioration. The church was not the only agency of redemption; other institutions carried religious functions as well and together brought about "the kingdom of God on earth." As Ely said, "The legislator in city, state or nation is likewise a minister in Christ's church, and he is guilty of violation of a sacred trust if he does not endeavor to bring to pass the kingdom of God in his sphere."[70]

What Ely and others saw was a disturbing gap between a comfortable Protestantism of the native middle to upper class population and the brutal working class world in which Protestantism was either irrelevant or unable to make a significant impact. Convinced that a Social Christianity possessed the power to hold together a disintegrating society, they launched a critique on the Protestant establishment and pointed the way to programmatic responses on the part of churches.

The Social Christianity that infused the social gospel movement had several distinctive doctrines. The most important was that of divine immanence. God was no longer remote, terrifying or even judgmental, but He was to be found within human experience, at work in the social environment, revealing himself in historical progress toward freedom and human dignity. This notion of God was not new in any sense for the awesome God of Puritan Calvinism had been under reconstruction for over two centuries. The orthodox interpretation of 19th century evangelicalism had already removed the sting of divine determinism (by modifying such ideas as predestination and election) and refocused the center of Christianity upon man's faith rather than the character and acts of God. With the emergence of evolutionary thought, particularly after the Civil War, traditional evangelicalism came under attack from a "New Theology" that questioned the static revelation of the Bible, the creation account, the emphasis on human depravity of any sort that required individual conversion, and the otherworldly focus of religion.[71] Liberal theologians updated these well-worn doctrines by adapting Christian truth to the current intellectual commitments, often accepting only that from Christianity which was compatible with a modernist outlook.[72]

Related to this view of God was the popular notion of the "kingdom of God on earth." While conservative Protestants tended to understand this in apocalyptic terms, those who accepted the New Theology saw the kingdom as the Christianizing of the social order along the lines of Christ's ethics (which in their view were quite consistent with democratic ideals). Those who called themselves Christians were partners, or co-workers, with Christ in this mission of penetrating the political and economic structures with the ideals of pure Christianity. Associated with this kingdom was a belief in the priority of social solidarity. As Ely argued,

> There is no such thing either as purely individual sin, or a purely individual righteousness. We are all responsible to a certain extent for all the poverty and sin and suffering about us. We fulfill our mission and develop our own true individuality...by bringing ourselves in body and mind into harmony with the laws of social solidarity.[73]

For Ely, this solidarity was expressed in the institution of the state so that religious laws in the truest sense were those which promoted the common good and secured the honest

administration of justice. Not all social gospellers were
interested in legislation, and very few in revamping or
overthrowing the existing structures, but all believed in the
possibility of social progress especially when the ethical
implications of religion were realized and practiced. Unity and
harmony would replace class strife as those who were blessed
with material wealth put their social responsibilty into action.
Though renouncing the individualist tone of orthodox
Christianity, the social gospel advocates still maintained a
commitment to individual redemption within the social context.
This incipient individualism eventually prevented the movement
from engaging in serious political reform and made their
strategies ineffective and naive.

The social gospel featured some articulate spokesmen.
Washington Gladden, a New York farm boy who learned the ways of
reform from abolitionists and prohibitionists before the Civil
War, became an early advocate during pastorates in
Congregational churches in Brooklyn and Springfield,
Massachusetts. When he arrived in Columbus, Ohio, in 1882 (where
he lived until his death in 1918), he was preaching the themes
of the New Theology: divine immanence, divine possibilities of
man, kingdom of heaven on earth, and an incessant faith in
progress.[74] Gladden scorned socialism but supported labor
unions and frequently spoke to employers and workers in
Columbus. For him, class warfare as evidenced at Haymarket
Square, or Homestead, or Pullman, would destroy the nation,

unless the church could become a context of social justice and
unity. Gladden remained a missionary for the Protestant faith,
sentimentalized with the "brotherhood of man and fatherhood of
God" as the ultimate solution.

The name most associated with the social gospel was that
of Walter Rauschenbusch, a German Baptist preacher who acquired
his credentials in New York's Hell's Kitchen, and then gave the
movement some systematic formulation while teaching at Rochester
Theological Seminary.[75] Influenced by the social philosophy of
Henry George, Edward Bellamy and Henry Demarest Lloyd,
Rauschenbusch adopted a strong anti-capitalist stance. A
commonwealth of justice could only be attained by the ideal of
the kingdom, the spirit of Christianity that was impeded
primarily by the creeds and structures of the churches. The
kingdom, for Rauschenbusch, was "the democratic spirit, which
the Church inherited from Jesus and the prophets" and if the
social gospel could put this spirit "in control of the
institutions and teaching of the Church," a society of
individuals would then find freedom through self-sacrificial
love.[76]

Rauschenbusch's mild socialism was not Marxist at all but
rather a blend of liberal humanism and radical New Testament
Christianity. His anti-capitalist rhetoric made him appear
pro-labor to conservatives, but he had little to say that
satisfied the working class.[77]

Presbyterian minister Charles Stelzle did penetrate the

labor movement on behalf of the social gospel. Once a unionist
and machinist, Stelzle received his meager theological training
at Moody Bible Institute. His interest in the working class
earned him a denominational post as a "home missionary" to
workingmen. He made the most of this opportunity by means of
lecturing, cultivating relations with unions, writing a weekly
column, and speaking in factories; within Presbyterian ranks, he
was often branded a socialist and by 1913, was pressured to
resign. His greatest achievement was the establishment of the
New York Labor Temple, an institutional church that maintained
connections with unionists and socialists as well as offering
social services to workers. But like his fellow social
gospellers, Stelzle detested class division, saw Christianity as
a source of reconciliation and worked to improve the status of
working men and women within the system.[78]

Several things can be noted about the social gospel
phenomenon. First, it was a movement dominated by clergymen.
Like the abolitionists, the eloquent, passionate preacher with a
ready audience gained public attention and influence. Second,
these clergymen never seriously questioned the existing
capitalist system; their socialism usually extended only to
public utilities. This may explain the occasional support of
social gospel causes by philanthropic millionaires, such as J.
Pierpont Morgan. Even Rauschenbusch received Rockefeller money
for his church building.[79] The failure of social gospel
advocates to develop effective ties with militant groups that

actually fought against the social order made them less than
threatening. Third, by ultimately reducing religion to ethics,
the social gospellers doomed their own cause. After World War I
and the crushing of liberal optimism, much of the progressive
reform zeal subsided. The religious motivation supplied by the
social gospel became an outmoded way of thinking. Fourth, the
social gospel became institutionalized in the denominational
structures. Each of the major denominations formed social
service departments. In 1908, at the formation of the
interdenominational superstructure, the Federal Council of
Churches, a "Social Creed of the Churches" was adopted that gave
the social gospel confessional status. However, these
bureaucratic responses did little to affect the lives of working
people.

Christian Socialism

If the social gospel in its hey-day before the First
World War was plagued by its upper class orientation, there were
Protestants willing to consider an overhaul of the political and
economic system. These were the Christian Socialists, who were
committed to a more radical application of the social gospel,
yet were hindered by many of the same problems.[80] Their track
record was as dismal as that of the various Socialist parties
that functioned from the 1880s until the Red Scare of the early
20s.+

As a religious ideology, Christian Socialism was a shaky
bridge between Christian social thought and the socialist

agenda. A similar attempt had been made in England and some of the literature produced there influenced American Protestants. W. D. P. Bliss, an Episcopal clergyman, who had begun an institutional church in Boston for workingmen, and became involved with the Knights of Labor in 1886, played a pioneering role.[81] In the 1890s, he and several other Episcopalians formed a pro-labor association to help arbitrate labor disputes, the Church Association for Advancement of Interests of Labor. Bliss also formed a Society of Christian Socialists, started publishing a journal and became infatuated with Edward Bellamy's Nationalist clubs. However, at this early stage, Bliss and his associates were simply social gospellers whose involvement with workers had given them a high respect for organized labor, the reform unionism espoused by the Knights and a vision for a Christian democracy that stressed social solidarity rather than capitalism. They were Christians showing interest in elements of the Socialist program.

However, Bliss refused to identify with the Socialist Labor Party and steered clear of utopian schemes, like the Christian Commonwealth Colony in Georgia which attracted 400 followers in 1896. None of these activities gained Bliss any friends among the socialists but neither were most Christian leaders interested in Bliss' radical positions.[82]

After 1900, Christian Socialism regained momentum, aided by Rauschenbusch's writings that were sympathetic to the socialist ideal of a classless society. In 1906, a Christian

Socialist Fellowship was organized with almost 25 chapters and over a thousand members. About 20 pastors in Chicago identified themselves as socialists around this time. A Methodist minister, E. M. Carr, edited the Christian Socialist for a number of years. Bliss was an active member and even wrote Sunday school lessons from a socialist viewpoint. The CSF endorsed the Socialist Party but also tried to articulate a Christian expression of socialism. Many of its members were active in Socialist Party activities and worked to preserve Socialist unity. At the same time, the CSF labored to gain acceptance among churches for the socialist alternative.

But this phase of Christian Socialism came to a rapid end when the United States entered the War in 1917. The Socialist Party's stance against American entry divided the party; the Christian Socialists were among those who withdrew. The Russian Revolution also created problems for the Socialist Party and led to a great loss in membership. The post-war reaction to all socialist groups made the political environment anything but friendly for Christian Socialists.

The socialist Christians were also hurt by internal weaknesses. One particular leader, George Herron, a minister and professor at Grinnell College (Iowa), whose visionary and sensational critique of capitalism earned him a national reputation, promoted the cause vigorously until many of his more extreme views and messianic complex offended even those most sympathetic. Herron's well-publicized divorce and remarriage to

his mistress brought shame to him and the CSF. Herron appeared
in Chicago occasionally to give lectures and was treated by the
press as an oddity. Eventually Herron abandoned Christianity
entirely and participated in Socialist Party functions until
1914, when he abruptly moved to Italy and became a recluse
intellectual.[83] To Bliss, Herron was an impractical idealist
and a socialist with no political sense. How much damage Herron
did to the cause is hard to determine. The fate of the CSF was
sealed with that of the Socialist cause.

The Fundamentalist Response

The social gospel was a movement of Protestant liberals
concerned about the church's relation to the world; an equally
distinctive movement was conservative evangelicalism, or
fundamentalism as it came to be called. Its primary concern was
with the church's relation to historic Christianity.[84] Like the
social gospel, fundamentalism's formative period of development
was the last two decades of the 19th century, but its most
obvious impact on Protestantism and on American culture occurred
after 1900. A variety of simplistic stereotypes have been
frequently attached to this phenomenon obscuring important
features of its origin and activity. Fundamentalism has been
labelled anti-intellectual, anti-modern science, a rural
southern reaction to urban culture, and a collective anxiety of
19th century Protestants unable to deal with secular or liberal
thought. All of these characterizations neglect abundant
evidence that northern urban pastors were in the forefront of

the movement, that modern business methods and contemporary public relations gimmicks were utilized by fundamentalist preachers, that its proponents advanced a variety of theological innovations of their own and that its most aggressive spokesmen did anything but abandon the cities.[85]

Clearly the heart of fundamentalism was continuous and consistent with 19th century evangelicalism: the revivalist emphasis on individual conversion, the belief in supernatural revelation located in the Bible, the supreme task of evangelistic activity by clergy and lay people, refraining from a host of worldly pleasures, and voluntary membership of believers in congregations were all carried into the 20th century church. The emergence of liberal doctrines was met by a conservative defense of such beliefs as the deity of Christ, human sin and divine judgment (many of these latter doctrines were eventually dubbed the "fundamentals" and separated the "true Christians" from the apostate). The first skirmishes were heresy trials of free-thinking pastors and were usually won by the conservatives; but as theologians in the Protestant seminaries became increasingly liberal, another generation of pastors and church leaders was produced that was able to take over the denominational machinery and eventually compel fundamentalists to leave. In the final analysis, the fundamentalist-modernist controversy became a political battle in the denominations. As the losers, the fundamentalists withdrew to form their own institutions and subculture.[86]

Several wealthy businessmen invested heavily in
fundamentalist programs, including Club trustee Henry Crowell.
The 1909 publication of a set of twelve volumes of conservative
scholarly writings known as The Fundamentals were distributed
free to three million persons in the United States and around
the world. The cost of this defense of the faith was borne by
two brothers, Lyman and Milton Stewart, Los Angeles millionaires
who owned the Union Oil Company. Stewart money also built the
fundamentalist Bible Institute of Los Angeles and published the
Schofield Reference Bible, a Bible with fundamentalist
commentary.[87] William Jennings Bryan's Bible Crusaders of
America organization was largely funded by hotel chain owner,
George Washburn.[88]

While these fundamentalists rejected the social gospel,
primarily because of the liberal theology it embodied, they were
not uninvolved in social concerns. They were probably as active
in urban work as the social gospellers.[89] But their
prescription for urban diseases was different. They continued to
emphasize the moral regeneration of the individual as the
starting point of social reform, a view widely rejected by
liberal activists. Christian conversion was the vehicle for this
personal renewal and evangelists, like Chapman, Sunday and
others of lesser renown, relentlessly preached that message. In
the same breath, they denounced booze, prostitution, gambling,
dancing, political corruption and other forms of wickedness. The
more sophisticated fundamentalist clergymen also proposed

various reform measures, many of which appeared in Progressive
platforms. Mark Mathews, William Riley and John Roach Straton
are examples of these socially-minded preachers.[90] But Socialist
proposals were completely foreign to their way of thinking.
Structural reform ignored the heart of their theological system:
the individual's personal and private relationship to God. Nor
were they able to comprehend evil in the system itself; societal
problems were caused by evil people. The social hierarchy was at
best neutral, if not actually good. It would certainly function
more righteously if more individuals were morally upright. This
naive social thought rendered much of their benevolent activity
in the cities of little long-term consequence (even though the
depth of their devotion may have affected individual persons).

William Jennings Bryan was an anomalous figure in the
story of fundamentalism. In the mid-twenties, after all his
political battles, he took up the cudgels on behalf of a
Protestant faith that he perceived to be under serious attack.
That he became the national spokesman for the fundamentalist
cause at a trial in the south over an issue not actually germane
to that cause illustrates the connection of this movement with
the broader Protestant culture. After the Scopes trial, at which
Clarence Darrow made a monkey out of Bryan, who providentially
passed away the week after, fundamentalism became associated in
the public mind with backwoods, rural, southern white culture.
Fundamentalism became the butt of the nation's jokes. The
political naivete of the northern fundamentalists had cost them

dearly. Bryan had not been a fundamentalist in strict theological terms. For him, Christianity was a social force that made a civilization great and as a Christian civilization, America could not afford to abandon its religion. Unlike some of his fundamentalist brethren, Bryan had not accepted pluralism in the American ethos. He was more intent on saving America than saving souls.

The most unusual figure in the fundamentalist pantheon was Princeton scholar, J. Gresham Machen, who was driven from the Seminary and the Presbyterian denomination in the late 20s because of his fundamentalist stance.[91] Intellectually, Machen towered over his fellow clergymen, having studied in Germany with the most liberal of Biblical scholars; socially, he came from an elitist southern family (associating in the same circles as Woodrow Wilson) and practiced many of the taboos condemned by other fundamentalists. Machen became the most articulate defender of historic Christianity and in his works, showed how liberal expressions of it vitiated the substance of Protestant religion. In Machen's orthodoxy, Christian experience rested on a set of truths (for Machen, Christianity was a religion based on facts open to scientific investigation); when liberals reversed this order, they ultimately sacrificed Christianity.

Machen perceived the fundamentalist-modernist controversy as an intellectual crisis, one in which Christianity's relationship to the culture was the issue.[92] Liberals had succumbed to the culture, he believed (not realizing how much conservatives had done the same); orthodox believers had to hold out for a Renaissance of Christian humanism, in which Christianity infused and penetrated the arts and sciences. By casting his lot with the fundamentalists (he was always squeamish about the label) whose posture toward the culture was one of attack, Machen lost the opportunity to address the culture with any hope of obtaining a hearing. His political conservatism which bordered on libertarianism also prevented his finding any common ground with his liberal foes. Yet Machen, like few others on the orthodox camp, had recognized the loss of intellectual power in American Christianity, a loss that was attributable to both liberals and conservatives.

Yet tens of thousands of Chicago Protestants were never active in the social gospel, or the fundamentalist-modernist debate, or had any acquaintance with the Pentecostal movements. For them, it would appear that religion comprised one compartment of their total life activities, primarily confined to Sundays, essentially a passive acquiescence to the truths espoused by the clergy who were viewed as the experts in religion. However, this description does not do justice to the private ruminations of many persons sitting in the pews, for as the individuals who are the subject of this study reveal, numerous laymen did have their own ideas about religion and they did attempt to integrate their religious vision with other dimensions of their lives. It would even appear that businessmen in particular were prone to take religion seriously.[93]

An explanation of this connection will be attempted in the following chapters but it is worth noting that men like the Club trustees were accustomed to achieving success and exerting their power. In the early part of this century, men involved in commercial affairs were folk heroes of a sort--despite the occasional drubbing they took at the hands of novelists, muckrakers and left-wing progressives. A far greater share of the population emulated them and took their amateur advice to heart. Thus, it should not be surprising that businessmen carried weight in religious circles.

The businessman was known as a man of action. He accomplished things. He dealt with facts and hard realities. A good businessman was one who had the resources, the right connections and the determination to get the job done. The problems of the marketplace continually challenged both his organizational skill and his spirit; he was inclined to cultivate both.

What worked in business should work in religion as well. Being a Christian was essentially a matter of how one acted, certainly more so than what one believed. Christianity was meant to be a practical religion that improved the quality of social life. Certainly, it was to be more than good deeds, but good deeds demonstrated its truthfulness more than anything else. Barnes once defined "religion pure and undefiled" as "a means of serving others to the limit of one's ability."[94]

But action itself was not sufficient for the modern

Christian; it had to be accompanied by character. Character implied moral convictions, determination, self-discipline and other similar traits. Interestingly, these were often considered the marks of a successful businessman. Religion was indispensable to the development of character, because of the model of a figure like Jesus and because of the ideals that religion promoted. The spiritual dimension was a safeguard against a soul-deadening materialism, according to Barnes, who hoped the Sunday Evening Club would "quicken the interest of us businessmen in eternal realities of life and religion."[95]

Theological questions became insignificant to this muscular Christianity. Truth was being continually discovered and one could hardly be dogmatic. Barnes criticized religious leaders who "go up and down the land, proclaiming as sacrosanct, hallowed and unchangeable, the doctrines and dogmas of the early church."[96] Even the Bible itself had to be read as literature and not necessarily compatible with modern scientific knowledge in all its details.[97]

If there was one word the business community used to describe its own agenda, it was "efficiency." Many of the corporate executives had experimented with various efficiency schemes that streamlined production and attempted to extract more work from the employees. The same techniques were eventually applied to religious enterprises. This standard of efficiency had a tendency to emphasize measurable results and encourage pragmatic decisions.[98] The efficient church kept

records of its accomplishments: the number of souls saved, or
dollars raised, or in Barnes' case, the number of brothels shut
down and honest politicians elected. Qualitative issues lost
their importance as the intangibles of the Christian experience
were discarded for more concrete demonstrations of moral
betterment.

NOTES

1. Thomas J. Riley, The Higher Life of Chicago (Chicago: University of Chicago Press, 1905), p.116.

2. For an excellent portrait of Mundelein and his impact on Chicago Catholicism, see Edward Kantowicz, Sole Corporation (South Bend: University of Notre Dame Press, 1983). Note also Joseph John Parot, Polish Catholics in Chicago, 1850-1920 (DeKalb: Northern Illinois University Press, 1981) for a fine treatment of Chicago Catholicism in one ethnic community.

3. Chicago Tribune, 17 October 1910.

4. Ford C. Ottman, J. Wilbur Chapman: A Biography (New York: Doubleday, 1920); William McLoughlin, Modern Revivalism from Charles G. Finney to Billy Graham (New York: Ronald Press, 1959), pp.377-378; both of these treatments reinforce Chapman's image as a business-minded evangelist. Chapman was a close friend of Philadelphia tycoon, John Wanamaker, and formerly the pastor of Wanamaker's Bethany Presbyterian Church.

5. Chicago Tribune, 15 March 1918.

6. Chicago Tribune, 10 January 1918.

7. Commerce (Chicago), 21 February 1918.

8. Chicago Tribune, 15 March 1918.

9. Thomas J. Dorst, "Sowing the Seeds of Reform: The Chicago Tract Society, 1889-1910," Chicago History 12:1 (Spring, 1983), pp.36-43.

10. Chicago Tract Society, Annual Report (1909).

11. Allan W. Bosch, "The Salvation Army in Chicago, 1885-1914" (Ph.D. dissertation, University of Chicago, 1965); Edward H. McKinley, Marching to Glory: The History of the Salvation Army in the United States 1880-1980 (San Francisco: Harper & Row, 1980); Herbert A. Wisbey, Soldiers Without Swords:

A History of the Salvation Army in the United States (New York: Macmillan, 1955).

12. Francis E. Clark, World-Wide Endeavor (Philadelphia: Gillespie, Metzgar & Kelley, 1895); Dwight Pratt, A Decade of Christian Endeavor 1881-1891 (Chicago: Fleming Revell, 1891).

13. "The Christian Endeavor Society" (Columbus, Oh.: International Society of Christian Endeavor, n.d.).

14. Chicago Tribune, 10 July 1915.

15. Chicago Tribune, 13 July 1915.

16. Emmot Dedmon, Great Enterprises: 100 Years of the YMCA in Metropolitan Chicago (Chicago: Rand McNally, 1957).

17. Record of Christian Work (East Northfield, Mass.), January, 1908. For biographical treatments of Mott, see C. Howard Hopkins, John R. Mott 1865-1955 (Grand Rapids: Eerdmans, 1979); Roger D. Woods, "The World of Thought of John R. Mott" (Ph.D. dissertation, University of Iowa, 1965).

18. George A. Salstrand, The Story of Stewardship (Grand Rapids: Baker Book House, 1956), pp.47-52. See also Robert Speer, "The Layman's Duty to Propagate His Religion" (New York: Board of National Missions, n.d.); John R. Mott, Liberating the Lay Forces of Christianity (New York: Macmillan, 1931); Stephen C. Neill and Hans-Ruedi Weber, The Layman in Christian History (Philadelphia: Westminster Press, 1963), pp.248-260.

19. The IWM story has been told by Eldon G. Ernst, "The Interchurch World Movement of North America 1919-1920" (Ph.D. dissertation, Yale, 1968). Charles E. Harvey claims that Ernst was led astray by Raymond Fosdick's successful attempts to obscure the involvement of John D. Rockefeller, Jr. in the IWM. Harvey traces Fosdick's machinations on behalf of Rockefeller to escape the embarrassment of the IWM collapse. See Harvey, "John D. Rockefeller, Jr. and the Interchurch World Movement of 1919-1920: A Different Angle on the Ecumenical Movement," Church History 51:2 (June 1982), pp.198-209.

20. Quoted in Harvey, "John D. Rockefeller," p.202.

21. Clifford Barnes in Church Federation Bulletin (Chicago), December 1925.

22. Chicago Tribune, 8 February 1912. See also Harry G. Lefever, "The Involvement of the Men and Religion Forward Movement in the Cause of Labor Justice, Atlanta, Georgia, 1912-1916," Labor History 14 (Fall 1973), pp.521-534.

23. Frederick F. Shannon, "A Study of Constructive Manhood," sermon preached at Central Church, Chicago, 1928. Chicago Historical Society.

24. Jenkin Lloyd Jones, "What Is It To Be A Christian?" (Chicago: Unity Office, n.d.), pp.10, 12.

25. Richard H. Thomas, "Jenkin Lloyd Jones: Lincoln's Soldier of Civic Righteousness" (Ph.D. dissertation, Rutgers University, 1967).

26. Andrew Stevenson, Chicago, Preeminently a Presbyterian City (Chicago: n.p., 1907).

27. Kenneth Wylie, ed. "Presbyterians in Chicago, 1833-1983" (Chicago: Presbytery of Chicago, 1983); Clifford M. Drury, Presbyterian Panorama: 150 Years of National Missions History (Philadelphia: Presbyterian Church of USA, 1952). For related discussion on Presbyterianism in Chicago, see Lefferts A. Loetscher, The Broadening Church (Philadelphia: University of Pennsylvania Press, 1954); William T. Hanzsche, The Presbyterians (Philadelphia: Westminster Press, 1934); Robert T. Nichols, Presbyterianism in New York State (Philadelphia: Westminster Press, 1963): Andrew C. Zenos, Presbyterianism in America (New York: Thomas Nelson, 1937).

28. Joan W. Moore, "Stability and Instability in the Metropolitan Upper Class" (Ph.D. dissertation, University of Chicago, 1959); Kathleen D. McCarthy, Noblesse Oblige: Charity and Cultural Philanthropy in Chicago, 1849-1929 (Chicago: University of Chicago Press, 1982).

29. Presbytery of Chicago, Minutes of December 2, 1918.

30. David R. Forgan, Sketches and Speeches (Chicago: n.p., 1925), p. 220.

31. Quoted in John Mulder, Woodrow Wilson: The Years of Preparation (Princeton: Princeton University Press, 1978), p. 231.

32. David Hugh Jones, "German Kultur and American Christianity," sermon preached at First Presbyterian Church, Evanston, May 19, 1918. Chicago Historical Society.

33. Continent (Chicago), 13 July 1911.

34. Continent (Chicago), 21 January 1915.

35. Charles Quirk, "A Statistical Analysis of the Signers of the Auburn Affirmation," Journal of Presbyterian Church 43:3 (September 1965).

36. Andrew C. Zenos, The Elements of Higher Criticism (New York: Funk & Wagnalls, 1896), p.46.

37. Nolan Best, Inspiration (Chicago: Fleming Revell, 1923), pp.80, 108.

38. Nolan Best, "The Relation of the Religious Press to Religious Education" in Proceedings of the Second Convention of Religious Education Association, 1904 (Chicago: Religious Education Association, 1904), p.427.

39. Arthur A. Hays, "Pilgrim: Puritan: Protestant," inaugural address delivered at McCormick Seminary, September 14, 1920.

40. Charles Erdman, Presbyterian Men (Chicago: Presbyterian Brotherhood, 1911), p.214.

41. Presbytery of Chicago, Minutes of September 10, 1917.

42. Continent (Chicago), 7 January 1915.

43. Andrew C. Zenos, "Vital Christianity," address at McCormick Seminary, September 11, 1923.

44. Presbytery of Chicago, Minutes of October 3, 1918.

45. Two of the better histories of the Protestant Episcopal Church are Raymond W. Albright, A History of the Protestant Episcopal Church (New York: Macmillan, 1964) and James T. Addison, The Episcopal Church in the United States 1789-1931 (New York: Charles Scribner's Sons, 1951). A more iconoclastic treatment of Episcopalianism is Kit and Frederica Konolige, The Power of Their Glory: America's Ruling Class, the Episcopalians (New York: Wyden Books, 1978). For a discussion of Episcopal lay organizations, see E. Clowes Chorley, Men and Movements in the American Episcopal Church (New York: Charles Scribner's Sons, 1946).

46. John Henry Hopkins, The Great Forty Years in the Diocese of Chicago 1893-1933 (Chicago: Centenary Fund of Diocese of Chicago, 1936).

47. The impact of Anglo-Catholicism in the U.S. Episcopal Church is examined in George DeMille, The Catholic Movement in the American Episcopal Church (Philadelphia: Church Historical Society, 1950). See also Eugene R. Fairweather, ed. The Oxford Movement (New York: Oxford University Press, 1964); R. W. Church, The Oxford Movement 1833-1845 (Chicago: University of Chicago Press, 1970).

187

48. Warren C. Platt, "The Reformed Episcopal Church: The Origins and Early Development of its Ideological Expression," Historical Magazine of the Protestant Episcopal Church 52:3 (September 1983).

49. C. G. Brown, "Christocentric Liberalism in the Episcopal Church," Historical Magazine of the Protestant Episcopal Church 37:1 (March 1968); Stephen H. Applegate, "The Rise and Fall of the Thirty-Nine Articles: An Inquiry into the Identity of the Protestant Episcopal Church in the U.S.," Historical Magazine of the Protestant Episcopal Church 50:4 (December 1981).

50. Clyde Griffin, "Rich Laymen and Early Social Christianity," Church History 36 (March 1967).

51. James O. Bennett, Saint James' Church, Chicago and Its Rector: A Study of a Metropolitan Pastor (Chicago: n.p., 1914).

52. These insights are garnered from Jackson Lears, No Place of Grace: Antimodernism and the Transformation of American Culture 1880-1920 (New York: Pantheon Books, 1981).

53. Hopkins, The Great Forty Years, p.187.

54. Quoted in Perry J. Stackhouse, Chicago and the Baptists (Chicago: University of Chicago Press, 1933), p.143.

55. Quoted in Frederick A. Norwood, The Story of American Methodism (Nashville: Abingdon, 1974), p.356. See also Almer Pennewell, The Methodist Movement in Northern Illinois (Sycamore: Sycamore Tribune, 1942).

56. Shailer Mathews' works include The Church and the Changing Order (New York: Macmillan, 1907); The Individual and the Social Gospel (New York: Laymen's Missionary Movement, 1914); The Spiritual Interpretation of History (Cambridge: Harvard University Press, 1916); The Faith of Modernism (New York: Macmillan, 1924).

57. For a discussion of the modernist-fundamentalist battle in the Northern Baptist Convention, see Robert Moats Miller, Harry Emerson Fosdick: Preacher, Pastor, Prophet (New York: Oxford University Press, 1985), pp.150-173.

58. Robert Moats Miller, How Shall They Hear Without a Preacher? The Life of Ernest Fremont Tittle (Chapel Hill: University of North Carolina Press, 1971).

59. Stackhouse, Chicago and the Baptists, p.203.

60. Northwestern Christian Advocate (Chicago), 7 February 1912.

61. Isabelle Horton, The Builders (Chicago: n.p., 1910) tells the story of the Chicago Training School for City, Home and Foreign Missions to which Norman Harris contributed over $100,000 and of which he was board president for at least six years. Frederick A. Norwood's From Dawn to Midday at Garrett (Evanston: Garrett Evangelical Theological Seminary, 1978) includes discussion of Harry Wheeler's leadership role in the development of the Biblical Institute.

62. W. E. B. DuBois, "The Religion of the American Negro" in Religion in the American Experience, ed. Robert Handy (Columbia: University of South Carolina Press, 1972), p.180. See also E. Franklin Frazier, The Negro Church in America (New York: Schocken Books, 1963); Seth Scheiner, "The Negro Church and the Northern City, 1890-1930" in Seven on Black: Reflections on the Negro Experience in America, ed. William Shade (Philadelphia: Lippincott, 1969).

63. U. S. Department of Commerce/Bureau of the Census, Religious Bodies (1916) Part Two: Separate Denominations (Washington: Government Printing Office, 1919).

64. Chicago Commission on Race Relations, The Negro in Chicago: A Study of Race Relations and a Race Riot in 1919 (Chicago: University of Chicago Press, 1922), pp.500-501.

65. David M. Reimers, White Protestantism and the Negro (New York: Oxford University Press, 1965); Andrew E. Murray, Presbyterians and the Negro - A History (Philadelphia: Westminster, 1966).

66. William McLoughlin argues that Negro churchgoers in America were overwhelmingly "fundamentalist" in outlook. By his definition, they were fringe sects whose "psychological frustrations and anxieties" due to their alienated status were released through the perfectionism, millenarianism and emotionalism of their religion. In this category, McLoughlin includes the northern fundamentalists. Omitting the psychological reductionism, Robert Handy notes certain parallel patterns: "the piety of the expanding black churches" was similar to white evangelicals who were "revivalistic and Bible-centered, emotional in tone, simplistic in theology, at home in lay-led Sunday schools and missionary societies" (p.272). William McLoughlin, "Is There a Third Force in Christendom?" Daedalus 96 (Winter 1967); Robert T. Handy, A History of the Churches in the United States and Canada (Oxford: Clarendon Press, 1977). See also Arthur E. Paris, Black Pentecostalism: Southern Religion in an Urban World (Amherst: University of Massachusetts Press, 1982).

67. Vinson Synan, The Holiness-Pentecostal Movement in the United States (Grand Rapids: Eerdmans, 1971). See also Grant Wacker, "The Holy Spirit and the Spirit of the Age in American Protestantism, 1880-1910," Journal of American History 72:1 (June 1985).

68. J. R. Washington, Black Sects and Cults (New York: Doubleday, 1973); Arthur H. Fauser, Black Gods of the Metropolis (Philadelphia: University of Pennsylvania Press, 1944).

69. Studies of the social gospel movement are plentiful. Charles Hopkins, The Rise of the Social Gospel in American Protestantism 1865-1915 (New Haven: Yale University Press, 1940); Paul Carter, The Decline and Revival of the Social Gospel:Social and Political Liberalism in American Protestant Churches 1920-1940 (Ithaca: Cornell University Press, 1954); Robert Miller, American Protestants and Social Issues, 1919-1930 (Chapel Hill: University of North Carolina Press, 1956); Robert Handy, The Social Gospel in America 1870-1920 (New York: Oxford University Press, 1966); William Hutchison, The Modernist Impulse in American Protestantism (Cambridge: Belknap Press, 1976).

70. Quoted in Handy, Social Gospel, p.242.

71. Winthrop Hudson, The Great Tradition of American Churches (New York: Harper, 1953), p.201. For contemporary expressions of this New Theology, see William Newton Clarke, An Outline of Christian Theology (New York: Charles Scribner's Sons, 1898); Edward S. Ames, Beyond Theology (Chicago: University of Chicago Press, 1959); Arthur Cushman McGiffert, The Rise of Modern Religious Ideas (New York: Macmillan, 1922).

72. Kenneth Cauthen's categories of "evangelical liberals" and "modernist liberals" are helpful in measuring the degree of adaptation that different theologians made. Among the former he includes Fosdick, A. C. Knudson and Eugene Lyman; these Christocentric liberals abandoned the foundation of Biblical authority for a progressive revelation that relied on the personal experience of the believer. The example and teachings of Jesus were still considered normative and the basis for the world's most developed religion. The modernists, on the other hand, such as Mathews, D. C. MacIntosh and Henry Wieman, dismissed revelation altogether and opted for a scientific methodology to assess the validity of religious content. Christianity itself was no longer unique in comparison to other religions, though Jesus was a model of revolutionary religious living. Kenneth Cauthen, The Impact of American Religious Liberalism (New York: Harper, 1962).

73. Quoted in Handy, Social Gospel, p.236.

74. Paul Boase, The Rhetoric of Christian Socialism (New York: Random House, 1969), pp.29-35.

75. Walter Rauschenbusch's four major works are Christianity and the Social Crisis (New York: Hodder & Stoughton, 1907); The Social Principles of Jesus (New York: Association Press, 1916); A Theology for the Social Gospel (New York: Macmillan, 1917); Christianizing the Social Order (New York: Macmillan, 1919).

76. Quoted in Ralph Gabriel, The Course of American Democratic Thought (New York: Ronald Press, 1956), p. 327.

77. John Aiken and James McConnell, "Walter Rauschenbusch and Labor Reform: A Social Gospeller's Approach," Labor History 11 (Spring 1970). See also David E. Harrell, The Social Sources of Division in the Disciples of Christ 1865-1900 (Atlanta: Publishing Systems, 1973), pp.99-105.

78. George Nash, "Charles Stelzle: Apostle to Labor," Labor History 11 (Spring 1970).

79. Robert Cross, The Church and the Social Order 1865-1910 (Indianapolis: Bobbs-Merrill, 1967), pp.322-327.

80. Robert T. Handy, "Christianity and Socialism in America, 1900-1920," Church History 21 (March 1952).

81. Richard Dressner, "William Dwight Porter Bliss' Christian Socialism," Church History 47 (March 1978).

82. Clyde Griffen, "Christian Socialism Instructed by Gompers," Labor History 12 (Spring 1971).

83. Phyllis Nelson, "George Herron and the Socialist Clergy 1890-1914" (Ph.D. dissertation, State University of Iowa, 1953).

84. Norman Furniss, The Fundamentalist Controversy 1918-1931 (New Haven: Yale University Press, 1954); Ernest Sandeen, The Origins of Fundamentalism: Toward a Historical Interpretation (Philadelphia: Fortress Press, 1968); Ferenc Szasz, The Divided Mind of Protestant America 1880-1930 (University, Ala.: University of Alabama Press, 1982); George Marsden, Fundamentalism and American Culture (New York: Oxford University Press, 1980); James D. Hunter, American Evangelicalism: Conservative Religion and the Quandary of Modernity (New Brunswick: Rutgers University Press, 1983).

85. Paul Carter, "The Fundamentalist Defense of the Faith" in Change and Continuity: The 1920's, ed. John Braeman

(Columbus: Ohio State University Press, 1965), pp.179-214.

86. Recent scholars have stressed the theological roots of fundamentalism that made it a positive force in Protestantism, not merely a negative reaction. Ernest Sandeen views fundamentalism as an alliance between two 19th century theologies, dispensationalism and the Princeton theology. Dispensationalism was a form of millenialism and historical interpretation developed by British pietists that claimed to read the Bible "literally" and that divided history into distinct eras, or dispensations, based on the Biblical text, arriving at a view of the imminent return of Christ, a millenial kingdom on earth and the rapid decline of world civilization. These ideas became very popular among conservative Protestant ministers as early as the 1870s. The other tributary was the rugged Calvinist brand of Protestantism staunchly maintained at Princeton Seminary with a new emphasis on Biblical inerrancy, the view that the Scripture was without error. This doctrine became central to the conservative position and placed its adherents on a collision course with liberals who preferred progressive revelation and the scientific account of evolution to an implausible creation story. But as Sandeen points out, the inerrancy idea was itself an application of inductive science, an attempt to demonstrate the validity of Christian belief on the basis of reason and the evidence of Biblical archaeology.

Paul Carter, who in earlier works treated fundamentalism as a dying gasp of an outmoded Protestantism, later agreed with Sandeen's emphasis, noting that "Fundamentalism is not simply the `old-time' religion" but is a "new" affirmation of the inherited tradition" ("The Fundamentalist Defense," p.188).

Critics of Sandeen's thesis, while agreeing on the theological innovations, have faulted him for neglecting the context in which fundamentalism became controversial. The battle for denominational control was the prevailing issue and theological differences were never faced squarely. Nor was the fundamentalist movement a mere quarrel among theologians. As George Marsden attempts to show, it was a broad national movement that gained a great deal of public attention and which was rooted in the mainstream of Protestant-American civil religion. Fundamentalists, according to Marsden, were trapped in an ambivalent relationship to American culture. They found themselves becoming a beleaguered minority as liberal Christianity flowered, but they were still faithful to a heritage in which they were the Establishment. They affirmed individualism, free enterprise, patriotism, moral standards and common sense. This identity paradox extended to their theological formulations: on the one hand, they looked for a millenial kingdom and judgment on a godless society, yet America was somehow unique in the divine economy and deserved the intense loyalty of the Christian. They wanted to be out of this world, yet at the same time, they wanted to be in a revived America.

Fundamentalism generally tapped the middle-class white segments of the Protestant constituency. In comparing the biographies of conservative and liberal clergy of this era of controversy, William Hutchison found a basic similarity in economic background. Both groups were overwhelmingly Anglo-Saxon, native-born, urban rather than rural, and from professional families. Conservatives were likely to come from families of wealth and in more cases, from the South.

Walter Ellis' study of specific Baptist congregations showed that lay fundamentalists when compared to those of modernist persuasion, tended to be younger, of lower middle-class socio-economic status and often immigrants from Protestant areas of Europe; the liberal Protestants were an older cosmopolitan crowd, already upwardly mobile and experiencing intellectual doubts. Ellis concludes that fundamentalism with its clear position on the authority and source of truth, its confident eschatology and its "plain man's theology" met the religious needs of younger lower middle-class Protestants more effectively. Ernest Sandeen, "Toward a Historical Interpretation of the Origins of Fundamentalism," Church History 36 (March 1967); Leroy Moore, "Another Look at Fundamentalism," Church History 37 (June 1968); Vernon Mattson, "The Fundamentalist Mind: An Intellectual History of Religious Fundamentalism in the United States" (Ph.D. dissertation, University of Kansas, 1971); William Hutchison, "Cultural Strain and Protestant Liberalism," American Historical Review 76 (April 1971); Walter Ellis, "Social and Religious Factors in the Fundamentalist-Modernist Schisms Among Baptists in North America" (Ph.D. dissertation, Pittsburgh, 1979); Everett Perry, "The Role of Socio-Economic Factors in the Rise and Development of American Fundamentalism" (Ph.D. dissertation, University of Chicago, 1959); Gregory H. Singleton, "Fundamentalism and Urbanization: A Quantitative Critique of Impressionistic Interpretations" in The New Urban History, ed. Leo Schnore (Princeton: Princeton University Press, 1975).

87. Marsden, Fundamentalism and American Culture, pp. 118-123.

88. Perry, "The Role of Socio-Economic Factors," p.111.

89. Norris Magnussen, Salvation in the Slums (Metuchen, N.J.: Scarecrow Press, 1977). For the impact of fundamentalism on immigrant Protestant groups, see Frederick Hale, Trans-Atlantic Conservative Protestantism in the Evangelical Free and Mission Covenant Tradition (New York: Arno Press, 1979); James D. Bratt, Dutch Calvinism in Modern America: A History of a Conservative Subculture (Grand Rapids: Eerdmans, 1984); Gary S. Smith, "Calvinism and Culture in America 1870-1915" (Ph.D. dissertation, Johns Hopkins, 1980); Lawrence B. Davis, Immigrants, Baptists and the Protestant Mind in America (Urbana: University of Illinois Press, 1973).

90. Ferenc Szasz, "Three Fundamentalist Leaders: Bryan, Straton and Riley" (Ph.D. dissertation, Rochester, 1969); Robert Wenger, "Social Thought in American Fundamentalism 1918-1933" (Ph.D. dissertation, Nebraska, 1973).

91. Ned J. Stonehouse, J. Gresham Machen: A Biographical Memoir (Grand Rapids: Eerdmans, 1954); Hutchison, The Modernist Impulse, pp. 258-281.

92. J. Gresham Machen, Christianity and Liberalism (Grand Rapids: Eerdmans, 1923, 1974 edition).

93. Edward C. Kirkland in "Divide and Ruin" in Interpretations of American History: Since 1965 (Volume 2), ed. Gerald N. Grob and George A. Billias (New York: Free Press, 1967) takes issue with the common view of businessmen compartmentalizing their lives.

94. Clifford Barnes, "Tentative Report of the Committee on a System of Teaching Morals in Public Schools," address delivered at the 1911 National Education Association convention. Chicago Historical Society.

95. Clifford Barnes, "Personal Notes," Chicago Sunday Evening Club Papers, Chicago Historical Society.

96. Jacksonville Daily Journal (Illinois), 11 June 1925.

97. Times-Herald (Chicago), 26 January 1901.

98. A book by Club speaker, Clarence Barbour, with the title of Making Religion Efficient (New York: Association Press, 1912), listed the survey results that were part of the Men and Religion Forward Movement. This data noted that 38.5 per cent of teachers in men's Sunday school classes were businessmen; they outnumbered all other categories (clergy, professionals).

CHAPTER 4

THE IDEOLOGY OF A BUSINESS CLASS

The previous chapters have depicted a group of
religiously-motivated businessmen pursuing a set of goals within
a specific historical context. Several observations can be made
about these individuals. First, they were among the most
successful industrialists, capitalists and lawyers in Chicago
during the period of 1900 to 1920, if success is measured by
prestige, wealth and positions of power. Secondly, they chose to
identify themselves with religious causes and to some degree
articulated their own religious ideas. Thirdly, they acted upon
their convictions about the type of society Chicago should be
and in the process revealed some of their fundamental values and
their perspective upon American society.

These convictions and values, however coherently they
were expressed, served to undergird the economic and political
behavior of this group of businessmen. They were a part of a
larger system of beliefs, or propositions, that these men held
about themselves and the world around them. Another word for
such a system is _ideology_. The reason for introducing this

concept is to place the question of religious belief and economic activity into the larger context of social values that govern a particular group's actions in the marketplace. The contribution of religion to this process should then become more obvious.

The Concept of Ideology

Since the use of the term _ideology_ has itself been the subject of several historical analyses, no attempt will be made to trace its origins.[1] Currently, the concept of ideology is used in several different ways: pejoratively, to indicate a false explanation of social reality fostered by a ruling class to protect its own interests;[2] inclusively, to describe the collective myths and "maps of reality" held by an entire cultural group;[3] cautiously, because it integrates the above two ways, to describe the dominant set of social beliefs which those in power use to defend their status and which are acknowledged as legitimate by those in more subordinate positions.[4]

For several reasons, the third definition will be the one used in this chapter. The pejorative use of ideology, still the most popular among scholars and the public at large, carries too many overtones of a conspiracy that reduces human actors to clever manipulators or unwitting dupes. The anthropological approach, though of much greater scholarly value, is extremely difficult to employ in analyzing pluralistic societies, and in the case of one stratified by distinct economic classes, pays too little attention to this crucial determinant. The last alternative seems to be free of both these weaknesses.[5]

Several points need to be added to this definition:
first, an ideology is always a simplified, often oversimplified,
set of propositions about human nature and the constitution of a
good society. These simple explanations of complex phenomena
function as codes to help make decisions, take sides, identify
friends and enemies, and reinforce one's own identity in the
larger social fabric.

Secondly, an ideology is in some ways a "popular
philosophy" which incorporates a wide range of opinions,
prejudices and assumptions shared by a large constituency of
people. It is somewhat amorphous and subject to continual
manipulation.

Third, an ideology is a public set of beliefs that are
used by individuals when engaged in public dialog. It is quite
possible that individuals will privately dissent from some
elements of the prevailing ideology and even entertain private
beliefs that are at variance with the cultural tradition. This
does not necessarily make them hypocrites; ideology serves
public purposes and its adherents may support it for the general
good it accomplishes.

Fourth, one cannot deduce the elements of an ideology
strictly on the basis of what people say. Their behavior must be
given equal weight. The reason may seem obvious: people do not
always act according to their professed beliefs. Yet the
historian cannot to be too cynical about these professions

otherwise he or she is left to merely speculate about why people acted as they did. The assumption must be made that people choose to act with a fair degree of sincerity, and that even if their explanations are inadequate, they do reflect what that person (or persons) is thinking at that time. However, their actions will be, in most cases, a more reliable gauge of their intentions.

Further, an ideology cannot be reduced to abstract formulations if the intention is to reflect the way people actually adopt them. An ideology is more accurately described as a constellation of symbols or images that carry a host of connotations and emotional responses. This does not mean an ideology is irrational; in fact, an ideology appears to be "common sense" to its adherents. Nevertheless, the ideology is formed by a clustering of impressions and convictions that are usually connected to personal experiences. Thus, explanations for social reality tend to be visualized in some way.

Thus, an ideology is never really explained; it is more like a presumption about the way things are and the way things should be. The burden of proof is not upon the adherent but upon the one challenging the ideology. Though it seems coherent to the one who accepts the elements of an ideology, it is not like religious doctrine that can be spelled out and defended.

Seventh, the development of an ideology is always an interactive process that involves numerous persons who find themselves continually coping with change and who must adjust their ideology in response to that change. Moments of crisis or periods of fundamental transitions in a society are especially pregnant with ideological expression and definition. Usually, an ideology will have its spokespersons who are more articulate and who have the opportunity to reflect upon that ideology. But it would be mistaken to imply that an "intelligentsia" handles the ideological work on behalf of a ruling class, at least in the definition adopted for this chapter. Rather, persons in positions of power contribute to the development of an ideology. As the portrait of the Club trustees and speakers in an earlier chapter showed, there tended to be a convergence of perspective between the two groups.

Rarely will an ideology be entirely consistent even though its adherents assume it is. In fact, there will be numerous contradictions that are simply overlooked or explained away. These internal tensions are often the key to change for they present the opportunity for critical reflection and alternative courses of action.

None of the above points address a central feature of the definition of ideology which is the role of the dominant class. This requires the introduction of another term, hegemony, defined by Italian neo-Marxist Antonio Gramsci as the "spontaneous consent" given by the masses to the general direction imposed on social life by the dominant group or groups.[6] In other words, the majority of people in a given society "agree" with the social perspective of those in power.

hey tend to believe that the ideology of the dominant class is
:he correct, or legitimate, one.

The notion of an hegemonic ideology assumes that other
.deologies can develop. Indeed, in most societies, there will be
numerous systems of social values, particularly in
heterogeneous, pluralistic cultures. Individuals may, in fact,
adhere to more than one ideology without sensing any real
:ension (e.g., the compartmentalization of religion makes it
possible for an individual to have multiple loyalties). The
critical issue in an industrialized, capitalist society in which
a heirarchy of economic classes exists, is the nature of the
ideology that serves to preserve those economic arrangements.
Ideological hegemony assumes that the ideology of the economic
elite is the controlling perspective and that it is able to
engineer the consent of the majority of society members.

This, of course, raises the question of manipulation. Is
the consent of the masses obtained by a combination of force and
propaganda? Theorists such as Gramsci answer with a categorical
No. In their view, such a mechanical interpretation simply does
not fit any capitalist society. The legitimation of a dominant
ideology is far more subtle and more tenuous, especially during
periods of rapid social change. This does not mean that those in
power will not resort to military force if they feel seriously
threatened but such measures are relatively rare.

Hegemony is preserved by less self-conscious means. For
example, a ruling class sets the parameters for public dialog by

determining the range of alternative views that will be permitted serious consideration. Thus, as has already been shown, socialist proposals for restructuring American economic life were gradually forced out of public discussion so that by 1920, the Red Scare phenomenon sanctioned the suppression of leftist political parties. (The fact that the A. F. L. labor unions joined in this suppression may indicate the degree to which organized labor had consented to the existing economic structure.)[7]

Even though free speech was seriously curtailed during World War I, there was still the opportunity for dissenting voices to be heard such as the socialists. The hegemony of a dominant ideology can usually tolerate numerous deviations from the norm provided they do not threaten the power base.

Another means by which hegemony is maintained is through the distribution of information. Again, one does not have to resort to accusations of propaganda to acknowledge the fact that the media is largely subject to the demands of the business community. Its reliance upon advertising dollars prevents any serious challenge against the societal structures. In early-century Chicago, the control was even more overt, for the newspapers were all owned by wealthy families (some of whom were quite willing to inject their political biases into their papers).[8]

Other institutions, besides the press, are equally effective in conveying the legitimacy of a governing ideology.

Schools are primary arenas for inculcating the predominant values and beliefs of the society; thus, it should be no surprise that business leaders showed so much interest in the public schools. Churches, community organizations, labor unions, and business associations are also able to communicate and reinforce the ideology.

Finally, hegemony is preserved by a large portion of the society simply because the existing social and economic structures are relatively beneficial to them. A ruling class may have a lion's share of the societal goods, but subordinate groups may have access to enough to satisfy them. In fact, dominant groups frequently accommodate the desires and demands of subordinate groups when it becomes necessary to preserve peace. The ideology of the dominant group is usually oriented to the maintenance of social stasis. For example, an individual like Booker T. Washington, was highly regarded by the business elite because he represented the desired kind of Negro: one who pulled himself up from poverty and ignorance and became a success through hard work, clean living and accepting the supremacy of white society over black. Whether Washington intended it or not, he became a vindication of the dominant ideology and the model of how all blacks could obtain economic well-being and political respect.[9]

One further application of the definition of ideology should be made. The transfer of a set of social values and beliefs from one generation to the next occurs through a process of _reproduction_.[10] The agencies (schools, churches, organizations) which serve to legitimate the prevailing ideology also help to educate their members. Both knowledge and skills are reproduced in the learners, whether they are children or adults, so that persons can not only identify the correct ways of thinking but also know the proper ways of acting. The interest of the Club trustees in industrial and commercial education provides a good example. The vocational training programs which they helped to establish in the Chicago public schools were designed to familiarize future workers with the opportunities and demands of the workplace, teach them some basic skills and cultivate the suitable work habits that would be needed. The reproduction of a working class thus included an ideological component; a similar process could likely be observed in the Ivy League colleges which many Club trustees attended where they learned how the upper class was to think and work.[11]

The role of religion in the development of an ideology is an important element in this discussion. As already noted, religion can be a legitimating force useful to the dominant groups in society. It can also be a source of a dissenting ideology; or at least it can stimulate individuals to rebel against the prevailing social values.

Normally, religion is one of several sources of content for an ideology. As this study will attempt to show, religion is far from a minor source in that it often provided the vocabulary, the images and the motivations needed to make a coherent system of beliefs. However, religion does not operate in a vacuum; it responds to material conditions and attempts to explain and cope with those conditions using its authoritative body of knowledge. So too an ideology is not detached from its social and economic context; rather, it is rooted in that context, generally subject to the limitations which that context imposes. Yet ideology is not completely bound. It can produce proposals to break out of those limitations, especially if one pays attention to its inner contradictions. Religion may be one of the most helpful sources for this critical reflection, simply because it claims to be supernatural, subject to demands from outside time and space.[12] Whether this is actually the case is a matter to be raised later.

The remainder of this chapter will include an examination of these dynamics between religion and the dominant ideology of Chicago's elite business community.

Elements of an Ideology

The preceding theoretical discussion sets the stage for a more systematic analysis of the dominant ideology in Chicago during the early decades of this century. This analysis will of necessity be incomplete since it will concentrate upon only one party in the formation and maintenance of the ideology. A study of several other groupings in Chicago (e.g., the working class as a whole, other Protestant groups, such as the large constituencies of German and Swedish Lutherans, not to mention

the significant, non-religious population) would provide a
fuller picture of the strength and significance of this
ideology.

One other admission must be granted. The ideology
cultivated by the businessmen, lawyers and bankers in this study
will be treated as representative of the larger business class
of the city. Given the prominence of the Club trustees in the
social order, this essay assumes some liberty in extending the
social values of these men to others with similar status. For
the sake of convenience, the phrase "business ideology" will be
used to identify the specific way in which these business
leaders formulated the dominant social perspective; the
assumption remains that this business ideology was fairly
pervasive in the minds of most Chicagoans, extending beyond its
application to the business world.

If the ideology of a group contains an implicit
self-definition, then one of the central elements of the Club
trustees' ideology was their <u>vision of personal success</u>. Their
image of the virtuous man was the individual who through
disciplined labor and personal integrity achieved material
success and the acclamation of his fellows. No other human
pursuit offered a better means of achieving this goal than a
career in business. This vocation contained all the necessary
elements: no limits on the amount of work an individual could
invest, the need for cooperative relationships with others that
relied on a level of trust, steadily increasing monetary

rewards, widespread public approval of business as the best choice for a person with high aspirations.

By and large, the Club trustees had fulfilled this vision and were happy to impart advice to the younger generation. A weekly Chicago Tribune column, "How to Become a Millionaire" published in 1912, gave Charles Hutchinson the opportunity to say, "Indifference is the principal cause of failure. Intense industry leads to success." (He added a tip: "Remain with a big corporation.")[13] Another Chicago millionaire told readers to "avoid the professions" and "go for manufacturing, mining, transportation or commerce."[14]

Both George Reynolds and A. C. Bartlett added warnings to withhold immediate gratification for future prosperity. "Keeping everlastingly at it, subordinating expenses to income and saving a certain amount every year, are three things every aspirant for success must remember," said Reynolds.[15] Bartlett noted that the "foundation of success is mental discipline." He urged young men to "lay aside their pride and work, then you'll become a captain of industry. The problem is lack of perseverance. And lavish expenditures instead of careful savings of money."[16]

This image of business success was reinforced by the idea of the self-made man. Many of the Club trustees believed that they had risen to the top primarily through their own efforts. Men like Norman Harris, Marvin Hughitt, John Shedd, David Forgan and Henry Crowell had begun at the lowest rungs of their respective enterprises. When they arrived at the highest

echelons, they were hailed by their colleagues and the press as
Horatio Algers of sorts. Shedd was introduced to Outlook readers
as a statesman of presidential timber; the interviewer noted
that "the attitude which baffles Mr. Shedd is one who stays at
the bottom for lack of enough ambition or courage or common
sense to climb any higher."[17]

Implicit in this praise of hard-working businessmen was a
glorification of work itself. Laboring was man's purpose and the
means to personal fulfillment. Theoretically, all work was
potentially ennobling if pursued with the right attitude.
Chicago businessmen were not especially successful at helping
their workers find the same delight in labor which they enjoyed,
but they were convinced it was possible. In 1911, the
Association of Commerce roundly applauded Congregational
minister, Frank Smith, who described what he thought was "the
supreme test of modern industry."

> I think it is to so build our factories, our mills, so
> establish our great commercial institutions, so relate and
> interrelate the men which come in touch and contact with
> them, so adjust wages and present all of these great
> elements that enter into them, that every man from president
> or stockholders down to the most menial toiler shall be
> strengthened, and shall be exalted and uplifted and be
> builded in his moral character.18

Of course, this meant that the opposite, idleness, was a
serious offense. Nor should excessive help be extended to those
who refused to work. To reap where one does not sow was not only
unjust but deprived that person of the satisfaction of enjoying
what he earned. Even a lukewarm Protestant could quote verses
from the Bible to support this conclusion.

Such Social Darwinism was not usually articulated in raw terms. Most of the trustees knew that the stark disadvantages under which many people began their careers needed to be mediated to some degree; nor could people be deliberately abused by those with greedy ambitions. Thus, many in the business class were quite prepared to give government a role in adjusting social conditions. In a speech to the Cook County High School Association, Club trustee Franklin MacVeagh portrayed this enlightened conservatism:

> Government has assumed, and undoubtedly will assume again, functions that it used to decline; and this is due to a new social instinct partly, at least, inspired by socialism. And from the socialist propaganda comes, undoubtedly, a good deal of the inspiration to grapple with the problems of poverty and social distress and social inequality, which is beginning to so distinctly mark the time. But this is all independent of the willingness of modern liberty at this early day to surrender wholly the ideas of democratic government and individual freedom. There is no sign of any such surrender or cataclysm.[19]

At the heart of this ideological component of success was a concern for a man's character. Usually, this was defined in terms of morality: honesty, reliability, respect for others, wholesome attitudes, loyalty to family and friends. Good character led to success in the marketplace because it fueled hard work and cooperative relationships.

Here also religion made a significant contribution, for the person who professed Christianity was expected to follow the example of Christ, who was perceived as having a perfect character. Christianity also espoused all of the personal ideals linked with good character and implied that God was an active force in a person's life to produce those qualities. Thus, for many business leaders, Christianity was indispensable for personal and public morality. No other religion or philosophy was as capable of affirming the ethic of success.

A second element of the ideology was the view these businessmen held toward their larger environment. The controlling image was America, a nation with a special destiny, operating under divine favor, built upon the Anglo-Saxon, Protestant heritage, dedicated to the freedom of the individual to work and achieve material success. These men were more than mere patriots; they infused the national agenda with a sense of divine mission. America, in their view, was the harbinger of Christian civilization, the one place on earth where people were living the way God intended man to live. Thus, entry into World War I was essential in order to preserve this republic against the dangerous threat of tyranny.

The sacred quality of the republican form of government was deeply felt by the corporate elite. One of their own, Edgar Bancroft, claimed that

> ...in a republic, organized government is but the mortal body--the principles of human rights and a quick and constant moral sense are its immortal sense. The animating theory of our government, that it embodies and expresses justice, rather than power, never was more impelling and vital than now. 20

In his mind, Bancroft linked the concept of organized republican government with the belief that America was a just and open society in which all had the opportunity to succeed.

John O'Leary, who represented management in the 1919

steel strike, went a step further with his notion of industrial Patriotism: "The nation has a splendid asset in its vast number of independent workmen, who, at the moment, are Americans first, and internationalists never." He went on,

> We must reawaken that spirit of patriotism that became to us such an asset through the war, and which is now almost dormant. After helping the world fight for democracy, we cannot sit by and see our nation lose it.21

The practical implications of this spiritualized nationalism soon became obvious: the "foreign element" in America posed a threat to the national identity and had to be Americanized; the brand of Christianity which created the divine destiny had to be exported to other parts of the world, making Protestant missionaries also the purveyors of American civilization; urban metropolises, like Chicago, were microcosms of the nation's problems and possibilities, endowing business leaders with the high calling of producing civic righteousness; the pseudo-religious nature of citizenship implied a concern for the welfare of others in American society to be expressed through innumerable forms of philanthropy and good will.

One way in which many business leaders expressed this aspect of their ideology was through their images of the era's Presidents, especially Roosevelt and Wilson. These men became larger-than-life symbols of the kind of America corporate leaders desired. Contemporary observer, Mark Sullivan, noted that this was a common phenomenon in the population at large.

> Roosevelt, Bryan, Wilson ... in them the people personified their convictions, visualized their aspirations ... they represented a common mood in which common man regarded

himself as oppressed, in danger of becoming stratified
economically, a mood of revolt against organized wealth and
the boss system in politics.22

Chicago business leaders had the advantage of meeting
Presidents in person on a fairly regular basis. No doubt they
were treated to heroic descriptions of America's destiny as well
as encouraging remarks about their role as men of business. Some
of the Club trustees were present at the Progressive Party
convention in Chicago in 1912 when Roosevelt delivered his
Armegeddon speech, though most remained loyal to Taft, who
earlier told the Union League Club, "the highest duty of the
Administration is to permit business to go on undisturbed."[23]

Roosevelt was by far the most attractive symbol (in spite
of his temporary break from the Republican Party). He
represented muscular Christianity to many, militant imperialism
for others, and hard-driving outspoken masculinity to most. His
personal religious faith was more show than reality; as he once
said,

The religious man who is most useful is not he whose sole
care is to save his own soul, but the man whose religion
bids him strive to advance decency and clean living and to
make the world a better place for his fellows to live in.[24]

But he was a firm believer in the doctrine of
Americanism. In his Fear God and Take Your Part, Roosevelt
wrote:

The larger Americanism demands that we refuse to be sundered
from one another along lines of class or creed or section or
national origin ... we judge each American on his merits as
a man. Only thus shall we stand erect before the world, high
of heart, masters of our own souls.[25]

Wilson, though a Democrat, was a popular figure in the

Chicago business community, no doubt facilitated by his Presbyterian ties. Wilson shared Roosevelt's vision of America, stating that "there is nothing that gives a man a more profound belief in Providence than the history of this country."[26] More refined and scholarly than Roosevelt, Wilson's image was still attractive as a representative of public morality and the responsible individual (the latter impression reflects the impact of political rhetoric, for Wilson was actually responsible for more of the major Progressive legislation than Roosevelt was; yet Wilson's "New Freedom" campaign branded him as an advocate of the individual).[27]

Clearly, Protestantism was borrowed to construct a kind of civil religion. Though the Bible did not have anything directly to say about America, the entire treatment of Old Testament Israel was adaptable. So the United States became God's chosen people, launched upon a pilgrimage to the Promised Land, called to live righteously in that Land, enjoying its fruits of "milk and honey" and overcoming the heathen who threatened its security. Christ was also Americanized (in some cases, converted into a successful salesman) to be the example for individuals to follow. According to this logic, if enough individuals determined to follow Christ's example, the result would be a moral America.[28]

Intimately connected to the images of personal success and American destiny was a notion of material progress. The measuring stick for both the personal and national ideals

described above was invariably the "bottom line." Just as the
sign of business success was profitability, so too the mark of
progress by the individual and society was increased wealth.
Money was viewed as a good in itself, to be desired and
acquired, to be used to accomplish noble purposes. The wealthy
man and the wealthy nation were revered in this ideology because
of the good they were capable of doing.

Perhaps nothing drilled the virtue of money into the
turn-of-the-century capitalist mind more than Russell Conwell's
hugely popular "Acres of Diamonds" speech. The Philadelphia
preacher (and founder of Temple University) delivered this
anecdotal homily over 6000 times (he was also a Club speaker)
for which he garnered more than $8 million. Conwell pulled no
punches in advocating the pursuit of wealth:

> Ninety out of every hundred people here have made that
> mistake this very day. I say you ought to be rich; you have
> no right to be poor. To live in Philadelphia and not be rich
> is a misfortune, and it is doubly a misfortune, because you
> could have been rich just as well as be poor. Philadelphia
> furnishes so many opportunities. You ought to be rich.
> Well does the man know, who has suffered, that there some
> things sweeter and holier and more sacred than gold.
> Nevertheless, the man of common sense also knows that there
> is not any one of those things that is not greatly enhanced
> by the use of money. Money is power. Love is the grandest
> thing on God's earth, but fortunate the lover who has plenty
> of money. Money is power; money has powers; and for a man to
> say, "I do not want money," is to say, "I do not wish to do
> any good to my fellowmen." It is absurd thus to talk.[29]

Clergymen like Conwell harnessed the Christian faith to
this goal, advising Protestants that "we ought to get rich if we
can by honorable and Christian methods, and these are the only
methods that sweep us quickly toward the goal of riches."[30] If

Christian methods were not sufficient to sanctify wealth,

donating that wealth to a Christian cause was. As one speaker

told the Laymen's Missionary Movement gathering in Chicago,

> I want to live a few more years and be in business for the
> Master's sake. I have not been in it that way yet. Isn't
> that enough of a motive for a man? I do not care so much now
> about mere wealth and its accumulation, but I do care about
> the use of wealth, and I would give anything if to-night my
> heart and my will were so at the disposal of Jesus Christ
> that I could look into his face and say: "My Master, I am in
> business for thee and thee only."31

The Episcopal bishop, William Lawrence, also a Club

speaker, rivalled Conwell in linking godliness with riches. Said

Lawrence,

> Put ten thousand immortal men to live and work in one
> fertile valley and ten thousand moral men to live and work
> in the next valley, and the question is soon answered as to
> who wins the material wealth. Godliness is in league with
> riches ... in the long run, it is only to the man of
> morality that wealth comes. We believe in the harmony of
> God's universe. We know that is only by working along His
> laws natural and spiritual that we can work with efficiency.
> Only by working along the lines of right thinking and right
> living can the secrets and wealth of nature be revealed. We,
> like the Psalmist, occasionally see the wicked prosper, but
> only occasionally.32

Though somewhat crass, these formulations only reinforced

the prominence of business in the pantheon of high callings. One

critic writing about America's "business civilization" described

the rise of the businessman:

> All other orders in society having been swept away, and a
> business career being the sole one that leads inevitably to
> power when successful, the business man's standard of values
> has become that of our civilization at large.33

Several Club trustees were in fact irritated with the

criticism of big business which often emanated from labor

leaders, more radical progressives and novelists. The

Association of Commerce provided a platform for these trustees

to react and reaffirm their status in American society. Harry

Wheeler, when he was U. S. Chamber of Commerce president in 1911

as well as head of the Commerce Association, stated:

> It seems to me, gentlemen, that the time has come when the
> business interests of this country for their own
> preservation if for no other motive should absolutely unite
> as a concrete force comparable in power and in strength to
> other national forces, and offset against these national
> forces sometimes enacting legislation inimical to commerce
> the voice that shall say: "Thus far and no farther shall you
> go."34

A. C. Bartlett repeated the frequent claim of business

expertise being the most capable of solving social problems

(partly because of knowledge and partly because of its unselfish

and neutral stance):

> When a great business problem is to be solved, not only the
> knowledge of experts, but their opinions and judgment are
> requisite to a satisfactory solution.
>   Every thinking man knows that the tariff is a great
> business problem; and outside of those having selfish
> interests to serve, all men desire to have that problem
> virtually solved by business experts, through a commission
> composed of uninfluenced and unbiased members.35

Actually, these men had little to fear, for the ethos of

business had permeated American culture, not the least of which

was the church and the practice of religion. Creating wealth was

distasteful to only a small minority of the population; the

masses were quite prepared to chase the siren of materialism,

assured that it was for a good purpose.

However, the business ideology did feature a spirit of

service to counter the negative consequences of materialism. For

Protestant businessmen, selfishness was simply unfitting for the image of personal success, the ideal of patriotism and the proper pursuit of wealth. Instead, social relationships were to be marked by generosity, friendliness and mutual respect. On a larger scale, citizens were to consider the needs of the nation above their own. Service rendered on behalf of the values America represented was the highest virtue. All of these values were continually extolled by businessmen.

At the Association of Commerce's annual dinner for the sons of its members in 1911, president Harry Wheeler raised the Association's standard of citizenship:

> We believe of all the functions given by the organization in the course of the year, none has greater significance than that dinner where the father leads his son and his son's friends under the influences of this association, and thereby impresses upon their minds as the men of tomorrow that there is a place in the ranks of this organization worthy to be filled by any man, worthy to be envied by any man, a place where service of great value may be rendered to the city and to the nation.36

The War provided a host of heroes for this ideology in the form of young men killed in battle. The rhetoric flowed unstintingly at Association gatherings. YMCA preacher Sherwood Eddy was as eloquent as any:

> God forgive us if we go back to the old life of ease, of selfishness, of materialism, forgetting humanity and God. We will meet this present crisis. Let us rise with the spirit of those men that died for us on that bloody western front, in that high spirit of service to humanity, true to our country and to our flag. Yes, we are going to do it, two almost superhuman tasks, but we can do them both, and we will. We are going to win the war. We are going to win the world.37

This spirit was needed on the civic front as well. Businessmen motivated by civic patriotism were expected to

invest time and money in projects that benefited Chicago.
Museums, parks, art, urban beautification, gifts to universities
and schools were just a few of the tangible evidences of the
civic spirit.

As described earlier, many businessmen took this service
ideal one step further by adopting a personal sense of duty for
the general welfare of the city. As the corporate elite with the
greatest amount of wealth, they perceived themselves as the
appropriate stewards to put this wealth to the best use. Those
who were Protestants were already familiar with the many
Scriptures urging brotherly love and service to others. Some
went so far as to reduce Christianity to an ethic of service.

Though a crusty capitalist who did not embody the
business ideology as faithfully as some, Andrew Carnegie did
reflect the pull of this ideology. An agnostic all his adult
life, he carried with him the ethos of the Calvinist Church of
Scotland which he knew as a boy.[38] His massive riches was
obtained by rather ruthless adherence to the ideal of unlimited
cultivation of wealth. Many of his opponents who stood in his
way were rudely cast aside. The crushing of the Homestead strike
in 1892 was only a more dramatic illustration of how he treated
his personnel and his competition (though his conscience was
tender enough that he left the country on vacation so he
wouldn't have to observe the strike in person).

No other prominent American was more infatuated with
Herbert Spencer's brutal social philosophy of a struggle for

existence that brooked no government interference or private
charity.[39] But Carnegie could not live by this ethic in such raw
terms and a kind of religion of philanthropy or stewardship of
the wealthy elite was necessary.

The disposal of his wealth--some $350 million, leaving
only $30 million for himself and his wife, all of which he gave
away in his years of retirement--was an idea he nurtured
throughout his career. He said,

> The man of wealth must become the mere agent and trustee for
> his poorer brethren, bringing to their service his superior
> wisdom, experience, and ability to administer, doing for
> them better than they would or could do for themselves.40

The pursuit of wealth for its own sake was
sacrilegious and degrading. How one obtained the wealth gave him
no moral qualms, but what one did with it was where values came
into play.

Carnegie's values were outlined in his famous Gospel of
Wealth articles and his Triumphant Democracy published in 1886.
These works ring with affirmations of individualism and
classical liberal notions of democracy which find their
fulfillment in material progress.[41]

Finally, the business ideology of the Club trustees
contained a form of racialism in which the supremacy of the
white male was a given. Though hardly made explicit by these
men, this element of the ideology was clearly evident in
attitudes toward American blacks and toward women. The masculine
emphasis in Protestant religion and the occasional references to
Anglo-Saxonism among Protestant businessmen have already been

mentioned. Several other aspects of this discrimination can be
observed.

First, women were considered important for the
advancement of Christianity. They were by nature more responsive
to religious truth and experience. What women needed was "soul
development" more so than the "modern education" being offered
to them. Their career choices were either to cultivate a
spiritual home or enter the front lines of overseas and home
missions work. Aggressive, worldly women were not appreciated by
leading Protestants. Even the wife of one prominent evangelist
moaned,

> We send missionaries to Europe, Asia and Africa to bring
> residents of those foreign countries to Christ, and then our
> American women tourists travel about the same countries
> smoking cigarets. God pity our country, if our women are
> coming to such a pass as that.42

Secondly, though blacks should not be denied their
political rights, they were inherently different from whites
(and this usually meant inferior). A common view was that "the
Negro is naturally a tiller of the soil." Booker T. Washington's
comment in Chicago in 1912 (speaking in Emil Hirsch's Sinai
Temple) that the hope for the Negro is in his agricultural
instinct only helped to reinforce that idea.[43] A major
Protestant publication, Record of Christian Work, carried a
lengthy article in 1908 on the "Negro soul" claiming that "the
Negro has a poetic soul" which gave him the ability to sing
under affliction.[44] The conclusion was that whites should be
careful not to educate the Negro's soul out of him. Chicago

Presbyterian minister, Joseph Vance, probably reflected the predominant view, when he preached,

> The negro must be lifted from African pagandom by the same processes through which other nations have risen. He must begin with training his hand, and grow from this to mental achievement, moral strength and aesthetic culture.45

The sheer absence of women and blacks from any of the arenas in which these businessmen made their corporate decisions or where they strategized a municipal reform or religious program can only be noted. With the exception of their churches and homes (even here biographical accounts of these men in Who's Who directories say nothing about their wives), these men seldom, if ever, interacted with women and blacks on equal terms. Not surprisingly, it may not have occurred to them that their Bibles stated that "there is neither Jew nor Greek, slave nor free, male nor female, for you are all one in Christ."[46]

Conclusion

The portrait of the ideology just sketched is by no means complete. Only five images have been isolated; there could easily be more and probably in a different configuration. But the objective was to outline a framework of values and beliefs that governed behavior and helped the subjects explain the world they lived in. Assuming this has been accomplished, what can be said about the significance of this ideology?

First, it is obvious that a religion provides content which ideological formulation absorbs. This "borrowing" may include the religious vocabulary, such as Theodore Roosevelt's

use of Armegeddon terminology; specific maxims, such as the
Biblical commands to work for one's own bread; and symbols, such
as the figure of Jesus as a model human being. It may be more
accurate to say that religious persons bring this content into
their reflections on the social order, often carelessly, but
with the conviction that this content has merit.

Secondly, it follows that the business ideology of these
individuals was enriched and strengthened by the religious
content. Its legitimacy within the larger Protestant population
was certainly enhanced. The religious support provided to the
various components of the ideology endowed them with universal
significance, or at least the semblance of it.

Yet, from the perspective of the religion, one might
conclude that the religious system was seriously compromised in
the transaction. Certain elements were given the status of
public values, while other doctrines and beliefs were ignored or
relegated to private religious activity. The implication is hard
to escape: what the dominant class considered socially
irrelevant about religion became, in fact, irrelevant.

On the other hand, the overlooked elements of a religion
may become the source of a challenge to the hegemonic ideology.
For example, there were Protestants, especially in the lower
classes, who did not share most of the primary emphases of the
business ideology (e.g., the vision of America, the cult of
self-made success through hard work, the supremacy of the white
male and material progress). The status of these Protestants in

the social order made a challenge an unlikely prospect, but under changed economic and social conditions, religion could have fueled an alternative ideology.

Third, the means by which certain elements of religion are selected and incorporated into an ideology has much to do with the needs and interests of the dominant group. Weber called this process elective affinity meaning the choice of symbols or beliefs according to their similarity or compatibility with the economic practice of a class. Thus, Biblical guidelines on work were grasped while Biblical themes of community life and celebration were ignored.

Fourth, because it was in part created by Protestant businessmen, this business ideology was immensely instrumental in legitimizing their economic practice. Rooted in certain facts about the social and economic system, it was not a mere illusion or lie. Rather it was a workable set of explanations. The fact that one detects almost no indication of personal anxiety or guilt on the part of the Club trustees may be a sign of its effectiveness.

Finally, the conditions of the marketplace helped to stimulate the development of this ideology and it would appear, they continued to shape it. As long as capitalistic business conditions thrived, the business ideology would remain intact. Only when the external conditions shifted (as they did one decade later in 1929) did certain elements of the ideology become problematic, and adjustments need to be made.

NOTES

1. George Lichtheim, The Concept of Ideology and Other Essays (New York: Random House, 1967); Job Dittberner, The End of Ideology and American Social Thought, 1930-1960 (Ann Arbor: UMI Research Press, 1979).

2. Karl Marx's The German Ideology (New York: International Publishers, 1972 edition) established the pejorative use of this term. Daniel Bell in The End of Ideology: On the Exhaustion of Political Ideas in the Fifties (Glencoe, Ill.: Free Press, 1960) adopts the pejorative version of this conception but claims we are in a post-ideological age. Bell views ideology as a "trap" and ideologists as "terrible simplifiers." He adds, "Ideology makes it unnecessary for people to confront individual issues on their individual merits. One simply turns to the ideological vending machine, and out comes the prepared formulae. And when these beliefs are suffused by apocalyptic fervor, ideas become weapons, and with dreadful results" (p.405).
Everett Carl Ladd, Jr. in Ideology in America: Change and Response in a City, a Suburb and a Small Town (Ithaca: Cornell University Press, 1969) claims that "it no longer makes much sense to describe the ideological confrontation as one between 'conservative' businessmen and 'liberal' labor leaders" (p.341). Setting aside traditional notions of political ideologies, Ladd introduces a Cosmopolitan-Parochial polarity which he believes more adequately explains ideational conflict.

3. Clifford Geertz, The Interpretation of Cultures: Selected Essays (New York: Basic Books, 1973) offers the best discussion of ideology as a cultural system. Though not in the same camp as Geertz, Karl Mannheim's Ideology and Utopia (New York: Harcourt, Brace & World, 1936) aims at a broader notion. See also Kenneth and Patricia Dolbeare, American Ideologies (New York: Markham, 1973).

4. Carl F. Kaestle, Pillars of the Republic (New York: Hill & Wang, 1983), pp.75-103; Kaestle, "Ideology and American Educational History," History of Education Quarterly 22 (Summer

1982); J. Philip Wogaman, The Great Economic Debate: An Ethical Analysis (Philadelphia: Westminster, 1977), pp.10-33; Francis X. Sutton, et al. The American Business Creed (New York: Schocken Books, 1956) are all illustrations of this definition.

5. A number of sociologists have called for refocusing the discipline of sociology of knowledge (pioneered by Mannheim in the 1930s), bracketing epistemological questions and historical treatments. The new concern must be with everything that passes for "knowledge" in society and particularly, "common sense knowledge" rather than ideas. This leads to a social theory that concerns itself with how individuals construct their view of "everyday" reality. Peter Berger and Thomas Luckmann credit Alfred Schutz for establishing this new agenda. Alfred Schutz, The Phenomenon of the Social World (Evanston: Northwestern University Press, 1967); Alfred Schutz and Thomas Luckmann, The Structures of the Life-World (Evanston: Northwestern University Press, 1973); Peter L. Berger and Thomas Luckmann, The Social Construction of Reality (New York: Doubleday, 1966).

6. Antonio Gramsci, Selections from the Prison Notebooks of Antonio Gramsci (New York: International Publishers, 1971). See also David L. Sallach, "Class Domination and Ideological Hegemony," Sociological Quarterly 15 (Winter 1974); Jurgen Habermas, Toward A Rational Society: Student Protest, Science and Politics (Boston: Beacon Press, 1970).
Jackson Lears' No Place of Grace: Antimodernism and the Transformation of American Culture 1880-1920 (New York: Pantheon Books, 1981) uses Gramsci's analysis of hegemonic ideology to depict the reinforcement of a dominant culture's hegemony. Lears points out that the private struggles of the custodians of the bourgeois class (a process he calls antimodernist) had unintended public consequences: their search for self-fulfillment served to promote accommodation to a secularized culture and to the existing class structure of American society. In a similar way, Helen Horowitz in Cultural Philanthropy in Chicago from the 1880s to 1917 (Lexington: University of Kentucky Press, 1976) links philanthropy to the preservation of class hegemony.
A vigorous attack against the Gramscian position is Nicholas Abercrombie, Stephen Hill and Bryan S. Turner, The Dominant Ideology Thesis (London: George Allen & Unwin, 1980). These authors claim that economic and political factors are sufficient to explain the class structure of a society and its self-preservation.

7. Robert K. Murray, Red Scare: A Study in National Hysteria, 1919-1920 (Minneapolis: University of Minnesota Press, 1955). See also John Higham, Strangers in the Land: Patterns of American Nativism 1860-1925 (New York: Atheneum, 1963).

8. John Tebbel, An American Dynasty: The Story of the McCormicks, Medills and Pattersons (New York: Doubleday, 1947); Lloyd Wendt, Chicago Tribune: The Rise of a Great American Newspaper (Chicago: Rand McNally, 1979); Jay Robert Nash, People To See: An Anecdotal History of Chicago's Makers and Breakers (Piscataway, N.J.: New Century Publishers, 1981); James W. Linn, James Keeley, Newspaperman (New York: Bobbs-Merrill, 1937); Charles H. Dennis, Victor Lawson: His Work and His Time (Chicago: University of Chicago Press, 1935).

9. Booker T. Washington, Up From Slavery: An Autobiography (New York: Dodd, 1903, 1965 edition); Louis Harlan, Booker T.Washington: The Making of A Black Leader 1856-1901 (New York: Oxford University Press, 1972) and Booker T. Washington: The Wizard of Tuskegee 1901-1915 (New York: Oxford University Press, 1983).

10. Henry Giroux, Ideology, Culture and the Process of Schooling (Philadelphia: Temple University Press, 1981); Pierre Bourdieu and Jean-Claude Passeron, Reproduction in Education, Society and Culture (Beverly Hills: Sage Publications, 1977); Samuel Bowles and Herbert Gintis, Schooling in Capitalist America: Educational Reform and the Contradictions of Economic Life (New York: Basic Books, 1976). Educational sociologists have begun to examine textbooks as one tool of ideological reproduction. See Michael Apple, Ideology and Curriculum (Boston: Routledge and Kegan Paul, 1979); Jerome Karabel and A. H. Halsey, ed. Power and Ideology in Education (New York: Oxford University Press, 1977); Michael Apple and Lois Weis, ed. Ideology and Practice in Schooling (Philadelphia: Temple University Press, 1983).

11. Cornelius H. Patton and Walter T. Field, A Study of New England College Life in the Eighties (New York: Houghton Mifflin, 1927); Thomas Le Duc, Piety and Intellect at Amherst College 1865-1912 (New York: Arno Press, 1946, 1969 edition). See also Burton J. Bledstein, The Culture of Professionalism: The Middle Class and the Development of Higher Education in America (New York: W. W. Norton & Company, 1976); E. Digby Baltzell, The Protestant Establishment: Aristocracy and Caste in America (New York: Random House, 1964).

12. For an excellent discussion of the relationship between religion and ideology, see Anthony Giddens, Capitalism, Socialism and Social Theory (London: Cambridge University Press, 1971), pp.205-223.

13. Chicago Tribune, 16 March 1912.

14. Chicago Tribune, 30 March 1912.

15. Chicago Tribune, 28 January 1912.

16. Chicago Tribune, 14 January 1912.

17. "The Views of John G. Shedd," Outlook, 13 January 1912. See also John G. Cawelti, Apostles of the Self-Made Man (Chicago: University of Chicago Press, 1965). William Miller in his Men in Business (New York: Harper & Row, 1952) observes that "if it be true, as leading American businessmen and leading American historians continue to assert, that, so to speak, anyone can become president of large business firms, it appears to be true also that at least in the early twentieth century most of the successful aspirants had certain social characteristics that distinguished them sharply from the common run of Americans of their time" (p.337).

18. Commerce (Chicago), 10 November 1911.

19. Franklin MacVeagh, "The Value of Certain Social and Economic Facts," address delivered to Chicago and Cook County High School Association, March 6, 1897. Chicago Historical Society.

20. Edgar Bancroft, The Mission of America and other War-Time Speeches (Washington: n.p., 1927), pp.16, 24.

21. Commerce (Chicago), 4 October 1919.

22. Mark Sullivan, Our Times: The Turn of the Century, 1900-1904 (New York: Charles Scribner's Sons, 1927), p.100.

23. Chicago Tribune, 10 March 1912. See also Paolo E. Coletta, The Presidency of William Howard Taft (Lawrence: University Press of Kansas, 1973); William Manners, TR and Will: A Friendship That Split the Republican Party (New York: Harcourt, Brace & World, 1969); Donald F. Anderson, William Howard Taft: A Conservative's Conception of the Presidency (Ithaca: Cornell University Press, 1968).

24. Quoted in Edward Wagenknecht, The Seven Worlds of Theodore Roosevelt (New York: Longmans, Green & Company, 1958), p.183.

25. Theodore Roosevelt, The Works of Theodore Roosevelt, Volume 18 (New York: Charles Scribner's Sons, 1926), p.259.

26. Quoted in John M. Mulder, Woodrow Wilson: The Years of Preparation (Princeton: Princeton University Press, 1978), p.230.

27. Woodrow Wilson, The New Freedom (New York: Prentice-Hall, 1913, 1961 edition). See also George Mowry, Theodore Roosevelt and the Progressive Movement (Madison:

University of Wisconsin Press, 1946).

28. Robert T. Handy in A Christian America (New York: Oxford University Press, 1971) argues that "most Protestants in the America of 1890 saw themselves as belonging to a national religion, a religion of civilization" but by the 1930s, a "second disestablishment of religion" was in progress in which the special identification of Protestant churches with American civilization was drawing to an end (p.210). Robert Bellah's Beyond Belief: Essays on Religion in a Post-Traditional World (New York: Harper & Row, 1970) includes his famous 1966 essay "Civil Religion in America" which launched an intense debate over the existence of an actual American civil religion. See also John F. Wilson, Public Religion in American Culture (Philadelphia: Temple University Press, 1979); Russell E. Rickey and Donald G. Jones, ed. American Civil Religion (New York: Harper & Row, 1974); Martin Marty, The Public Church: Mainline-Evangelical-Catholic (New York: Crossroads, 1981).

29. Russell H. Conwell's "Acres of Diamonds" in Agnes Ruch Barr, Russell H. Conwell and His Work (Philadelphia: John C. Winston Company, 1926), p.414.

30. Ibid., p.415.

31. Alfred E. Marling, "Money and the Kingdom" in Men's National Missionary Congress (New York: Laymen's Missionary Movement, 1910), p.236.

32. William Lawrence, "The Relation of Wealth to Morals," World's Work 1 (January 1901), pp.286-292. See also John W. Clark, Religion and the Moral Standards of American Businessmen (Cincinnati: Southwestern Publishing, 1966).

33. James Truslow Adams, Our Business Civilization (New York: Albert and Charles Boni, 1929), p.15.

34. Commerce (Chicago), 21 June 1912. Another Chicago capitalist who reacted to the critics of big business was J. Ogden Armour. See his The Packers, the Private Car Lines and the People (Philadelphia: Henry Altemuste, 1906). For a scholarly defense, see Emily Stipes Watts, The Businessman in American Literature (Athens: University of Georgia Press, 1983). Watts gives too much credence to "anti-business" novelists like Upton Sinclair, Theodore Dreiser, Jack London and Robert Herrick, and fails to recognize the overwhelming positive press businessmen did receive in the Progressive era.

35. Commerce (Chicago), 5 December 1910.

36. Commerce (Chicago), 29 December 1911.

227

37. Commerce (Chicago), 5 July 1918.

38. Joseph F. Wall, Andrew Carnegie (New York: Oxford University Press, 1970).

39. Ibid., pp.376-397.

40. Quoted in Sidney Fine, Laissez-Faire and the General Welfare State (Ann Arbor: University of Michigan Press, 1956), p.115. See also Robert McCloskey, American Conservatism in the Age of Enterprise (New York: Harper & Row, 1951).

41. Andrew Carnegie, Triumphant Democracy (Port Washington, N.Y.: Kennikat Printers, 1886, 1971 edition); Carnegie, The Gospel of Wealth, and other Timely Essays (Cambridge: Belknap Press, 1965).

42. Chicago Tribune, 19 October 1910.

43. Chicago Tribune, 13 March 1912.

44. Record of Christian Work (East Northfield, Mass.), June and July, 1908. The writer, Thomas Nelson Baker, a black, called for the "re-Negronization" of the American Negro.

45. Chicago Tribune, 7 January 1901.

46. Galatians 3:28.

CHAPTER 5

PROTESTANTISM AND CAPITALISM: STILL CONNECTED

The core issue in this study has been the interaction between religion and economic practice. The preceding portrait of the Chicago Sunday Evening Club trustees has shown that religion was a factor in their activities as leading capitalists in the city. It also became obvious that these same individuals engaged in reshaping their Protestant faith to fit the urban industrial society in which they operated.

The concept of ideology was added to the discussion because the religion of these businessmen can be understood better as a component of a larger framework of social values and beliefs. Furthermore, an ideology must be analyzed in relation to the distribution of power and wealth in a given society in order to properly assess its development and influence. Thus, in the case of the Club trustees, Protestant religion became a contributor to a dominant ideology that legitimized capitalistic enterprise.

This final chapter will attempt to draw out some of the implications of this phenomenon of Protestant religion in a capitalist society. One place to begin is with the classic debate, largely instituted by Max Weber, over Protestantism's relationship to capitalism.

Weber's Protestant Ethic Thesis

The question which Weber asked himself was: why were Protestants at the forefront of rational, capitalistic enterprise? Why was the Western bourgeois class so dominated by Protestants (as opposed to Catholics)?

Weber answered these questions in his famous essay, The Protestant Ethic and the Spirit of Capitalism published in 1904 (though it did not appear in English until 1930).[1] This work was part of a much larger study of the sociology of the major world religions which did not appear until after his death.[2] Weber had several concerns which need to be kept in mind as we evaluate his work. First, he was trying to explain the emergence of Western civilization, particularly its rational, technical and liberal character, which distinguished it from Buddhist, Hindu, Islamic and Jewish cultures. He observed that religious beliefs indirectly influenced economic activity and that in the case of the West, Protestants were prominent among the rising middle classes of the capitalist nations.

Secondly, Weber was intrigued with the consequences of religious belief upon people's secular affairs. "We wish to ascertain," he wrote in reference to Western capitalism, "whether and to what extent religious forces have taken part in the qualitative formation and quantitative expansion of that spirit over the world."[3] He was doing battle in both the scholarly and the political arenas with Marxian materialists who held that all values and ideas were economically determined. In other words, religious systems were developed by classes of people to explain, justify and rationalize their place in the economic order. Though Weber agreed with much of this, he firmly held to the opposite: that ideological factors were just as important as economic considerations.[4]

Third, he was interested in how individual people made sense of the world they lived in, how they internalized beliefs and operated according to various psychological sanctions which rested on those beliefs. He was breaking new ground in sociological theory by looking for connections between formal beliefs, ethical norms and social class. This partly explains why his writings were always suggestive but never thorough.

Weber's Protestant ethic thesis can be summarized briefly. Modern capitalism, defined by Weber as "the pursuit of profit, and forever renewed profit, by means of continuous, rational, capitalistic enterprise," received its impetus in the Protestant Reformation primarily through Calvinist theology.[5] The call to an ascetic way of life was transferred from the monastery to the earthly vocations of all believers thus ennobling ordinary work to become a means of glorifying God. Said Weber, "The Protestant conception of calling gave everyday worldly activity a religious significance."[6] Calvin's doctrine of predestination, in which God ordains who will be saved, was

modified by his descendents to include a frugal, sober lifestyle
of diligence and hard work as a means of demonstrating one's
election. For Weber, these theological shifts provided the
psychological sanctions needed for middle class entrepreneurs
to earn profits and then use these profits to enhance further
economic growth. The consequence of Calvinist theology was a
"spirit of capitalism" which became the motive force in the
expansion of modern capitalism. This spirit was not sufficient
in itself, of course; the economic conditions had to be present
such as technological advances, available capital and the
rational structures of law and administration (such as
bookkeeping procedures), for capitalism itself to develop. But
for Weber, this spirit took priority:

> The question of the motive forces in the expansion of modern
> capitalism is not in the first instance a question of the
> origin of the capital sums which were available for
> capitalistic uses, but, above all, of the development of the
> spirit of capitalism.[7]

Eventually, according to Weber, capitalism as a
rationalized, bureaucratic form of economic life became
self-sustaining, leaving the Protestant faith largely
irrelevant. The "spirit of religious asceticism" vanished
leaving a residue of pure utilitarianism.[8] Modern capitalism was
for him an "iron cage" in which human creativity and autonomy
are slowly crushed by the bureaucratic control of a state
economy.[9]

Weber's thesis provoked intense discussion that has not
subsided among sociologists and economists interested in the

sociology of religion. Criticisms of his position have been
varied but persistent. A more detailed examination of these
attacks will help to draw out the subtle aspects of Weber's
work.

A frequent criticism has been that Weber misrepresented
Calvin and his followers who never condoned the pursuit of
wealth as a means of proving one's salvation. Others have
pointed to Catholics and Jews during and after the Reformation
who were just as capitalistic as the Protestants. Moreover,
Weber seems to treat Puritanism as a monolithic entity and fails
to consider the significant differences between English Puritans
of the 16th and 17th centuries (not to mention the fact that
these Puritans, who were Weber's first cases of Protestants
engaged in business, lived over a century after the
Reformation). If he had, he would have discovered that Calvinist
doctrine was itself evolving. Puritans of a later era were less
rigorous in their discipline of worldliness than their
forbearers had been.

Weber was certainly vulnerable in his historical
analysis; he provided little, if any, empirical documentation
for his assertions. He failed to study Protestant capitalists to
see why they engaged in profitable ventures and if their
religion had any effect on their business practices. But several
things can be said in his defense. He was not blaming John
Calvin for starting capitalism, nor was he saying that Calvinism
"caused" capitalism. Weber is quite clear on this point.

...we have no intention whatever of maintaining such a
foolish and doctrinaire thesis as that the spirit of
capitalism could only have arisen as the result of certain
effects of the Reformation, or even that capitalism as an
economic system is a creation of the Reformation. In itself,
the fact that certain important forms of capitalistic
business organizations are known to be considerably older
than the Reformation is a sufficient refutation of such a
claim.10

He adds, "We are thus inquiring only to what extent
certain characteristic features of this culture can be imputed
to the influence of the Reformation."[11] His analysis was
actually far more subtle. He was suggesting that Calvinist
theology was instrumental in developing a capitalist mentality.
Weber's interest was in

...the influence of those psychological sanctions which,
originating in religious belief and the practice of
religion, gave a direction to practical conduct and held the
individual to it. Now these sanctions were to a large extent
derived from the peculiarities of the religious ideas behind
them.12

This influence was largely unintended; that is, the
psychological motivations that derived from Calvinist doctrine
were not foreseen by Calvin or his associates. Yet the Calvinist
brand of Protestantism became an important ingredient in
creating incentives that favored the rational pursuit of
economic gain.

A recent study of 17th century Scottish Calvinist
industrialists who built the first large-scale factories in
Scotland attempted to do some of the historical work Weber
should have done. Gordon Marshall concluded that despite the
limitations on available data, there were enough instances in
which actors explicitly related their capitalist activities to

Calvinist premises that

> ...there are reasonable grounds for suggesting that it is
> likely Weber, rather than the Marxists, who has correctly
> identified the relationship between the two world-views, by
> attributing the development of the capitalist ethos to the
> nature of Calvinist teaching rather than vice versa.13

Weber's use of Benjamin Franklin as a prototype of the
capitalist spirit has bothered many critics who point to
Franklin's obvious irreverence and agnosticism. But Weber's
argument is that even though the religious content of "Puritan
worldly asceticism" had died away by Franklin's time, the
sanctions which it produced continued to be operative and
powerfully effective in the most capitalistic of cultures, the
United States.[14]

Another line of criticism was that Weber missed the point
of the Reformation's influence on the emergence of capitalism in
the West. Instead of attributing the rise of the capitalist
spirit to Calvinism, he should have observed the negative effect
of the Catholic Counter-Reformation upon commercial
development.[15] The conditions for the growth of capitalist
organization were ripe throughout Europe, not just where the
Protestant movement took root; what hindered the rise of
capitalism in Catholic territories was what Herbert Leuthy
called "the shadow cast by the Inquisition and heresy trials
across the lands." He adds,

> During these centuries, in one half of Europe, an
> intellectual ferment, general and active throughout the
> whole continent on the eve of the Reformation, was
> extinguished and destroyed. The existential minimum of a
> free society, without which neither intellectual nor
> industrial pioneers, neither scientific research nor

economic progress, are possible, was there totally uprooted.16

The implication of this rebuttal to Weber was that capitalism did not need any form of ideology to trigger its emergence, assuming that the necessary factors of capital, technology and international trade were all in place. H. M. Robertson in his critique of Weber takes a similar position: "The rise of the capitalist spirit is the same as the rise of economic rationalism - something which took place independently of Church teaching, on the basis of commercial experience."17 All that the church, Protestant or Catholic, could do was make concessions to the spirit of the age if it wished to retain any influence at all.

Either out of defense of religion or disregard of its relevance, many critics have rejected Weber's interest in Protestantism and posited the rise of capitalism to other factors: material conditions, as noted above, or bourgeois liberalism and Enlightenment thought. The secularizing influence of 18th century rationalism which undermined the other-worldly perspective of the religiously-dominated Western culture seems to many to be a more plausible explanation for the upsurge of economic activity and the rise of a capitalistic middle class. Protestantism can then be viewed as a more rationalized religion than Catholicism, thus more receptive to this new middle class.

Some historians have taken further steps from this Enlightenment thesis to explore the rise of modern science and technology. George Grant claims "there was in the theology of

the Calvinist Protestants a positive element which made it
immensely open to the empiricism and utilitarianism in the
English edition of the new sciences."[18] He goes on to state that

> ...the connection was from the side of the Protestants who
> found something acceptable in the new ideas so that often
> they were the instruments for these ideas in the world,
> almost without knowing the results for their faith. At the
> least, Calvinist Christianity did not provide a public brake
> upon the dissemination of the new ideas as did Catholicism
> and even sometimes Anglicanism.19

Students of Weber, like Reinhard Bendix and Lewis Coser,
have generally agreed with Grant's position. They believe that
Weber was really attempting to explain the phenomenon of
"increased rationalism in various phases of social life."[20] The
key was the "disenchantment" of the world that made intense
economic activity a virtue rather than a vice. Among other
things, the Calvinist brand of Protestantism served to foster
this disenchantment. (Weber's mistake was in focusing only upon
Calvinism.) Once this process had occurred, religion was no
longer significant for this rationalism had a life of its own,
in fact, one that led into a dehumanizing bureaucratization of
all social life.

While there is substance to these re-interpretations of
Weber, he did exhibit a particular interest in the social and
economic effects of religion. His claim was really quite modest.
For Weber, there existed "an affinity between economic
rationalism and certain types of rigoristic ethical religion."[21]
Elements in the Protestant faith resonated with the pattern of
middle class economic life and each reinforced the other. He

also noted in passing that the Protestant religion had
influenced the working classes as well; for example, in the case
of British Methodism, Protestantism helped to create a docile,
pliable, hard-working and steady labor force. Though allowing
for far greater emotional expression, Methodism was essentially
Calvinistic and reinforced the idea of calling. John Wesley's
own fear of wealth (earned through hard work) leading devout
Methodists astray only helped to stimulate the same Protestant
ethic. Weber observed,

> ... the full economic effect of those great religious move-
> ments, whose significance for economic development lay above
> all in their ascetic educative influence, generally came
> only after the peak of the purely religious enthusiasm was
> past. Then the intensity of the search for the Kingdom of
> God commenced gradually to pass over into sober economic
> virtue; the religious roots died out slowly, giving way to
> utilitarian worldliness.22

The reason for introducing these Weberian insights into
the sociology of Protestant religion is not to prove or disprove
his claims about the origin of capitalism. While that was the
burden of Weber's Protestant ethic thesis, it is not the concern
of this study. Instead, this essay has attempted to highlight
another dimension of this relationship: the impact of capitalism
on Protestant faith. Viewed from this perspective, the dynamic
relationship of capitalism and Protestantism which fascinated
Weber continues to be a vital issue for understanding both the
development of capitalist societies and the evolution of
Protestantism in the 20th century. The evidence presented in
this study of religious activities by Chicago businessmen at the
turn of the century establishes both the contribution of

Protestant religion to a governing ideology of a business class
and the incorporation of business values and structures into
Protestant religion. (While these issues were not of apparent
interest to Weber, they can be explained more adequately by re-
ferring to Weber's theoretical work.)

Protestantism and Business Ideology

To summarize, these representatives of a capitalist
class found within mainline American Protestantism particular
beliefs that reinforced their vision of society and sanctified
their efforts to shape that society. As members of an
economically and socially privileged group, they gravitated
toward those beliefs that legitimized their place in society.
They selected out of a religious system those elements that best
explained the world in which they found themselves. What sort of
Protestantism did these wealthy industrialists create? Some have
characterized it as "muscular Christianity" because of its
accent on decisive action. The individual who boldly confronted
social problems - whether it be the notorious saloon or
corruption in municipal government - had grasped the essentials
of Christianity. Theological speculation was of little value.
What counted was the spirit that compelled the Christian to
apply his faith in practical ways.

The essence of this brand of Protestantism was a moral
force. Christianity provided ideals to live by. It guided human
relations and transcended class differences. Conflicts between
labor unions and their employers were to be resolved by men who

acted righteously and sympathetically in their personal behavior.

Such Protestantism did not seriously question the striking contrast of extremely wealthy capitalists and hosts of starving immigrant workers consigned to all sorts of dehumanizing work. These men were on the top because they had worked hard, acted honestly and fairly and reaped the benefits of common sense and heroic action. In America, anyone could make it to the top on the same terms.

None of this diminishes the sincerity and dedication of this Protestant faith. A large proportion of these Protestants were more than mere church attenders. They swelled the ranks of the Sunday school movement, fought the battles for prohibition and clean government, revered the Bible and the Sabbath as symbols of a vibrant Christianity that made their nation strong. Their piety was aggressive and while contained within the limits of respectability, did serve to stimulate their pursuit of financial success.

This study has shown Protestants gripping certain aspects of the Christian faith and missing entirely other elements. Evidence for this can be seen in their propensity to define problems in terms of the individual. Poverty and crime were traced to the victim's own failures and the solution was always a personal affair, starting with conversion to Christian faith and then living up to Christian ideals and moral standards. While some social gospellers concentrated on reforming societal

structures, aiming their message at wealthy capitalists whom
they believed had Christian consciences, the majority of
Protestant laymen were preoccupied with populating the urban
industrial environment with good Christian people.

But the system itself was a given; it was not perceived
as problematic. The industrial workplace was a reality that
could not be changed. Though cognizant of the corporate
dimensions of Christianity, these Protestant laymen could not
appreciate the implications of it for themselves. They did not
see it as a way of life that was partially at odds with the
whole business mentality. Rather, for them Christianity affected
the person in a more private manner. Jesus himself would have
worn a three-piece suit in their view as he delivered his
message of good will and brotherhood. Certainly, he would have
attacked the corrupt, pharisaical politicians and the selfish
plutocrats, but he would not have required his followers to live
in defiance of the economic system. The frequent comparison of
Theodore Roosevelt to Christ eloquently expressed this
adaptation of Protestant religion.[23]

Not all Protestants shared these images of successful
Christianity. There were hosts of immigrant Lutherans and
pietistic Pentecostals, black and white, who nurtured visions of
Christian community that differed from the prevailing model. But
even they could not ignore that larger ideological amalgam of
Protestantism, American patriotism and upper class materialism.
Protestantism itself had become part of the mechanism for

maintaining social order. It was embedded in the language of the dominant forces in American society.

Indeed, in the hands of these religiously-inclined businessmen, Protestantism itself began to resemble the environment in which they operated. As already noted several times, one of the key words of those decades was _efficiency_. The source of that idea was obvious. The mammoth factories and sprawling corporate conglomerates that emerged in the late 19th century needed to organize and streamline their operations to reduce costs and maximize profits. This applied to human beings as well as to machines and management procedures. Not surprisingly, the same emphasis on efficiency surfaced in Protestant church life. Denominational hierarchies became corporate giants attempting to establish organic, if not organizational, unity by merging programs through such agencies as the Federal Council of Churches.[24]

As already shown, these individuals were motivated by a paternalistic sense of stewardship. In their perception of themselves, their superior talent, astuteness and perseverance had garnered their wealth for them and made them eminently qualified to distribute it wisely and for the good of the most people. Many glorious church edifices were erected with their money as were schools, seminaries and benevolent organizations. These men breathed a spirit of pragmatism and accountability into church activities. They expected results from their investment. These results had to be measured and counted. To them, and to most people in the pew, religion was more a matter of what people did, not what they believed.

Unfortunately, this evangelical pragmatism contributed to the demise of theological vigor. Tough intellectual problems that were thrown up by the new sciences and a growing spirit of infidelity were not tackled by the churches. Theological disputes that raged in denominational seminaries and annual conventions hardly touched most church members who couldn't see what difference these issues made to their daily routines. Yet those issues did make a difference. A critical leg of their ideological framework was crumbling, losing its integrity and vitality as a religious system. A source from which a social critique could be launched was slipping away leaving them blinded to all the compromises they had made.[25]

If this analysis of a businessmen's religion has some foundation, the question still remains: what difference did it make? Did it contribute to the growth or decline of Protestant religion? To speak of a religious decline or demise requires some caution. While numerous intellectuals and academics abandoned religious faith, and for many others religious observance became a mere formality, larger segments of the population continued to be active participants in church life.

Nevertheless, one can speak of a loss of influence or power. Religion increasingly became a private affair that respectable people kept more or less to themselves and subject to their own interpretation. The attitude of Sinclair Lewis'

Babbitt had become pervasive: you didn't talk about religion.
Nor was it allowed on center stage of the public arena with the
same degree of acceptance. As Peter Berger observed in The Noise
of Solemn Assemblies, the paradox is that when religion achieves
social functionality, it also becomes socially irrelevant. While
"religion appears as a prominent symbol of public life," for the
individual "religion is relegated pretty exclusively to his
private life, a leisure-time activity."[26]

What was missing was that "in a culture where religion is
functional both sociologically and psychologically," there was
"no confrontation with the God who stands against the needs of
society and against the aspirations of human hearts."[27] Without
the confrontation, there could be no judgment, no acknowledgment
of failures and gross sin, no admission that Protestantism had
helped to create idols. And without this judgment, there could
be no speaking a word of judgment to American society.
Protestant leaders were now its priests; any prophets would more
than likely be dismissed as fanatics or sectarians.

The dominant strain of the Protestant faith had become in
many ways a domesticated religion. It was useful for the average
citizen but without any intellectual prowess. The denial of the
importance of theology in the end sapped the church of its one
source of truth; without theology, religious persons could make
their faith almost anything they desired.

Protestantism became absorbed into the mores and values
of an industrialized culture and took on the priorities of that

world. They abandohed the position of tension with the culture and overlooked that greater tension that ought to have existed between themselves and the God they claimed to know. In so doing, the mainstream Protestant bodies forfeited the opportunity to speak prophetically to a society which they eventually acknowledged was less than Christian.

Most historical accounts of this domestication of Protestantism concentrate on the thought of prominent theologians and clergymen; one of the aims of this study has been to show that the class structure of American society and especially those in positions of power and influence by virtue of financial wealth had just as much to do with the process. In making religion efficient, these laymen helped to make it irrelevant.

NOTES

1. Max Weber, <u>The Protestant Ethic and the Spirit of Capitalism</u> (New York: Charles Scribner's Sons, 1930, 1958 edition).

2. Max Weber, <u>The Sociology of Religion</u> (Boston: Beacon Press, 1922, 1963 edition).

3. Weber, <u>Protestant Ethic</u>, p.91.

4. One of the major problems with Weber's thesis is that it cannot easily be proved or disproved. He posits a capitalist mentality which is necessary to produce a capitalist order. This capitalist mentality represents a theoretical commitment to the independent influence of ideas. To agree with Weber, one is compelled to accept his starting point. Thus, instead of proof, one can expect only plausible explanations realizing there are alternative ones.

One alternative is the Marxist one. For Marx, religion was an ideal but distorted expression of the relationship between dominant and subordinate groups (the standard pejorative use of the term ideology). Calvinism, for example, was a convenient justification for an ascending capitalist class, just as Methodism with its emphasis on discipline and a religion of the heart served the needs of an exploited working class. A strict Marxist will not take religious claims very seriously. The real reasons for a person's behavior are not religious but economic. To a Marxist, a capitalist is only religious because it gives him or her psychological reassurance. Religious explanations serve to legitimize their privileged status in the social order.

Weber differed with Marx in that he considered religious ideas to have an autonomous influence. He did not believe that theological statements could be dismissed so easily. They clearly influenced economic activity.

Some scholars have argued that Weber and Marx were actually closer to each other than their disciples have thought. In some of his later works, Marx seemed to recognize that ideology was needed by persons to form a set of meanings for their actions, though these meanings were largely shaped by economic factors. If this is so, then the two sociologists have much in common. For Weber's position was that reality for a person is both external and internal. One has to respond to the actual conditions in one's environment but one copes with these conditions according to some ideological framework. This means that social relations are "religiously sensitive." A person's economic class and religious orientation interact with each other. It is to Weber's credit for focusing sociological study on this more dynamic and far more complex relationship.

5. Weber, Protestant Ethic, p.17.

6. Ibid., p.80.

7. Ibid., p.68.

8. Ibid., p.181.

9. Several biographical treatments of Weber include discussion of his pessimistic view of bureaucratic rationalism in an advanced capitalist society. See Arthur Mitzman, The Iron Cage: An Historical Interpretation of Max Weber (New York: Alfred A. Knopf, 1970); Reinhard Bendix, Max Weber: An Intellectual Portrait (New York: Doubleday, 1960).

10. Weber, Protestant Ethic, p.91.

11. Ibid., p.90.

12. Ibid., pp.97-98.

13. Gordon Marshall, Presbyteries and Profit: Calvinism and the Development of Capitalism in Scotland, 1560-1707 (New York: Oxford University Press, 1980), p.261. See also Gordon Marshall, In Search of the Spirit of Capitalism: An Essay on Max Weber's Protestant Ethic Thesis (New York: Oxford University Press, 1982). See also H. J. Demerath and Phillip E. Hammond, Religion in Social Context: Tradition and Transition (New York: Random House, 1969); H.R. Trevor-Roper, Religion, the Reformation and Social Change (London: Macmillan, 1967), pp.1-45. R. H. Tawney is also sympathetic to Weber's basic position and elaborates upon it in Religion and the Rise of Capitalism (New York: Harcourt, Brace & World, 1926). See also Ross Terrill, R. H. Tawney and His Times (Cambridge: Harvard University Press, 1973).

14. Weber, Protestant Ethic, p.180.

15. W. Fred Graham, The Constructive Revolutionary: John Calvin and His Socio-Economic Impact (Richmond: John Knox Press, 1971), p.198.

16. Herbert Leuthy, "Once Again: Calvinism and Capitalism" in Max Weber, ed. Dennis Wrong (Englewood Cliffs: Prentice-Hall, 1970), p.134.

17. H. M. Robertson, "A Criticism of Max Weber and His School" in Protestantism, Capitalism and Social Science: The Weber Thesis Controversy, ed. Robert W. Green (Lexington, Mass.: D. C. Heath, 1973), p.80.

18. George Grant, "Technology and Empire" in Carl Mitchum and Robert Mackey, Philosophy and Technology: Readings in the Philosophical Problems of Technology (New York: Free Press, 1972), p.190.

19. Ibid., p.190.

20. Lewis Coser, Masters of Sociological Thought (New York: Harcourt, Brace Jovanovich, 1971), p.9. See also Bob Goudzwaard, Capitalism and Progress (Toronto: AACS, 1979).

21. Weber, Sociology of Religion, p.94.

22. Weber, Protestant Ethic, p.176. See also E. P. Thompson, The Making of the English Working Class (New York: Pantheon Books, 1963); Wellman Warner, The Wesleyan Movement in the Industrial Revolution (London: Longmans, Green & Company, 1930). V.A. Demant in Religion and the Decline of Capitalism (London: Faber, 1952) takes a different tack by arguing that the capitalist experiment has failed partly because of the corroding effects of religion. See also Robert N. Bellah, The Broken Covenant: American Civil Religion in Time of Trial (New York: Seabury Press, 1975), pp.114-116; Daniel Bell, The Cultural Contradictions of Capitalism (New York: Basic Books, 1976).
For some contemporary studies of religion and its interaction with economic life, see Herbert Gutman, Work, Culture and Society (New York: Random House, 1966); Liston Pope, Millhands and Preachers: A Study of Gastonia (New Haven: Yale University Press, 1942); Kenneth Underwood, Protestant and Catholic: Religious and Social Interaction in an Industrial Community (Boston: Beacon Press, 1957); Paul E. Johnson, A Shopkeeper's Millenium: Society and Revivals in Rochester, New York 1815-1837 (New York: Hill & Wang, 1978).

23. The critique of Protestantism offered in this chapter has been made by others. See H. Richard Niebuhr, The Kingdom of God in America (New York: Harper & Brothers, 1935); Niebuhr, The Social Sources of Denominationalism (Hamden, Conn.: Shoe String Press, 1929); Henry May, Protestant Churches and Industrial America (New York: Harper & Brothers, 1949); Donald B. Meyer, The Protestant Search for Political Realism 1919-1941 (Berkeley: University of California Press, 1960).

248

24. Gibson Winter, "Religious Organizations" in The Emergent American Society, Volume 1, ed. W. Lloyd Warner (New Haven: Yale University Press, 1967), pp.408-484.

25. Some might argue that the Protestant faith exerted a distinctly humanizing influence on the industrial scene. Those who took their religion seriously, and there were many, were not immune to the sufferings and injustices that surrounded them. By and large, they were busy workers devoting vast amounts of energy to establishing the Kingdom of God on earth and preparing people for the one in the future. They did not run away from urban ills but were in the forefront of almost every campaign to improve the lot of those who lived in the metropolis. Laboring with a determined but optimistic sense of urgency, they tried desperately to correct the problems of rapid urban growth.

But they failed to see that they themselves were partly the cause for the problems they were trying to solve. Those victims who aroused their sympathy suffered because of an economic structure that relegated them to the bottom of the social order where their deprivation permitted Anglo-Saxon Protestants to enjoy abundant wealth. While these well-meaning individuals entertained the myth that the system was open to all who persevered, the reality that it was closed and inherently unequal eluded their consciences.

26. Peter Berger, The Noise of Solemn Assemblies (New York: Doubleday, 1961), p.38.

27. Ibid., p.123.

APPENDIX A

CHICAGO SUNDAY EVENING CLUB TRUSTEES 1908-1920

Charles Alling, Jr. (1865- ?)

Schooling: University of Michigan
Church: First Presbyterian, Chicago
Occupations: President, Chicago Business Law School
    Alderman, 2nd Ward
Affiliations: South Side Business Association
    Cook County Sunday School Association
    State Board of Health
    New Charter Convention
    Legal Aid Society
    Masons

Frank H. Armstrong (1853-1920)

Schooling: Cornell (Iowa)
Church: First Presbyterian, Evanston
Occupation: President, Reid, Murdoch & Company
    (wholesale grocers)

Affiliations: Association of Commerce
    City National Bank
    Merchants' Loan & Trust
    Commercial Club
    Evanston YMCA
    Presbyterian Hospital
    Chicago Lying-in Hospital
    Chicago Bureau of Charities
    Art Institute
    Cornell College

Edgar C. Bancroft (1857-1925)

Schooling: Knox College
           Columbia Law School
Church: ?
Occupations: International Harvester (general counsel)
             Atchison, Topeka & Sante Fe (general
             counsel)
             U. S. Ambassador to Japan

Affiliations: Butler Brothers
              Chicago Bar Association
              Belt Line Railway Company
              Chicago & Western Indiana Railway
              Chicago Law Club
              Chicago Race Commission
              Cliff Dwellers
              Chicago Literary Club

Adolphus C. Bartlett (1844-1922)

Schooling: Danville Academy (New York)
           Clinton Liberal Institute (New York)
Church: Central Church/St. James Episcopal
Occupation: Hibbard, Spencer & Company (wholesale
            hardware)

Affiliations: Northern Trust Bank
              First National Bank
              Chicago & Alton Railway Company
              Legislative Voters' League
              Committee of Fifteen
              Home for the Friendless
              Chicago Relief & Aid Society
              Chicago Board of Education
              University of Chicago
              Beloit College
              Art Institute
              Chicago Athanaeum
              Cliff Dwellers
              Chicago Literary Club

Charles L. Bartlett (1860-?)

Schooling: Brown University
Church: Episcopalian
Occupation: President, Chicago Title & Trust

Lloyd W. Bowers (1859-1910)

Schooling: Yale University
Columbia Law School
Church: Fourth Presbyterian Church, Chicago
Occupations: Chicago Northwestern Railway (general
counsel)
U. S. Solicitor-General

Affiliations: Chicago Law Club
Chicago Nursery and Half-Orphan Asylum

Eugene J. Buffington (1863-1937)

Schooling: Vanderbilt
Church: Congregational
Occupations: President, American Steel & Wire
President, Illinois Steel and Indiana
Steel Companies
President, Gary Land Company

Affiliations: Continental and Commercial Bank
U. S. Fuel Company
Gary State Bank
American Iron and Steel Institute
H. C. Fricke Coke Company
Chicago YMCA
Interchurch World Movement
Committee of Fifteen
Community Trust
Vanderbilt

Edward B. Butler (1853-1928)

Schooling: Boston public high schools
Church: Central Church
Occupation: President, Butler Brothers

Affiliations: Corn Exchange Bank
Legislative Voters' League
Chicago Orphan Asylum
Hull House
Erring Women's Refuge
Bureau of Associated Charities
Illinois Manual Training School
Illinois Industrial School for Girls
Cliff Dwellers
Rockford College

George E. Cole (1845- ?)

Schooling: Michigan public schools
Church: ?
Occupation: President, Cole Stationers

Affiliations: Municipal Voters' League
Legislative Voters' League
Citizens' Association

J. Lewis Cochran (1857-1923)

Schooling: Louderback College (Pennsylvania)
Church: St. James Episcopal, Chicago
Occupations: President, Edgewater Coal Company
             Cochran & McCluer Company (real estate)

Affiliations: Chicago Title & Trust
              Northwestern Elevated Railway Company
              Sons of American Revolution

Henry Parsons Crowell (1855-1944)

Schooling: Greylock Institute (Massachusetts)
Church: Fourth Presbyterian Church, Chicago
Occupations: President, Quaker Oats Company
             President, American Cereal Company

Affiliations: Association of Commerce
              Continental Illinois Bank
              Moody Bible Institute
              Laymen's Evangelistic Council
              McCormick Seminary
              Presbyterian Brotherhood
              Church Extension Committee (Chicago
              Presbytery)
              Committee of Fifteen
              Legislative Voters' League
              Illinois College

Abel Davis (1874-1937)

Schooling: Northwestern Law School
Church: Sinai Temple
Occupations: Chicago Title & Trust
Cook County Recorder
Illinois General Assembly

Affiliations: Chicago Real Estate Board
Chicago Bar Association
Association of Commerce
Chicago Plan Commission
Community Trust
Illinois National Guard
American Legion
Masons
Chicago Historical Society
Art Institute

Frederic Delano (1863- ?)

Schooling: Harvard
Church: Unitarian
Occupation: President, Wabash Railway Company

Affiliations:Chicago, Burlington & Quincy Railway
Company
American Unitarian Association
Unitarian Laymen's League
National Park Commission
Wacker Plan
Chicago Lying-in Hospital
University of Chicago
Chicago Literary Club
Harvard University

Jacob M. Dickinson (1851-1928)

Schooling: University of Nashville
          Columbia Law School
Church: Fourth Presbyterian Church, Chicago
Occupations: Illinois Central Railway (general
          counsel)
          Secretary of War (1909-1911)

Affiliations: American Bar Association
          American Society of International Law
          Chicago, Rock Island & Gulf Railway
          Chicago Literary Club
          Cliff Dwellers
          Izaak Walton League

Thomas E. Donnelley (1867-1955)

Schooling: Yale
Church: First Baptist Church, Chicago
Occupations: President, R. R. Donnelley Company
          President, Lakeside Press
          Chicago Directory Company

Affiliations: Association of Commerce
          International Harvester
          Commonwealth Edison
          First National Bank of Evanston
          Employers Association of Chicago
          War Industries Board
          Protection Mutual Insurance Company
          Interchurch World Movement
          Landis Award Committee
          Chicago Smoke Abatement Committee
          Cliff Dwellers
          Chicago Literary Club
          Art Institute
          University of Chicago

Bernard Eckhart (1852- ?)

Schooling: Wisconsin public schools
Church: ?
Occupations: President, Eckhart & Swan Milling Company
        President, Chicago, Terre Haute &
        Southern Railway Company
        Illinois Senate
        U. S. Food Administrator

Affiliations: Association of Commerce
        Continental National Bank
        Harris Trust & Savings
        Chicago Title & Trust
        Illinois Manufacturers' Association
        Railroad and Warehouse Commission
        Chicago Board of Trade
        Chicago Charter Convention
        Chicago Civic Federation
        West Chicago Park Commission
        Illinois National Guard
        Sanitary District of Chicago
        Illinois College

John V. Farwell, Jr. (1858-1938)

Schooling: Yale
Church: First Presbyterian Church, Lake Forest
Occupation: President, John V. Farwell Company
        (wholesale dry goods)

Affiliations: Chicago Northwestern Railway Company
        Employers' Association of Chicago
        State Pawners' Society
        Commercial Club
        Chicago Trust Company
        War Exemption Board
        Chicago YMCA
        Hyde Park Protective Association
        Chicago Plan Commission
        Municipal Voters' League
        Legislative Voters' League
        National Citizens' League
        Chicago Literary Club
        Lake Forest University
        World's Columbian Exposition

David R. Forgan (1862-1931)

Schooling: Common schools in Scotland
Church: First Presbyterian Church, Evanston
Occupation: President, National City Bank

Affiliations: Association of Commerce
              Religious Education Association
              United Charities
              Citizens' Street Cleaning Bureau
              Illinois College

William A. Gardner (1859-1916)

Schooling: Illinois public schools
Church: First Congregational Church, Evanston
Occupations: President, Chicago Northwestern Railway
             Company
             President, St. Paul, Minneapolis & Omaha
             Railway Company

Affiliations: Superior Coal Company
              Merchants' Loan & Trust Company

Richard C. Hall (1858- ?)

Schooling: Boston high schools
Church: St. Mark's Episcopal, Chicago
Occupation: President, Duck Brand Rubber Company

Affiliations: Association of Commerce
              Chicago YMCA
              Evanston YMCA
              Legislative Voters' League

Thomas A. Hall (1849-1911)

Schooling: Oberlin College
Church: Woodlawn Park Presbyterian Church
Occupations: President, Thomas Hall Real Estate
　　　　　　　Company
　　　　　　　Dearborn Power Company

Affiliations: Association of Commerce
　　　　　　　Office Building Managers Association
　　　　　　　Presbyterian Social Union
　　　　　　　Foreign Missions Committee (Chicago
　　　　　　　Presbytery)
　　　　　　　Church Extension Committee (Chicago
　　　　　　　Presbytery)
　　　　　　　Hyde Park Protective Association

Albert W. Harris (1867-1958)

Schooling: Gem City Business College (Quincy,
　　　　　　　Illinois)
Church: St. James Methodist Episcopal
Occupation: President, Harris Trust & Savings

Affiliations:　Association of Commerce
　　　　　　　Chicago Clearing House
　　　　　　　Chicago Railway Company
　　　　　　　Harris, Forbes & Company
　　　　　　　Chicago YMCA
　　　　　　　Community Trust
　　　　　　　Chicago Boys Club
　　　　　　　Art Institute
　　　　　　　Field Museum of Natural History

Norman Wait Harris (1846-1916)

Schooling: Westfield Academy (Massachusetts)
Church: St. James Methodist Episcopal
Occupation: President, Harris Trust & Savings

Affiliations: American Telephone & Telegraph Company
Michigan State Telephone Company
Chicago Training School for City and
Foreign Missions
International YMCA
Halsted Street Institutional Church
Northwestern University Settlement
Wesley Memorial Hospital
Northwestern University
Art Institute

Charles S. Holt (1855-1918)

Schooling: Williams College
Harvard Law School
Church: Second Presbyterian Church, Chicago
Occupation: Holt, Wheeler & Sidley (law firm)

Affiliations: Holt Lumber Company
Presbyterian Brotherhood
McCormick Seminary
Religious Education Association
Church Extension Board (Chicago
Presbytery)
Chicago Orphan Asylum
Williams College
Chicago Literary Club

James L. Houghteling (1855-1910)

Schooling: Yale
Church: St. James Episcopal, Chicago
Occupations: Peabody, Houghteling & Company (banking house)
Mackinaw Lumber Company
Black River Lumber Company

Affiliations: Brotherhood of St. Andrew
Chicago YMCA
Municipal Voters' League

Marvin Hughitt (1837-1928)

Schooling: Common schools in New York
Church: First Presbyterian Church, Chicago
Occupations: President, Chicago Northwestern Railway Company
Chicago, St. Paul, Minneapolis & Omaha Railway Company

Affiliations: Illinois Merchants' Trust Company
Northern Trust Company
American Sunday School Union
McCormick Seminary
Chicago Home for the Friendless
John Crerar Library

Charles L. Hutchinson (1854-1924)

Schooling: Chicago high schools
Church: St. Paul's Universalist Church, Chicago
Occupations: President, Corn Exchange National Bank
            President, Chicago Board of Trade

Affiliations: Northern Trust Company
              State Bank of Chicago
              Universalist National Convention
              Religious Education Association
              Chicago YMCA
              Chicago Orphan Asylum
              Chicago Relief & Aid Society
              Hull House
              Sanitary District of Chicago
              American Vigilance Association
              Chicago Peace Society
              Art Institute
              Cliff Dwellers
              University of Chicago
              Lombard College
              South Park Commission
              Chicago Historical Society
              Manual Training School
              Chicago Literary Club

William F. Hypes (1861-1931)

Schooling: Ohio high schools
Church: First Presbyterian Church, Chicago
Occupation: Marshall Field & Company

Affiliations: Towlet Hypes Company
              Chicago YMCA
              YMCA College
              Art Institute
              North Shore Music Festival

Noble Judah (1884-1938)

Schooling: Brown, Northwestern Law School
Church: St. Paul's Universalist Church, Chicago
Occupations: Chicago Title & Trust
           U.S. Ambassador to Cuba

Affiliations: American Bar Association
           United Charities
           Old Peoples Home
           Reserve Officers Association

Chauncey Keep (1853-1929)

Schooling: Chicago public schools
Church: St. James Episcopal, Chicago
Occupation: Illinois Merchants Trust Company

Affiliations: Marshall Field estate (trustee)
           Chicago Telephone Company
           Illinois Trust & Savings
           U.S. Trust Company
           Pullman Company
           Chicago Northwestern Railway Company
           Elgin Watch Company
           Chicago Historical Society

John B. Lord (1848-1936)

Schooling: Wesleyan Academy (Massachusetts)
Church: Kenwood Presbyterian Church, Chicago
Occupation: President, Ayer & Lord Tie Company

Affiliations: Harris Trust & Savings
           Presbyterian Hospital
           Washington & Jane Smith Home
           Legislative Voters' League
           Hyde Park Protective Association

Cyrus H. McCormick (1859-1936)

Schooling: Princeton
Church: Fourth Presbyterian Church, Chicago
Occupation: President, International Harvester

Affiliations: Chicago Northwestern Railway Company
     McCormick Seminary
     International YMCA
     Lake Forest University
     Princeton University
     Chicago Historical Society
     Field Museum of Natural History

Andrew MacLeish (1838-1928)

Schooling: Common schools in Scotland
Church: Fourth Baptist, Chicago
   First Baptist, Evanston
Occupation: Carson, Pirie, Scott & Company

Affiliations: American Baptist Foreign Missions
     Society
     Baptist Education Society
     Northern Baptist Convention
     Baptist Social Union
     University of Chicago
     Rush Medical College

Franklin MacVeagh (1837-1934)

Schooling: Yale, Columbia Law School
Church: Central Church
      St. James Episcopal, Chicago
Occupation: Whitaker, Harmon & Company (wholesale
      grocers)
      Secretary of Treasury

Affiliations: Commercial National Bank
      Chicago Bureau of Charities
      National Civic Federation
      American Civic Association
      Citizens' Association
      University of Chicago
      Cliff Dwellers
      Municipal Art League
      Chicago Literary Club
      Chicago Historical Society
      World's Columbian Exposition

John Nuveen, Jr. (1864- ?)

Schooling: Public schools in Holland
Church: Immanuel Baptist Church, Chicago
Occupation: John Nuveen & Company (municipal bonds)

Affiliations: Chicago YMCA
      Pacific Garden Mission
      Baptist Young People's Union
      Cook County Sunday School Association
      Chicago Baptist Social Union
      American Baptist Publication Society
      Kalamazoo College
      Chicago Literary Club

John W. O'Leary (1875- ?)

Schooling: Armour Institute, Cornell
Church: Methodist
Occupations: Arthur O'Leary & Son (iron works)
            Chicago Trust Company

Affiliations: Association of Commerce
              Illinois Manufacturers Association
              National Metal Trades Association
              First Englewood State Bank
              Illinois Car & Manufacturing Company
              U. S. Chamber of Commerce
              Chicago YMCA
              Chicago Church Federation
              Interchurch World Movement
              Committee of Fifteen
              Chicago Crime Commission
              National Guard Commission
              Infant Welfare Society
              Wesley Memorial Society

John T. Pirie, Jr. (1871-1940)

Schooling: Polytechnic Institute of Brooklyn
Church: First Presbyterian Church, Lake Forest
Occupation: Carson, Pirie, Scott & Company

Affiliations: Northern Trust Company
              First National Bank of Evanston
              Municipal Voters' League
              Lake Forest Hospital
              Citizens' Street Cleaning Bureau
              Chicago Zoological Society

George M. Reynolds (1865- ?)

Schooling: Iowa high schools
Church: Second Presbyterian Church, Chicago
Occupation: President, Continental & Commercial Bank

Agnecies: American Bankers' Association
            Federal Reserve Bank
            Peoples Trust & Savings
            Union Carbide & Carbon
            Chicago Clearing House Association
            Chicago Community Trust
            Citizens' War Board

A. M. Schoyer (1859- ?)
Schooling: Pennsylvania public schools
Church: ?
Occupation: Pennsylvania Railway Company

Affiliations: International YMCA
              Chautauqua

Howard Van Doren Shaw (1869-1926)

Schooling: Yale, Massachusetts Institute of Technology
Church: First Presbyterian Church, Lake Forest
Occupation: architect

Affiliations: United Charities
               Illinois College
               Art Instiute
               Municipal Museum of Chicago

John G. Shedd (1850-1926)

Schooling: New Hampshire common schools
Church: Kenwood Presbyterian Church, Chicago
Occupation: President, Marshall Field & Company

Affiliations: Illinois Centtral Railway Company
Illinois Trust & Savings
Mutual Life Insurance Company
Commonwealth Edison
Association of Commerce
Committee of Fifteen
Chicago Community Trust
Shedd Aquarium

William P. Sidley (1868-1958)

Schooling: Williams
Harvard Law School
Church: Christ Episcopal, Winnetka
Occupations: Williams, Holt & Wheeler (law firm)
Western Electric

Affiliations: Association of Commerce
Illinois Bell
Chicago YMCA
American War Claimants' Association
Chicago Literary Club
Newberry Library
Art Institute
Williams College

Solomon Smith (1877-1963)

Schooling: Yale
Church: First Presbyterian Church, Lake Forest
Occupation: President, Northern Trust Bank

Affiliations: Chicago Clearing House Association
Association of Commerce
Commonwealth Edison
Illinois Tool Works
U. S. Gypsum
Elgin National Watch Company
Presbyterian St.Luke's Hospital
American Red Cross
Chicago Natural History Museum

Ezra J. Warner, Jr (1877-1933)

Schooling: Yale
Church: First Presbyterian Church, Lake Forest
Occupation: President, Sprague, Warner & Company
(wholesale grocers)

Affiliations: Association of Commerce
Employers' Association
Northern Trust Bank
McCormick Seminary
Chicago YMCA
Committee of Fifteen
Chicago Bureau of Public Efficiency
American Red Cross
Illinois Children's Home Society
Hospital Association of Lake Forest
Chicago Institute of Social Science

Towner K. Webster (1849-1922)

Schooling: New York public schools
Church: First Presbyterian Church, Evanston
Occupations: Webster Manufacturing Company
             Webster Engineering
             Webster Electric

Affiliations: Association of Commerce
            Groene Home Movie Camera Company
            Northwestern University Settlement
            National Civic Federation
            Legislative Voters' League
            Civil Service Association

Harry A. Wheeler (1867-1960)

Schooling: Brooklyn public schools
Church: St. James Methodist Episcopal
Occupations: President, Union Trust Company
             President, U.S. Chamber of Commerce
             Federal food administrator (1917)

Affiliations: Association of Commerce
            Federal Reserve Board
            Mercantile Trust & Savings
            Garrett Biblical Institute
            Chicago Plan Commission
            Vassar College
            Northwestern University
            Public Library Commission

John E. Wilder (1861-1932)

Schooling: Massachusetts Agricultural College
Church: First Presbyterian Church, Evanston
Occupation: President, Wilder & Company (tanners)

Affiliations: Illinois Manufacturers Association
            Association of Commerce
            National Association of Tanners
            National Bank of Republic
            Evanston YMCA
            Beloit College

NOTE: Five Club trustees for whom biographical data
was not   available:

       William C. Boyden (lawyer)
       James Douglas (Quaker Oats)
       Philip James (Marshall Field & Company)
       George Ranney (International Harvester)
       Norman Williams (railroad machinery
       manufacturer)

APPENDIX B

CHICAGO SUNDAY EVENING CLUB SPEAKERS 1908-1920

Name	Affiliation	No. of Invitations*
Lyman Abbott	Editor, The Outlook	2
John Douglas Adam	Professor (New Jersey)	3
Jane Addams	Hull House (Chicago)	5
Charles F. Aked	Henry Ford European Peace Conference	1
Henry J. Allen	Governor (Kansas)	2
Charles P. Anderson	Bishop, Episcopal Diocese (Chicago)	11
E. Benjamin Andrews	Chancellor, Univ. of Nebraska	1
G. Glenn Atkins	First Congregational Church (Detroit)	5
James Henry Balmer	F.R.G.S. (South Africa)	1
Clarence A. Barbour	President, Brown University	5
Andreas Bard	Professor (Germany)	1
Charles E. Barker	M. D. (Washington, D. C.)	2
John Barrett	Int. Bureau of American Republics	1
W. A. Bartlett	First Congregational Church (Chicago)	1
Henry M. Beardsley	National Congregational Council	1
Samuel C. Benson	Ambulance Corps, France	1
Louis J. Bernhardt	Yale Hope Mission (New Haven)	1

Louis J. Bernhardt	Yale Hope Mission (New Haven)	1
Eli Bertalot	Waldensian Pastor (Italy)	1
Arthur Bestor	Chautauqua Institute (New York)	3
William C. Bitting	Second Baptist Church (St. Louis)	4
Hugh Black	Union Theological Seminary (New York)	18
Howard Bliss	Syrian Protestant College (Beirut)	1
Eva Booth	Salvation Army (New York)	2
Maud Ballington Booth	Salvation Army (New York)	2
Ballington Booth	Salvation Army (New York)	2
W. H. Wray Boyle	First Presbyterian Church (Evanston)	2
Nehemiah Boynton	Clinton Ave. Congregational (Brooklyn)	2
Henry Stiles Bradley	Piedmont Congregational (Worcester)	1
Hugh Brickhead	Emmanuel Church (Baltimore)	3
Fletcher S. Brockman	General Secretary for China (YMCA)	1
Charles R. Brown	Yale University (New Haven)	34
William J. Bryan	American political leader	3
William Lowe Bryan	President, University of Indiana	2
Robert J. Burdette	Author, clergyman (Pasadena)	1
David J. Burrell	Marble Collegiate Church (New York)	1
Willis H. Butler	Old South Congregational (Boston)	1
S. Parkes Cadman	Central Congregational (Brooklyn)	3
W. J. Calhoun	Lawyer, diplomat (Chicago)	1
Reginald J. Campbell	City Temple (London)	1
Charles F. Carter	Park Congregational Church (Hartford)	2
Lorenzo D. Case	St. Paul's Universalist, Chicago	1
Charles E. Cheney	Bishop, Reformed Episcopal Church	2

S. H. Clark	Professor, University of Chicago	1
Russell H. Conwell	President, Temple University	1
William C. Covert	First Presbyterian Church (Phila.)	4
Frank Crane	Union Church (Worcester)	2
Dan Crawford	Missionary (Central Africa)	1
Samuel M. Crothers	Professor, Harvard University	2
Charles S. Cutting	Judge (Chicago)	1
Josephus Daniels	Secretary of the Navy	2
Ralph B. Dennis	Professor, Northwestern University	1
A. C. Dixon	Moody Memorial Church	1
Edward D. Eaton	President, Beloit College	1
George Sherwood Eddy	Secretary for Asia (YMCA)	6
Samuel A. Eliot	Nat'l Federation of Religious Liberals	12
William A. Evans	Instructor, Moody Bible Institute	1
Samuel Fallows	Bishop, Reformed Episcopal Church	2
W. H. P. Faunce	President, Brown University	5
William W. Fenn	Dean, Harvard Divinity School	2
George H. Ferris	First Baptist Church (Phila.)	1
Hollis B. Fissell	Principal, Hampton Institute (Virginia)	2
Albert Parker Fitch	President, Carleton College (Minn.)	16
Joseph W. Folk	Governor (Missouri)	1
Harry E. Fosdick	Union Theological Seminary	26
Raymond B. Fosdick	League of Nations (New York)	4
William H. Foulkes	Rutgers Presbyterian Church (New York)	1
James E. Freeman	Bishop, Methodist Episcopal Church	24
Thomas F. Gailor	Bishop. Methodist Episcopal Church	7

Harry A. Garfield	President, Williams College	1
James R. Garfield	Secretary of the Interior	2
Henry George, Jr.	U.S. Congressman, journalist (New York)	1
Charles W. Gilkey	Hyde Park Baptist Church (Chicago)	9
James G. Gilkey	South Congregational Church (Mass.)	7
Charles L. Goodell	St. Paul's Church (New York)	2
Thomas P. Gore	U. S. Senator (Oklahoma)	1
James M. Gray	Dean, Moody Bible Institute	1
Thomas E. Green	American Red Cross	1
Wilfred T. Grenfell	Medical missionary (Labrador)	5
Sydney L. Gulick	Missionary (Japan)	1
John W. Gulland	Member of Parliament (England)	2
Frank W. Gunsaulus	Central Church (Chicago)	15
Frank Oliver Hall	Church of the Divine Paternity (N.Y.)	2
Richard C. Hall	Association of Commerce (Chicago)	1
J. Frank Hanly	Governor (Indiana)	2
Norman Hapgood	Editor, Colliers	1
William P. Hapgood	Columbia Conserve Co. (Indianapolis)	1
Edgar P. Hill	Presbyterian Church (Chicago)	4
Newell Dwight Hillis	Plymouth Church (Brooklyn)	9
Emil G. Hirsch	Sinai Temple (Chicago)	1
Richmond P. Hobson	Congressman (Alabama)	1
Edward W. Hoch	Governor (Kansas)	2
Charles S. Holt	Presbyterian Brotherhood of America	1
Hamilton Holt	Editor, The Independent	1
Ernest M. Hopkins	President, Dartmouth College	1

Lynn Harold Hough	President, Drew Theological Seminary	26
O. O. Howard	Founder, Howard University	1
Edwin H. Hughes	Bishop, Methodist Episcopal Church	20
John Hunter	Trinity Congregational (Scotland)	1
George Jackson	Professor, Victoria College (Toronto)	1
Charles E. Jefferson	Broadway Tabernacle Church (New York)	4
Jeremiah Jenks	Professor, New York University	1
David Hugh Jones	First Presbyterian Church (Evanston)	9
John P. Jones	Missionary (India)	1
Jenkin Lloyd Jones	All Souls Church (Chicago)	3
David Starr Jordan	President, Stanford University	1
Marcus A. Kavanagh	Judge of the Superior Court (Chicago)	1
James Keeley	Editor, Chicago Herald Examiner	1
John Kelman	St. George's Church (Scotland)	1
Henry Churchill King	President, Oberlin College	2
J. H. Kirkland	Chancellor, Vanderbilt University	2
Cosmo Gordon Lang	Archbishop of Canterbury (England)	1
William Lawrence	Episcopal Bishop of Massachusetts	1
J. Hamilton Lewis	Senator (Illinois)	2
Ben B. Lindsey	Judge of the Juvenile Court (Denver)	3
Owen R. Lovejoy	National Child Labor Committee	1
Frank O. Lowden	Governor (Illinois)	2
Hamilton W. Mabie	Editor, The Outlook	1
J. A. MacDonald	Editor, The Globe (Toronto)	11
Henry B. MacFarland	International Conference of YMCA's	1
John MacNeill	Walmer Road Baptist Church (Toronto)	2

Theodore Marburg	U.S. Minister to Belgium	1
Edwin Markham	Poet	1
Thomas R. Marshall	Governor (Indiana)	4
Shailer Mathews	Dean, University of Chicago	2
Mark A. Matthews	First Presbyterian Church (Seattle)	1
Cleland B. MacAfee	Professor, McCormick Seminary (Chicago)	2
Albert J. McCartney	National Presbyterian Church (Wash.)	8
James G. K. McClure	President, McCormick Seminary	5
Lee S. McCollester	Dean, Tufts College	1
Francis J. McConnell	Bishop, Methodist Episcopal Church	22
William F. McDowell	Bishop, Methodist Episcopal Church	20
William T. McElween	First Congregational (Evanston)	3
Alexander J. McKelway	National Child Labor Committee	1
Charles P. Medbury	University Church of Christ (Iowa)	1
William P. Merrill	Brick Presbyterian Church (New York)	14
Carl E. Milliken	Governor (Maine)	1
Utaki Minakuchi	Evangelist (Japan)	3
Charles B. Mitchell	Bishop, Methodist Episcopal Church	4
William R. Moody	Headmaster, Northfield Schools	1
R. R. Moton	Principal, Tuskegee Institute	2
John R. Mott	International Secretary, YMCA	12
Johnston Myers	Immanuel Baptist Church (Chicago)	1
Thomas Nicholson	Bishop, Methodist Episcopal Church	6
John W. O'Leary	Association of Commerce (Chicago)	1
Ernest Wray Oneal	First Methodist Episcopal (Chicago)	1
Chase S. Osborn	Governor (Minnesota)	1

Robert J. Patterson	Belfast, Ireland	1
Francis G. Peabody	Professor, Harvard University	13
Gifford Pinchot	National Conservation Association	1
Louis F. Post	Assistant Secretary of Labor	1
Edward D. Powell	First Christian Church (Loiusville)	1
John T. Proctor	President, Baptist College (China)	1
William A. Quayle	Bishop, Methodist Episcopal Church	2
William Radar	Calvary Presbyterian Church (S.F.)	1
Walter Rauschenbusch	Professor, Rochester Seminary	1
Robert Renard	Lieutenant, 341st Infantry (France)	1
Erman Ridgway	Publisher, Everybody's Magazine	1
Jacob A. Riis	Sociologist, journalist	4
Raymond Robins	Men and Religion Forward Movement	2
Franklin D. Roosevelt	Assistant Secretary of the Navy	1
David Ross	Free Church (Scotland)	3
Edward A. Ross	Professor, Univ. of Wisconsin	1
G.A. Johnston Ross	Professor, Presbyterian College	4
Henry Martin Sanders	New York	1
James Schermerhorn	Editor, The Detroit Times	1
Jacob G. Schurman	President, Cornell University	1
C. Anderson Scott	Professor, Westminster Seminary	1
Frederick F. Shannon	Central Church (Chicago)	2
Charles M. Sheldon	Central Church (Topeka)	1
Marion D. Shutter	First Universalist Church (Minneapolis)	1
Frank G. Smith	Warren Ave. Congregational (Chicago)	1
Fred B. Smith	World Alliance for Int.Friendship	11

Theodore G. Soares	Professor, University of Chicago	4
Robert E. Speer	Presbyterian Board of Foreign Missions	26
William Spurgeon	Evangelist (London)	2
Edward A. Stainer	President, Grinnell College	17
Charles Stelzle	Presbyterian Board of Home Missions	7
J. Ross Stevenson	President, Princeton Seminary	2
Leroy T. Steward	Colonel, Illinois Reserve Militia	1
George Black Stewart	Professor, Auburn Seminary	1
James S. Stone	St. James Episcopal (Chicago)	1
John Timothy Stone	Fourth Presbyterian Church (Chicago)	8
Walter T. Sumner	Dean, Cathedral of Saints Peter & Paul	1
Willaim Howard Taft	President, United States	1
Robert B. Taylor	President, Queen's University	6
Charles F. Thwing	President, Western Reserve Univ.	2
Ernest F. Tittle	First Methodist Episcopal (Chicago)	6
George W. Truett	First Baptist Church (Dallas)	1
Joseph A. Vance	Moderator, Presbyterian Church of USA	4
Henry Van Dyke	Professor, Princeton University	11
S. R. Van Sant	Commander in Chief, G. A. R.	1
Ambrose W. Vernon	Harvard Church (Brookline, Mass.)	1
George E. Vincent	Rockefeller Foundation	3
John H. Vincent	Founder, Chautauqua Institute	2
Booker T. Washington	President, Tuskegee Institute	2
Willaim O. Waters	Grace Episcopal (Chicago)	1
Benjamin I. Wheeler	President, University of Chicago	2
J. Campbell White	Laymen's Missionary Movement	1

John E. White	Second Baptist Church (Atlanta)	2
Brand Whitlock	Mayor (Toledo)	1
John L. Whitman	Superintendent, The Bridewell (Chicago)	1
Herbert L. Willett	Professor, University of Chicago	3
Charles D. Williams	Bishop, Protestant Episcopal Church	12
T. Rhhonda Williams	English Editor, The Christian Work	2
Frank H. Willis	Governor (Ohio)	1
Stephen S. Wise	Free Synagogue (New York)	8
Charles F. Wishart	President, College of Wooster	3
Cornelius Woelfkin	Fifth Avenue Baptist Church (New York)	5
Charles Wood	Church of the Covenant (Washington)	1
Leonard Wood	Major General, United States Army	2
John G. Wooley	Anti-Saloon League (Chicago)	1
Charles Zueblin	Publicist, lecturer	1

* Indicates total number of times individual spoke at the Club including occasions past 1920.

BIBLIOGRAPHY

Archival Materials

Clifford Barnes Papers, Chicago Historical Society, N. Clark & W. North, Chicago, Illinois 60610.

Chicago Sunday Evening Club Papers, Chicago Historical Society, N. Clark & W. North, Chicago, Illinois 60610.

Commerce (1910-1920), Chicago Association of Commerce and Industry, 130 S. Michigan, Chicago, Illinois 60603.

Henry Parsons Crowell Papers, Moody Bible Institute Archives, 820 N. LaSalle, Chicago, Illinois 60610.

Charles L. Hutchinson Papers, Newberry Library, 60 W. Walton Street, Chicago, Illinois 60610.

Hyde Park Protective Association Papers, Chicago Historical Society, N. Clark & W. North, Chicago, Illinois 60610.

Men At Work (1910-1912), Presbyterian Historical Society, 425 Lombard Street, Philadelphia, Pennsylvania 19147.

Minutes of Chicago Presbytery (1900-1920), McCormick Theological Seminary, 1464 E. 55th Street, Chicago, Illinois 60615.

Billy Sunday Papers, Billy Graham Center Archives, Wheaton College, Wheaton, Illinois 60187.

Primary Sources

Addams, Jane. Twenty Years At Hull House. New York: Macmillan, 1935.

Bancroft, Edgar A. The Mission of America and other War-Time Speeches. Washington: n.p., 1927.

Barbour, Clarence. Making Religion Efficient. New York: Association Press, 1912.

Carnegie, Andrew. The Gospel of Wealth and other Timely Essays. Cambridge: Belknap Press, 1965.

Chicago Commission on Race Relations. The Negro in Chicago: A Study of Race Relations and a Race Riot in 1919. Chicago: University of Chicago Press, 1922.

Forgan, David R. Sketches and Speeches. Chicago: n.p., 1925.

Haley, Margaret A. Battleground: The Autobiography of Margaret A. Haley. Urbana: University of Illinois Press, 1982.

Harris, A. W. The First Seventy-Five Years of the Harris Organization 1882-1957. Chicago: Harris Trust & Savings, 1957.

Harrison, Carter. Stormy Years. Indianapolis: Bobbs-Merrill, 1935.

Hopkins, John Henry. The Great Forty Years in the Diocese of Chicago 1893-1933. Chicago: Centenary Fund of Diocese of Chicago, 1936.

Lippmann, Walter. A Preface to Politics. Ann Arbor: University of Michigan Press, 1914.

Mathews, Shailer. The Church and the Changing Order. New York: Macmillan, 1907.

_____. The Individual and the Social Gospel. New York: Laymen's Missionary Movement, 1914.

_____. The Spiritual Interpretation of History. Cambridge: Harvard University Press, 1916.

Merriam, Charles E. The Rise of Urban America. New York: Arno Press, 1929.

Patterson, William B. Modern Church Brotherhoods. New York: Fleming Revell, 1911.

Speer, Robert. The Stuff of Manhood. New York: Fleming Revell, 1917.

Stevenson, Andrew. Chicago, Preeminently a Presbyterian City. Chicago: n.p., 1907.

Sullivan, Mark. Our Times: The Turn of the Century, 1900-1904. New York: Charles Scribner's Sons, 1927.

Sutherland, Douglas. Fifty Years on the Civic Front. Chicago: Civic Federation of Chicago, 1943.

Taylor, Graham. Pioneering on Social Frontiers. Chicago: University of Chicago Press, 1930.

_____. Chicago Commons Through Forty Years. Chicago: Chicago Commons Association, 1936.

Weber, Max. The Protestant Ethic and the Spirit of Capitalism. New York: Charles Scribner's Sons, 1958.

_____. The Sociology of Religion. Boston: Beacon Press, 1963.

Zenos, Andrew C. The Elements of Higher Criticism. New York: Funk & Wagnalls, 1896.

Secondary Sources

Baran, Paul and Sweezy, Paul. Monopoly Capital. New York: Monthly Review Press, 1966.

Bendix, Reinhard. Max Weber: An Intellectual Portrait. New York: Doubleday, 1960.

Berger, Peter. The Noise of Solemn Assemblies. New York: Doubleday, 1961.

Boyer, Paul. Urban Masses and Moral Order in America, 1820-1920. Cambridge: Harvard University Press, 1978.

Brody, David. Labor in Crisis: The Steel Strike of 1919. Philadelphia: J. B. Lippincott, 1965.

Buder, Stanley. Pullman: An Experiment in Industrial Order and Community Planning 1880-1930. New York: Oxford University Press, 1967.

Burgess, Ernest W. and Newcomb, Charles. Census Data of the City of Chicago, 1920. Chicago: University of Chicago Press,

1931.

Casey, Robert J. and Douglas, W. A. S. Pioneer Railroad: The
Story of the Chicago and Northwestern System. New York:
McGraw-Hill, 1945.

Cauthen, Kenneth. The Impact of American Religious Liberalism.
New York: Harper, 1962.

Cawelti, John G. Apostles of the Self-Made Man. Chicago: University of Chicago Press, 1965.

Counts, George S. School and Society in Chicago. New York:
Harcourt, Brace & World, 1928.

Crunden, Robert M. Ministers of Reform: The Progressives'
Achievement in American Civilization 1889-1920. New York:
Basic Books, 1982.

Davis, Allen. Spearheads for Reform: The Social Settlement and
the Progressive Movement. New York: Oxford University
Press, 1967.

Dedmon, Emmot. Great Enterprises: 100 Years of the YMCA in Metropolitan Chicago. Chicago: Rand McNally, 1957.

Diner, Stephen. A City and Its Universities. Chapel Hill: University of North Carolina Press, 1980.

Douglas, Ann. The Feminization of American Culture. New York:
Alfred A. Knopf, 1977.

Duis, Perry. The Saloon and the Public City: Chicago and Boston,
1880-1920. Chicago: University of Chicago Press, 1975.

Eaton, Leonard. Two Chicago Architects and Their Clients. Boston: MIT Press, 1969.

Edwards, Richard. Contested Terrain: The Transformation of the
Workplace in the 20th Century. New York: Basic Books,
1979.

Fine, Sidney. Laissez-Faire and the General Welfare State. Ann
Arbor: University of Michigan Press, 1956.

Ginger, Ray. Altgeld's America 1890-1905. Chicago: New Viewpoints, 1958.

Giroux, Henry. Ideology, Culture and the Process of Schooling.
Philadelphia: Temple University Press, 1981.

Goodspeed, Thomas W. University of Chicago Biographies, Volume 1 and 2. Chicago: University of Chicago Press, 1924.

Grant, Bruce. Fight for a City: The Story of the Union League Club. Chicago: Rand McNally, 1955.

Handy, Robert T. A Christian America. New York: Oxford University Press, 1971.

Hays, Samuel. The Response to Industrialism. Chicago: University of Chicago Press, 1957.

Heilbroner, Robert L. The Limits of American Capitalism. New York: Harper & Row, 1965.

_____. The Nature and Logic of Capitalism. New York: W. W. Norton & Co., 1985.

Horowitz, Helen. Cultural Philanthropy in Chicago from the 1880s to 1917. Lexington: University of Kentucky Press, 1976.

Hutchison, William. The Modernist Impulse in American Protestantism. Cambridge: Belknap Press, 1976.

Jaher, Frederic C. The Urban Establishment: Upper Strata in Boston, New York, Charleston, Chicago and Los Angeles. Urbana: University of Illinois Press, 1982.

Kaestle, Carl F. Pillars of the Republic. New York: Hill and Wang, 1983.

Karier, Clarence J. Shaping the American Educational State, 1900 to the Present. New York: Fress Press, 1975.

King, Hoyt. Citizen Cole of Chicago. Chicago: Horders' Inc., 1931.

Kogan, Herman and Wendt, Lloyd. Big Bill of Chicago. Indianapolis: Bobbs-Merrill, 1953.

Kolko, Gabriel. The Triumph of Conservatism. New York: Free Press, 1963.

Lane, Jack C. Armed Progressive. San Rafael, Cal.: Presidio Press, 1978.

Lears, Jackson. No Place of Grace: Antimodernism and the Transformation of American Culture 1880-1920. New York: Pantheon Books, 1981.

Lubove, Roy. The Professional Altruist: The Emergence of Social Work as a Career, 1880-1930. Cambridge: Harvard University Press, 1965.

Magnussen, Norris. Salvation in the Slums: Evangelical Social Action 1865-1920. Metuchen, N.J.: Scarecrow Press, 1977.

Marquette, Arthur. Brands, Trademarks and Goodwill: The Story of the Quaker Oats Company. New York: McGraw-Hill, 1967.

Marsden, George. Fundamentalism and American Culture. New York: Oxford University Press, 1980.

Marshall, Gordon. Presbyteries and Profit: Calvinism and the Development of Capitalism in Scotland, 1560-1707. New York: Oxford University Press, 1980.

_____. In Search of the Spirit of Capitalism: An Essay on Max Weber's Protestant Ethic Thesis. New York: Oxford University Press, 1982.

May, Henry. Protestant Churches and Industrial America. New York: Harper & Brothers, 1949.

McCarthy, Kathleen. Noblesse Oblige: Charity and Cultural Philanthropy in Chicago, 1849-1929. Chicago: University of Chicago Press, 1982.

McCloskey, Robert. American Conservatism in the Age of Enterprise. New York: Harper & Row, 1951.

McLoughlin, William. Modern Revivalism from Charles G. Finney to Billy Graham. New York: Ronald Press, 1959.

Miller, Robert Moats. How Shall They Hear Without A Preacher? The Life of Ernest Fremont Tittle. Chapel Hill: University of North Carolina Press, 1971.

Newell, Barbara. Chicago and the Labor Movement: Metropolitan Unionism in the 1930's. Urbana: University of Illinois Press, 1961.

Niebuhr, H. Richard. The Social Sources of Denominationalism. Hamden, Conn.: Shoe String Press, 1929.

_____. The Kingdom of God in America. New York: Harper & Brothers, 1935.

Noble, David. Forces of Production: A Social History of Industrial Automation. New York: Alfred A. Knopf, 1984.

_____. The Paradox of Progressive Thought. Minneapolis: University of Minnesota Press, 1958.

Ozanne, Robert. A Century of Labor-Management Relations.

Madison: University of Wisconsin Press, 1972.

Pennewell, Almer. The Methodist Movement in Northern Illinois. Sycamore, Ill.: Sycamore Tribune, 1942.

Rader, Benjamin. The Academic Mind and Reform: The Influence of Richard T. Ely in American Life. Lexington: University of Kentucky Press, 1966.

Reissman, Leonard. Class in American Society. New York: Free Press, 1959.

Schmidt, Stephen A. A History of the Religious Education Association. Birmingham: Religious Education Press, 1983.

Seligman, Ben B. Economics of Dissent. Chicago: Quadrangle Books, 1968.

Shade, William, ed. Seven on Black: Reflections on the Negro Experience in America. Philadelphia: Lippincott, 1969.

Spear, Allan H. Black Chicago: The Making of the Negro Ghetto, 1890-1920. Chicago: University of Chicago Press, 1967.

Stackhouse, Perry J. Chicago and the Baptists. Chicago: University of Chicago Press, 1933.

Stover, John F. The Life and Decline of the American Railroad. New York: Oxford University Press, 1970.

Strickland, Arvarh. History of the Chicago Urban League. Urbana: University of Illinois Press, 1966.

Strout, Cushing. The New Heavens and the New Earth: Political Religion in America. New York: Harper & Row, 1974.

Tawney, R.H. Religion and the Rise of Capitalism. New York: Harcourt, Bruce & World, 1926.

Tuttle, William M. Race Riot. New York: Atheneum, 1972.

Twyman, Robert W. History of the Marshall Field & Company. Philadelphia: University of Pennsylvania Press, 1954.

Tyack, David. One Best System. Cambridge: Harvard University Press, 1974.

Violas, Paul. The Training of the Urban Working Class. Chicago: Rand McNally, 1978.

Vitrano, Steven P. An Hour of Good News. Chicago: Chicago

Sunday Evening Club, 1974.

Watts, Emily S. The Businessman in American Literature. Athens: University of Georgia Press, 1983.

Wiebe, Robert. The Search for Order, 1877-1920. New York: Hill & Wang, 1967.

Weinstein, James. The Corporate Ideal in the Liberal State, 1900-1915. New York: Beacon, 1968.

Wheeler, George. Pierpont Morgan & Friends: The Anatomy of a Myth. New York: Prentice-Hall, 1973.

Wogaman, Philip. The Great Economic Debate. Philadelphia: Westminster Press, 1977.

For Product Safety Concerns and Information please contact our EU
representative GPSR@taylorandfrancis.com
Taylor & Francis Verlag GmbH, Kaufingerstraße 24, 80331 München, Germany

www.ingramcontent.com/pod-product-compliance
Lightning Source LLC
Chambersburg PA
CBHW050631280326
41932CB00015B/2598